The Beach Beneath the Streets

The Beach Beneath the Streets

Contesting New York City's Public Spaces

Benjamin Shepard
and
Gregory Smithsimon

excelsior editions

State University of New York Press
Albany, New York

Cover illustration courtesy of Caroline Shepard, www.carolineshepard.com

Published by State University of New York Press, Albany

For information, contact State University of New York Press, Albany, NY
www.sunypress.edu

Production by Kelli W. LeRoux
Marketing by Michael Campochiaro

Library of Congress Cataloging-in-Publication Data

Shepard, Benjamin.
   The beach beneath the streets : contesting New York City's public spaces /
Benjamin Shepard and Gregory Smithsimon.
      p. cm.
   Includes bibliographical references and index.
   ISBN 978-1-4384-3619-7 (hardcover : alk. paper) — ISBN 978-1-4384-3620-3 (pbk.
: alk. paper) 1. City planning—New York (State)—New York. 2. Public spaces—
New York (State)—New York. 3. Plazas—New York (State)—New York. I. Smith-
simon, Gregory. II. Title.

HT168.N5S54 2011
307.1'21609747—dc22

                                                     2010032059

                          10 9 8 7 6 5 4 3 2 1

Contents

Acknowledgments

The name for this book was hatched in one of New York's great public spaces, Prospect Park in Brooklyn, during the birthday party of Scarlett, Ben's younger daughter. In much of the United States, public birthday parties are unusual, but New York's small apartments and big parks mean that a sunny day can find three or four kids' parties going on in sight of each other. Kids were hula hooping and chasing each other with squirt guns. The two of us were taking a break from the action, standing in the shade of a tree and talking to another parent when we hit upon the title of the book. That moment captures the many debts we owe: to our families, to the intellectual fecundity of New York's public spaces, and to the many people who provided interviews, insight, inspiration, and action that made this book possible.

Much of *The Beach Beneath the Streets* was born of conversations during play dates, in New York's parks and streets, its art galleries and restaurants—with our kids, Dodi and Scarlett, Eamon and Una. It is their creative energy and our need to find abundant space for them to play and grow in a healthy, imaginative way, which propelled this project from idea to book. Caroline Shepard and Molly Smithsimon, our wives, were there to support the project as we moved from play dates to dinners and ongoing conversations, and occasional struggles just to move forward. Caroline also provided us with early photos of the streets of New York as well as the cover art for this project (www.carolineshepard.com). Other artists, activists from FIERCE and RTS, and photographers, contributed historic images that are just as irreplaceable. The Times Up! archive as well as activist photographers were tremendously generous with their time and photos.

The research on the history of bonus plazas relied on interviews from people who could have felt no compulsion to be as generous as they were. Among the many architects interviewed, the meetings with Richard Roth in an Upper West Side diner stand out as particularly revealing and representative of a classic use of public space: of how a generation of influential New York city builders eschew their offices or homes and set up meetings in bustling diners. There the sound quality is poor, but the energy of New York's street life energizes the interview. Likewise, the help of Philip Schneider, who continues to advocate for better plazas in the offices of the Department of Planning (although he has nominally retired) was invaluable.

Moving to the Hudson River Piers, we would like to thank Kate Crane, Michael Fabricant, Kerwin Kaye, and Bob Kohler for their close readings of Chapter 4. Thanks to Barton Benes for sharing his story and allowing us to republish copies of photos from his 1978 work *Pier 48: Letters from My Aunt Evelyn*. Several interviewees, including the legendary Bob Kohler, told their stories in some of the final days of their lives. Two interviewees were sent back to jail. And two of the chroniclers of life on the piers, Allan Bérubé and David Wojnarowicz, died before their time. They are sorely missed.

We could only write this book because earlier writers, theorists, and activists created the questions, stories, and movements of New York's public spaces. Activists welcomed us as participant observers into their meetings, and walked us through their movements. People like Alex Vitale could walk through a crowded event on Broadway, explaining how the activists' perception of police practices had influenced how they planned an event and organized a group. Groups such as RTS, FIERCE, Time's Up! and its Bike Lane Clowns marched, danced, and pedaled across Manhattan's streets to establish our right to the city. They in turn were building on the insights from queer theorists, the generation of 1968, Emma Goldman, and others who helped invent the idea of a pulsing democratic public space by and for the people. Only because they dreamed there could be a beach beneath the streets could we see it for ourselves.

Our respective academic departments, both vital parts of New York's besieged yet still thriving public sphere, the City University of New York, were just as helpful and just as present in public space. The Brooklyn College sociology department, Gregory's home base, has been a model of an academic department engaged in public space, whether playing softball or participating in a road race together in Brooklyn's parks. Their support, intellectual and collegial, has made working on this book a pleasure. The offices of the Department of Human Services at City Tech are surrounded by some of downtown Brooklyn's best public spaces, and have been the starting point from which Ben has investigated New York—from its activism to its waterfront.

We benefited immensely from discussions with colleagues. Dave Madden can parse a sentence like no one else, even while walking across 34th Street after hours spent in a local bar discussing friends' manuscripts. Among the many people whose input have made this book better are Herbert Gans, Sudhir Venkatesh, Charles Tilly, Sharon Zukin, Harvey Molotch, and Cuz Potter. Gregory also wants to thank Michael Donnelly at Bard College, who pressed me to explain the significance of my bonus plaza research. Though it is a delayed response, this book is the answer. We also benefited from reviews from *Urban Affairs Review, Liminalities, Working USA,* and the *Journal of Aesthetics and Protest,* and the book *Altered States: Politics after Democracy,* where earlier versions of some of these chapters were published.

We'd like to thank Larin McLaughlin and Kelli W. LeRoux of SUNY Press for first seeing promise in the proposal and for supporting, guiding and helping us pull together the book. We also thank the anonymous reviewers for their prescient suggestions for the project. We would also like to thank the PSC-CUNY 63251-00 41 University Committee on Research Award for support to complete the final production of this manuscript.

And finally, our debt of gratitude to the people who use and bring alive New York's public spaces. New Yorkers have an undeserved reputation for being hard. Conditions in the city are hard, but the people retain their humanity through it all, and let it shine in our shared spaces. We will always have something to share, and to struggle for, in public space.

For updates and reviews on this project, see www.benjaminheim shepard.com.

PART ONE

REPRESSION

Control, Exclusion, and Play in Today's Future City

Beneath the Screen? (handwritten)

The title for our work—The Beach Beneath the Streets—refers to the French May '68 slogan. "Sous les pavés, la plage!" often translated as "Beneath the pavement—the beach!" The anonymous graffiti from Paris 1968 conjures up any number of images—a subaltern vitality, the control of something unruly, the dominance of nature, and a possible return of the repressed. The expression also speaks to a new kind of social imagination, a right to view the city as a space for democratic possibilities, a social geography of freedom. "All power to the imagination," is perhaps the most famous bit of street graffiti from 1968. Throughout the period, the Situationists, a highly influential French avant-garde group who took part in the street demonstrations, argued urban space created room for one to consider and conceive of new perspectives on the very nature of social reality. Within such a politics, the rules of everyday life would be turned upside down and restored into a "realm for play" (Vaneigeem 1994, 131).

The Situationist response to the privatization of public space included innovations in approaches to activism. Two primary tactics utilized by the Situationists included interventions termed "détournement" and "dérive." Détournement refers to the rearrangement of popular signs to create new meanings (Thompson 2004). "An existing space may outlive its original purpose . . . which determines its forms,

"The city is burning tonight (Sous les pavés, la plage!)" Photo by view-askew, mural by Seth Tobocman, Norway.

3

functions, and structures; it may thus in a sense become vacant, and suscepti-
ble of being diverted, reappropriated and put to a use quite different from its
initial one," French Marxist philosopher and sociologist Henri Lefebvre would
explain. He described the way the process changed a local produce market in
1969. "The urban centre, designed to facilitate the distribution of food, was
transformed into a gathering-place and a scene of permanent festival—in
short, into a centre of play rather than of work—for the youth of Paris"
(LeFebvre 1974, 167). Dérive refers to short meandering walks designed to
resist the work- and control-oriented patterns of Georges Haussmanns
redesign of Paris (Thompson 2004). This approach anticipated today's Critical
Mass bike rides—a current "best practice" in playful, prefigurative community
organizing. "The dérive acted as something of a model for the 'playful creation' of all human relationships," writes theorist Sadie Plant (1992, 59). The
point of dérive is active engagement between self and space. It changes the
way one sees the streets (60). Such forms of play reveal a sense of agency, of
control of the way one wants to participate within the world. While play takes
place in all human cultures, its roots in movement activity can be found in the
works of the Surrealists and Dadaists (Plant 1992). The Situationists built on
this trajectory, which in turn found its way into modern movements ranging
from queer direct action ACT UP zaps to Reclaim the Streets (RTS) and Pink
Silver style tactical frivolity of the street parties of today's global justice movement (Jordan 1998; Shepard 2009; Shepard 2011).

Dérive and détournement also highlight something important about public
space and its relation to the social imagination, the topic of this book. Public
space is a source of contestation. It is intricately associated with any number
of notions: democracy, public debate, Shakespeare's "all the worlds a stage,"
Elizabethan theatre, comedy, and tragedy. Such thinking finds its way into the
very geography of the public commons. Take the town of Arakoulos, just a
few kilometers east of Delphi, the ancient home of the mythical oracle. Today
streets still ring with their own chorus. On summer evenings, chairs are set
out ten and twelve deep in front of the cafes that line the only significant
street in town. They overflow with occupants. Outside, the chairs and conversations of all the cafés intermingle in a daily social ritual that goes on for
hours. The agoras in the center of the ancient city states of Greece have long
been presented as the absolute ideal of public space. Coupled with the equally
engaged and lively use of public space in a Greek town like Arakoulos, the
moment is inspiring for a student of public spaces. But it quickly fills an
American observer with the simple question: how come streets in the United
States no longer feel like this?

The comparison is misleading. The United States does have vibrant,
diverse public spaces. There is no single ideal type of public space, yet the
bucolic Mission Dolores Park overlooking downtown San Francisco confirms

that there are vibrant examples here as well. In this compressed, urban park only a couple blocks long, there is marvelous integration of different users of the space, but simultaneously firm self-segregation as well. On any given day, one might find in the park twenty-four hour drug dealing down the hill from male sunbathers, kids on the unenclosed playground next to dogs running off their leashes, cops in their squad cars across the field, a political rally next to a basketball game—picnickers, tennis players, people waiting for the trolley, and even the anarchist direct action group Food Not Bombs serving free meals. The park seems like just the kind of space William H. Whyte would linger over as an ideal space of diverse, self-regulating interaction. Yet, the integration of these different uses hinges on a degree of self regulation: chaos would erupt if any of these groups infringed on the space of any of the others.

The segregation is not all voluntary: people have been assaulted for crossing into the drug dealers' space, disputes erupt between parents and dog owners, cops roar down the walkways. The risk of danger is real, as is exclusivity even in this most ideal of public spaces. Public space, even at its best, is a complex balance. And while advocates of public space often are strong opponents of police surveillance or corporate control, the space described here could not exist without order and social control. But control is not emanating from the squad car. Order in public space is generated primarily, though not exclusively in this case, by users. Despite the priority of self-regulation in public space, police increasingly play a role in filtering, controlling, and segregating access to public space. Competing liberatory and controlling visions of public space run throughout this book.

Though these opening vignettes offer glimpses of the recreational possibilities of such spaces, the purpose of the book is serious. Public space has attracted wide ranging attention from far-flung perspectives and disciplines; it is claimed like a battlefield, mourned as a dying species, embraced as the very incubator of democracy. Work coming out of these varied concerns is all valuable, but very difficult to rectify with each other. Three factors are considered here: exclusion, control, and play. In their own ways, each highlights the central features of public space, its repression and resistance, and provides the means by which students of public space can think coherently about the different traditions of the study of public space. Juxtaposing control and resistance, one locates a dialectic in the most passionate examinations of public space—comprised of alarms sounded at the privatization of public space, even the impending death of public space, and celebrations of the singular liberatory potential of the politics of public space. As opposition to privatized space becomes more sophisticated, and activists' interest in the potential of public space becomes more widespread, both the defense of public space and the strategic value of public space benefits from a framework with which to understand the ongoing threats to the future of public space. This book seeks to provide a framework that can relate insights about recent elite domination of public space as well as breakthroughs in the strategic use of public space for emancipatory purposes.

While the opening examples (as well as a few to follow) come from different sides of the globe, this examination of public space centers on New York. That is useful in part because the politics of space are strongly influenced by elites who seek to shape space and direct its uses—large-scale real estate developers, politicians, and bankers capable of moving large amounts of capital into and out of a region or project. Part of what makes New York an intriguing global city is the way that transnational social and cultural capital infuses its neighborhoods with a distinct glocal—global and local—dimension. Developers hold positions of particular influence in New York City and its politics, making this a particularly productive place to examine spatial trends that are nonetheless influential elsewhere. Thus, while public space takes shape in a local physical geography, the capital behind the bricks and mortar is connected to a neoliberal economic project aimed at the privatization and commodification of countless aspects of life, from water to air to the lands of cities around the world (Klein 2003). When New York faced a fiscal crisis in the mid-1970s, its reorganization served as a kind of trial run for the impact of these neoliberal policies on local space. In the years since, New Yorkers have had to contend with one crisis after another, with various camps promoting policy solutions involving still more privatization. Much of the work of New York activists, radicals, revolutionaries, queers, and community organizers has been a response to the threats borne of the 1975 restructuring. Given this, a brief review of New York City history since its fiscal crisis is instructive.

The Transformation of New York City in Power and Space

The transformation of space that this book examines parallels transformations in capitalism. For some time, authors who monitor the accessibility of public space have linked the loss of public space to the more aggressive turn in capitalism beginning around the early 1970s as the postwar consensus was stagnated by inflation and then replaced by a more ruthlessly profit-seeking global capitalism (Zukin 1991; Sorkin 1992; Davis 1990; Castells 1989; Sassen 2001). That global change had particular manifestations in individual cities, and New York's have been well-documented (Fitch 1993; Abu-Lughod 1999). As capitalists privatized public commons, eliminated programs guaranteeing public welfare, and launched vengeful raids on working class prosperity, elites first backed away from the city, then returned to disemboweled democratic spaces—building within their gentrified, eviscerated shells either elite playgrounds, upper-middle class consumerist shopping festival marketplaces, or "bread and circus" distractions from the economic restructuring going on all around.[1]

Recently, several important works have delved into the last forty years of New York history to consider the story of its vexing transformation. While Vitale (2008) considered the change in terms of policing, and Fitch (1993) viewed them via real estate, Freeman (2000) and Moody (2007) considered the city's changes from the vantage point of labor relations and shrinkage of the public sector, and Greenberg (2008) considered how New York was rebranded after the crisis. Zukin (2010) examined how the soul of the city has been threatened as the city is redeveloped on the foundation of a commodifiable, gentrified culture. And Marshall Berman (1982; 2007) considered what New York tells us about modernism. Berman, of course, was not the first to view the city as a narrative for our age. "Here I was in New York, city of rose and fantasy, of capitalist automotion, its streets a triumph of cubism, its moral philosophy that of the dollar," Leon Trotsky wrote in his autobiography. "More than any city in the world, it is the fullest expression of our modern age" (quoted in Moody). Implicit is a recognition of the cultural and economic influence of a distinct urban space. Over the past four decades, a transnational, neoliberal revolution in financing, policing, and real estate has shifted the way the city lives, works, and understands itself. Our view of the city begins with a glimpse of the space from the street to the sidewalk, between commerce and pleasure, at the intersection of work and play.

A common thread running through the writing about New York is the flux in public space and by extension the public sector. Here, one is invited to consider the ways the city is organized to preserve, privatize, profit from—sometimes support, and even defend public spaces. Borrowing from this rich tradition of scholarship, we consider changes in the urban environment via its public spaces, the work located within them, the ways people play, build communities, and make lives for themselves here. Much of the recent changes in New York's public spaces originate from the profound economic and demographic dislocation of deindustrialization. New York's deindustrialization really began with the post war era. Years before globalization, technological advances, including containerization, robbed New York's waterfront of some thirty thousand jobs from the 1950s to the 1970s (Freeman 1990; Levinson 2008). In 1966, the Brooklyn Naval Yard closed, robbing the city of some sixty thousand jobs (Freeman 2000). In the years to follow, many of these workers found employment at Kennedy Airport, as New York become more and more connected to the world. The shift was significant. "Changes in the waterfront divorced the city from its past," wrote labor historian Joshua Freeman (1990, 164). As ships increasingly docked in New Jersey, sailors stopped even coming to the city to work, linger, or loiter, leaving the city without a presence dating back to the earliest settlements in the city. "By the 1970s, much of New York's glorious waterfront lay abandoned," Freeman continued. "Decaying piers on Manhattan's West Side routinely burnt up in spectacular fires. Some docks were used as parking lots, others as bus barns and sanitation department garages. A few served as impromptu sunbathing decks" (164–65). Chapter 4 of this work considers the ways a different set of communities reoccupied abandoned piers on Manhattan's West Side.

Still, people continued to come to New York in search of industrial work. Throughout this period, a "generation of blacks and Latins were conscientiously following the American immigrant model—just when the American immigrant–industrial city was crumbling," Marshall Berman (2007, 17) notes. The new arrivals sometimes had difficulty finding jobs or bank loans to support their neighborhoods. Redlining increased, furthering a capital crisis draining resources from neighborhoods inhabited by minorities (Wilder 2000). Streets and buildings in the Bronx began to disintegrate in front of the world's eyes.

By the early 1970s, the post war business-labor accord, in which business agreed to compensate workers in exchange for labor stability, began to crumble. And the fiscal crisis witnessed a rebellion against the city's social democratic polis. "If we don't take action now, we will soon see our own demise," a New York financier confessed during a closed door meeting of business executives in 1973. "We will evolve into another social democracy" (quoted in Moody 2007, 17). Fearing New York City was becoming a European model welfare state with budgets and entitlements too generous for their liking, New York's bankers, business elite, and Governor Rockefeller pulled the plug, turned right, and sketched a path for the city's neoliberal rebirth. To pull off their coup, New York's business elite built on a series of financial crises.

In the years after 1968 and more intensely after 1972, a well-connected elite comprised of a triumvirate of America's social upper classes, corporate communities, and policy formation organizations called for a shift in direction for US social policy. An oil embargo, cheap foreign labor and goods, and a business downturn had all reduced the dominance of the United States within the world economy, resulting in diminished profits for US companies. While business leaders had once considered social welfare policies an effective means to co-opt social movements and keep the labor force literate, healthy, and productive, by the early 1970s, these same corporate leaders began to reconsider this view. Many in the business community felt these social policies helped cultivate movements that destabilized power hierarchies in the United States (Abramowitz. 2000). "It's clear to me that the entire structure of our society is being challenged," argued David Rockefeller in 1971 (quoted in Moody 2007, 17). With the export of jobs abroad, business interest in the health and safety of US workers began to diminish. Business leaders formed a coalition with the increasingly influential new right. Together, this elite class lobbied to restrict policies which: 1) created jobs for the unemployed, 2) made health and welfare policies more generous, and 3) helped employees gain greater workplace protections (Domhuff 1998). The years to follow brought a series of social and economic policies, which redistributed income upward, cheapened the cost of labor, shrunk social programs, weakened the influence of social movements, and limited the role of the federal government (Abramovitz 2000).

By 1975, the crisis reached its apex in New York. While pensions, substantive municipal wages, unions, and social diversity were not unusual, "among American cities, only New York was broke," notes Robert Fitch (1993, viiv). "As the recession gathered pace, the gap between revenues and outlays in the New York City budget increased" (Harvey 2005, 45). Banks initially planned to honor New York's debt, but Harvey notes, "in 1975 a powerful cabal of investment bankers (led by Walter Wriston at Citibank) refused to roll over the debt and pushed the city into technical bankruptcy" (45). (Three and a half decades later, Citigroup was more than willing to take in over fifty billion dollars from the Troubled Asset Relief Program when banks faced their own fiscal crisis [CBO 2010]. But we're getting ahead of ourselves.)

The city formed a Municipal Assistance Corporation (MAC) in 1975. "Its the fucking blacks and Puerto Ricans. They use too many city services and they don't pay any taxes," a spokesman for MAC explained at the time. "New York's in trouble because it's got too many fucking blacks and Puerto Ricans" (quoted in Fitch 1993, vii). Every crisis requires its scapegoats. So the city scripted a model of "planned shrinkage" to rid its streets of undesirables.[2] "Our urban system is based on the theory of taking the peasant and turning him into an industrial worker," New York Housing Commissioner Roger Starr, one of the plan's architects argued. "Now there are no industrial jobs" (quoted in Fitch 1993, viii).

Marshall Berman was teaching at City College at the time. "[M]any of the elites whose power was supposed to protect us against predators identified with the predators. They polarized the city into us and them," Berman remembers. "Starr's idea for dealing with the fiscal crisis was to divide the city's population into a 'productive' majority that deserved to be saved and an 'unproductive' minority that should be driven out" (22). Planned shrinkage would "strive to eliminate not bad individuals but bad neighborhoods" (Ibid.).

The MAC formed an austerity plan to flatline wages, reduce welfare services, and curtail the influence of unions in exchange for federal aid. Its business leaders started organizing to create an economy based around finances, insurance, real estate (FIRE) rather than industrial jobs. "The bail out that followed entailed the construction of new institutions that took over the management of the city budget," Harvey (2005, 45) continued. "They had first claim on tax revenues in order to first pay off bondholders: whatever was left was paid to essential services." The net result included a wage and hiring freeze, service and hiring cuts, and new fees for services, including tuition at City University for the first time. (Ibid.). Subways services declined. "The results could be seen on every street and in every institution of working class New York" (Freeman 2000, 270).

Most of the advances, which working class New Yorkers had helped create, including a thriving public sector, would be lost. The federal government was able to get back most all of the loans provided to New York City with Ford's signing of the Seasonal Financing Act of 1975. In retrieving the money, the lenders "strip[ped] the city government, the municipal labor movement, and working-class New York of much of the power they had accumulated over the previous three decades" (Ibid.). Those workers who could fit into the post industrial workforce would be welcomed. Those who could not would have a hard time maintaining a life in the city. "We have balanced the budget on the backs of the poor," Felix Rohaytn, of the MAC, candidly confessed, as the crisis waned (quoted in Berman 2007, 24). New York would not be the same.

Many observers argue that New York's mid-1970s social and economic transformation served as a dress rehearsal for the neoliberal reorganization of government and politics set in motion with Thatcher, Reagan, Clinton, and Bush (Moody 2007). In this way, the chain of events served as an example of what the neoliberal economics of the next two decades would look like. "The management of the New York fiscal crisis pioneered the way for neoliberal practices both domestically under Reagan and internationally through the IMF in the 1980s," Harvey explained. "It established the principle that in the event of a conflict between the integrity of financial institutions and bondholders' returns, on the one hand, and the well-being of citizens on the other, the former was to be privileged." The crisis established the new precedent that government policy was best aimed "to create a good business climate rather than look to the needs and well-being of the population at large" (Harvey 2005, 48).

New York was a significant candidate for this project. As much a part of the world as the States, New York and its business elite were profoundly influenced by global trends. Their response to the fiscal crisis can be understood as the financial elite protecting their investment in New York's financial sector (Moody 2007). "This amounted to a coup by the financial institutions against the democratically elected government of New York City, and it was every bit as effective as the military coup that had earlier occurred in Chile," argued David Harvey (2005, 45–46). Within this new battle, wealth moved from the middle classes back into the hands of elites. And the world learned a simple, brutal lesson from New York's experience: "[W]hat was happening to New York could and in some cases will happen to them" (Ibid.). "The fiscal crisis constituted a critical moment in the history of privatization, spreading the belief that the market could better serve the public than the government, that government was an obstacle to social welfare rather than an aid to it," wrote Joshua Freeman (2000, 272). "[T]he corporate world, if left alone, would maximize the social good," (Ibid.). "They seized the opportunity to restructure it in ways that suited their agenda," (Harvey 2005, 47). "Because New York served as the standard-bearer for urban liberalism and the idea of a welfare state, the attacks on its municipal services and their decline helped pave the way for the national conservative hegemony of the 1980s and 1990s" (Freeman 2000, 272).

This trend has been described as "neoliberalizing urbanism," notes sociologist Alex Vitale. "Uneven development inherent in neoliberal entrepreneurial economic development strategies favor concentrated capital at the expense of the poor and middle classes" (2008, 14). And social inequality expands. "Urban development creates social polarization which leads to a large underclass, who in turn must be socially and spatially restricted from newly developed spaces," (Ibid.). Hence the impetus to control, police, segregate, privatize, and overdevelop urban public space. Fixated on "the city's land use and value, taxing and spending priorities, and general business climate," New York's highly integrated business "complex" focused on maximizing the profitability of New York City's redevelopment in the years after the crisis (Moody, 27). "Nowhere in the country is land so valuable as in New York City," Moody elaborated. "And virtually all the components of the corporate headquarters complex have a deep interest in these values" (17). New York's urban neoliberalism found expression in policies and policing approaches aimed at maximizing social control of public spaces, including, "closed-circuited video surveillance systems, anti-homeless laws, and gated communities" (Vitale 2008 25). They were basically "responses to a social crisis" that the business elite helped orchestrate (Ibid., 24).

In *Remaking New York*, William Sites (2003) argues the use of state powers to redistribute resources away from the poor towards elite interests serves as a form of "primitive globalization." This concept echoes Marx's "primitive accumulation," in which the state distributes large portions of capital into the hands of a small elite few. Primitive accumulation is Marx's description for the crude concentration of wealth, which takes place in capitalist economic development. "The basis of the whole process," Marx explains, is a violent, coercive use of force by the state to displace the peasantry from lands where they have worked, followed by "bloody legislation" used to regulate the consequences of jarring separations from traditional ways of life. The beggars and vagrants tend to bear the brunt of the process (Sites 2003, 13). Skipping ahead from feudalism to mercantilism to the present era's transition into cross border economic integration, Sites argues today's mode of *primitive globalization* follows a similar pattern of reactive politics. Ad hoc corporate welfare policies and business subsidies displace the urban poor as the state dismantles the welfare state safeguards, while displacing the poor. Vitale

(Photo by Caroline Shepard.)

A hot August day in 1987, under the Brooklyn Bridge. (Photo by Caroline Shepard.)

concurs, "The entrepreneurial pursuit of centralized corporate economic development strategies therefore are responsible for the rise of the new urban underclass that has destabilized urban neighborhoods and public spaces," (2008, 26).

"On the one side, neoliberal housing and employment markets were increasing the numbers of people who were displaced and homeless," Frances Fox Piven succinctly explained (quoted in Vitale, 2008). "The failure of government on all levels to regulate the market forces driving this development, or to intervene to provide alternatives for the people affected, meant that people coped as they always have." This included sleeping outside, supporting themselves within a black market economy, peddling for cash, and of course self-medicating before another night on the mean streets. Piven concludes, "These behaviors in turn created popular political support for the coercive social controls that came to characterize city policy in the nineties. But neither the homeless nor the public were responsible for the limited alternatives which drove this mean result."

Yet, there is another side to this story. Resistance to neoliberal social controls comes in countless forms. Part of the story of New York's recovery includes the efforts of those who helped organize against the grinding forces

As more and more people found themselves displaced from their homes, the city's parks and public spaces became filled with those who had nowhere else to lay down their bodies. This was certainly the case in Tompkins Square Park in the 1980s when Tompkins Square Park Riot photographer Clayton Patterson took this photo.

of neoliberalism and the hypercontrol of public space. Marshall Berman writes about the ways his students, neighbors, and citizens in New York City resisted the patterns of spatial displacement, redlining, and disintegration, which characterized life during and after the fiscal crisis. With public spaces up for grabs, new art forms—including hip hop and graffiti—brought a range of colors to the panorama of New York's public spaces. Throughout the 1970s, graffiti artists, "developed a vibrant new visual language," Berman recalled. "They made themselves in a drab and disintegrating environment, and infused that environment with a youthful exuberance, bold designs, adventurous graphics." Eclectic and optimistic, urban space in New York also became a site for joyous improvisation—"some playful and insouciant, other existentially desperate; some projecting spontaneous overflows of powerful feeling" (Berman, 26).

Berman, who taught about the interconnections between Marxism and modernism, remembers the first time he saw a DJ spin records at his school. "It was the late '70's, during club hours, somebody would bring out turn tables and a DJ would scratch and collage dozens of records together while kids in the audience took turns playing MC, rapping over an open mike" (27). The result was a dance party ideally situated for the streets and sidewalks of

Graffiti, East Village, 1988. (Photo by Caroline Shepard.)

New York's public commons. Berman was particularly excited about the do-it-yourself ethos of these efforts by students, many whom could not afford music lessons. In between scratches and samples, they brought to the creation of both a new "music povera" and by extension an urban culture of resistance. Between the graffiti and hip-hop, Berman recognized signs of regeneration among the rubble of burning buildings. Berman muses:

> Their voices became the voice of New York Calling. . . . Their capacity for soul making in the midst of horror gave the whole city a brand new aura, a weird but marvelous bank of bright lights. They, and all New York with them, succeeded in the task that Hegel defined for modern man just 200 years ago: if we can "look the negative in the face and live with it," then we can achieve a truly "magical power" and "convert the negative into being" (29)

In the decades following the crisis, residents continued to cope with an ongoing attack on the public sector.

Many of these changes were first seen in New York's public spaces. Here, tolerance for the displaced masses wore thin. "The backlash against the socially marginal in New York began with the increased social disorder of the 1970's," notes Vitale. Compounding the issue, the 1972 Supreme Court decision in Papachristou v. Jacksonville, declared vagrancy ordinances unconstitutionally vague. Shop owners were no longer able to arrest loiterers. And the iconic image of a homeless man in front of a Madison Avenue department store became a sign of a city which leaned too heavily on the side of civil liberties rather than order. "Squeegee men, panhandlers, and people sleeping in public spaces came to be the most visible symptoms of an urban environment that many people felt was out of control" (Vitale 2008, 70).

As the cracks in social safety grew, those locked out of the new global economy flooded the streets. "[P]ublic spaces throughout these cities became gathering places for the newly dispossessed," Vitale continues. "Homeless people, unemployed youth, and others excluded from regular participation in housing and labor markets became an omnipresent visible statement about the condition of losers in the new global economy" (102).

While New York has traditionally been viewed as a liberal town, by the mid-1980s, a pro-development ethos came to supersede all other political regimes. It would continue to define governing coalitions in New York (Sites 1997). After the crisis years of the 1970s, "The creation of a 'good business climate' was a priority" (Harvey 2005, 47). "This meant using public resources to build appropriate infrastructures for business." Part of this infrastructure included increased police forces. And gradually, a liberal emphasis on prevention of social problems waned in favor of a get-tough approach. During the Koch and Dinkins administrations, neighborhood and business groups pushed the city to utilize order maintenance modes of policing (Vitale, 2008, 117). The trend was built into a very architecture of the city.

Take Donald Trump's Trump Tower. Completed in 1983, this fifty-eight-story skyscraper drew widespread praise. By its very nature, it embodied a model of exclusion. "To gain the right under zoning regulations to build a larger structure, he put a shopping plaza in Trump Tower with an indoor waterfall and even more marble, this time pink," notes Joshua Freeman (1990, 293). This included an atrium billed as public space few social outsiders ever access. While the space was hailed as the "epitome of Sophistication, the atrium merely brought the suburban shopping mall to New York, as the city stopped setting trends and began playing catch up" (293). Trump Tower would serve as a harbinger of New York's suburbanized, gated future (Hammett and Hammett 2007).

In the years to follow, space in New York became a site in a class war between those who lived, worked, and played in public and those who sought to control, curtail, and privatize this space. Shortly after his election as mayor in 1993, Giuliani's police chief William Bratton released a blueprint for policing focused on reclaiming New York's public spaces from the presence of the impoverished, the poor, and other social outsiders (Smith 1996; Vitale 2008). This involved a "broken windows" style of policing that included no tolerance for the smallest of infractions, profiling, stop-and-frisk policing of those who fit certain police profiles, flexible deployment, and the ongoing genera-tion of new rules and regulations all combining to create micromanaged public space (Vitale 2008, 121). "[A]uthorities responded by criminalizing whole communities of impoverished and marginalized populations," observed David Harvey (2005, 48). "The victims were blamed, and Giuliani was to claim fame by taking revenge on the increasingly affluent Manhattan bour-geoisie tired of having to confront the effects of such devastation on their own doorsteps" (ibid.). Critics noted that the underside of "quality of life" policing was increased police brutality and social control (McArdle and Erzen 2001; Levitt 2009; Sites 2003). Recent histories of police violence in New York City dedicate considerable attention to this aggressive policing approach (Johnson 2003; Levitt 2009).

Giuliani opponents would note that Mayor Giuliani's Quality of Life Cam-paign hinged on his definition of quality-of-life. Few suggested their own def-inition included:

> Community gardens bulldozed throughout the five boroughs; community centers auc-tioned off to profit-driven developers; aggressive police intrusion into peaceful assem-blies; thousands of cyclists and pedestrians hit every year; parks rigged with police video cameras; rents soaring (which profits whom?); sanitized chain stores and remote corpora-tions reshaping every neighborhood in their own image.

The broadsheet was written by Reclaim the Streets (RTS), a direct action affinity group of the Lower East Side Collective (LESC)—an influential New York group, whose struggle for public space is chronicled in Part 2 of this book. While Giuliani took a restricted view of public space, RTS suggested there was more to urban citizenship than going to and from work.

The group's goal was to "reinvigorate inner-city public life. Our definition of 'quality of life' does not mean conventional, homogenized, capitalized life, working 80 hours a week to pay the rent. . . We want real, eclectic democracy, not the brand that's being tossed our way." The broadsheet argued that open public space was a vital ingredient of democratic life. "The Mayor's campaign has been combined with efforts to privatize public spaces . . . already in short supply. If Giuliani is successful, his vision of a whitewashed, Disneyfied New York . . . will replace the diverse, exuberant, exciting New York of the pres-ent." It was time for those left out of the three-decades of fiscal restructuring and the more-recent mayoral quality-of-life politics to reassert their right to the city. "Help us counteract Giuliani's 'Quality of Life' campaign by celebrat-ing the real quality of life in New York with an all-inclusive, fun, takeover of Astor Place—after all, if we can't dance, its not a revolution!" Inserting play into the struggle for public space, RTS called for a return of the dispossessed for their first street action in 1998. "We hope to fill Astor Place with all those 'undesirables' that have come (or will soon come) under attack of Giuliani's homogenizing vision. *We need you to be there.*"

Over the next decade, a class war between the DIY (do-it-yourself) ethos, described by Berman, Lefebvre, and Reclaim the Streets and the neoliberal urbanism of Giuliani and Bloomberg became more pronounced. At the center of the conflict was a question about public space. *The Beach Beneath the Streets* highlights the struggle within the city between those who seek to enjoy and those who seek to control its public spaces. "New York City feels like a very different place today," Marshall Berman concludes in his introduction to *New York Calling*. Thirty years after Roger Starr's planned shrinkage, the city is more diverse than ever. "It is more saturated with immigrants, more ethnically diverse and multicultural than it has ever been, more like a microcosm of the whole world," Berman (2007) explains. "[A]nd thanks to New York's distinctively configured public space, you can see this whole world right out there on the streets. Its mode of multiculturalism is sexy—and threatening to the ultra orthodox in every religion" (32). Perhaps this is why the Giulianis of the world have sought to curtail and contain the abundance of its public spaces.

As even this brief review of recent New York history suggests, efforts to understand the threats and alterations to public space can benefit from the comparison to change in the economic and political sphere. For while the study of capitalism has identified a series of historical eras and forms, the study of space is much younger. One could view the transformation of public space as involving a single shift from public to private. But such a description would oversimplify the situation. If one links these transformations to shifts in economic and political power, a richer picture takes shape. Just as capitalists reinvent social relations in a series of historically identifiable periods—so that, for instance, for some decades capitalists built cities, then they disinvested from them, today they are selectively reinvesting in them again—so threats to public space have changed over time, from efforts to privatize space entirely, to designs that selectively filter it, to spaces that fully exclude and displace less privileged potential users. Thus, rather than bemoaning public space as something that existed in ideal form and which the public now risks having taken from it, it is useful to see the transformation of public space in the same way transformations to capitalism are understood. Public space faces an evolving threat, as the objectives of various actors who do not support or protect its public character change over time in response to their own material and social needs.

Defining Public Space

Though the term is only thirty years old, the definitions of *public* space are as varied, shifting, imprecise, and contradictory as any. Steven Carr and the other authors of *Public Space* provide a comprehensive definition of *pure* public space as "responsive, democratic and meaningful," places that

protect the rights of user groups. They are accessible to all groups and provide for freedom of action but also for temporary claim and ownership. A public space can be a
place to act more freely. . . . Ultimately, public space can be changed by public action,
because it is owned by all. . . . In public space, people can learn to live together. (Carr et
al. 1992, 19–20)

Similarly, Lewis Dijkstra suggests public space be classified according to three
criteria: that it be used by all (highlighting the issue of control), be accessible
by all (that is, how exclusive it is), and that it have a history for all (Dijkstra
2000; Orum and Neal 2010, 1).

These definitions avoid legalistic characterizations of public space ("gov-
ernment-owned property to which the public has access," for instance) that
are too narrow to be useful in an era of public-private partnerships. In a landmark ruling that has long disturbed First Amendment and public space advocates, the Supreme Court ruled in *Pruneyard v. Robins* (1980) that shopping
malls are not public spaces but private ones. Yet, for many people, they are
the most frequent site of public interaction. Rather than ignore malls, advocates have included them in their examination of contemporary public spaces.
In doing so, they have challenged the court's conception and argued that free
speech rights should be better protected there (as they are in some states).
Similarly, a legalistic definition would simply eliminate from consideration a
"public" space whose management or ownership had been transferred into
private hands, rather than generate questions about how such changes
affected the space.

A third understanding involves the intimate connection between notions
of public space, civil society, and democracy. It builds on De Toqueville's
arguments that democracy in the United States thrives to the extent that it
mediates between three distinct sectors of national life: government, the
market, and civil society in between. Thus, without community space, there
can be no democracy (Shepard 2002). Without public space, there is little
hope for community change or renewed civic engagement. Warner's (2002)
conception of a "counter public" used by those excluded by barriers to the
public sphere builds on this recognition.

A fourth conception of public space involves notions of a public sector.
Joshua Freeman (1990) describes such space as "social democracy." Such
public spaces are supported by public policies, which assume a commitment
to public education, health, housing, and social welfare provisions (Daniel
2000). In an era of a dwindling welfare state, such a sector is increasingly
embattled (Harvey 2005). Yet, critics argue the decline of neoliberalism opens
up space for resurgence of a public sector. Tensions over the privatization of
this sector inspire a range of social movements (Klein 2003).

Because so much of what is experienced as "public" space is in fact carefully controlled by private interests (and is not, therefore, "owned by all," and

cannot be "changed by public action"), we use a broader definition, based on how people experience a given space. Public spaces are places in which a range of people can interact with other people they don't necessarily know, and in which they can engage in a range of public and private activities— though both the users and the uses are inevitably limited. This conception incorporates spaces like malls, parks, and plazas built around retail space— including both spaces that approximate the ideal of public space and that thumb their noses at it.

Paradoxically, for public spaces, which are celebrated for being inclusive and accommodating, the sources of control of the space and the nature of exclusion from the space are what differentiate and define any public space. Just as important, what brings most of these users together, and what carves the space out as public and liberating, is something just as familiar to the wielders of giant political puppets at the rally as to the kids coming down the sliding board: play and public performance. The ludic, joyful, temporarily uninhibited physical engagement with the space itself is both an opportunity to act out one's identity and life and a means to declare and expand the boundaries of accepted behavior. It is an opportunity to explore and experiment with reality, identity, and possibility. At its core, play is truly free activity (Huizinga 1950; Shepard 2009; Shepard 2011; Winnicott 1971).

As play serves as a distinct countervailing force to the privatization of public space, a brief review of the concept is useful. For many, play is viewed as a resource with many applications for social movement activity. Our interest is in its capacity to aid social actors in eluding social controls and reimagining social relations. At its most basic level, play is an intuitive performance in freedom. The meanings of such performances take countless permutations. In the face of duress, social movement activity is perhaps most useful in helping social actors cultivate and support communities of resistance. Here, these new communities support social actors in engaging power rather than cowering in the face of often insurmountable political opponents. Within its very opposition to worlds of work, linear thinking, and social order, play subverts much of the logic of neoliberal urbanism (Shepard 2009: Shepard 2011).

To make sense of these shifting uses, we employ an autoethnographic approach, integrating both participant observation and theoretical understanding in order to cultivate an understanding of play in public space within a series of current social movements (see Butters 1983; Hume and Mulock 2004; Juris 2007; Lichterman 2002; Tedlock 1991). This lens takes increasing shape in Part 2. In contrast, Part 1 utilizes a mixed methodology—including interviews, field observations, and quantitative analysis—to consider class-based exclusivity versus democratic inclusion in public space.

Most importantly for students of public space, the parameters in which authentic play takes shape often extend beyond the boundaries of public and private space, where social norms find themselves in flux. While the English

Diggers failed to hold St. George's Hill in 1649, "what these outcasts of Cromwell's New Model Army did hold dear was the community created in their act of resistance; it was a scale model of the universal brotherhood they demanded in the future" (Duncombe 2002a, 17). Play is an ingredient in which to mix people and communities.

There are many forms of play, including the famous Diggers' land occupation or drag ACT UP zaps, the use of food and mariachi bands in Latino communities, dance dramaturgy, culture jamming, the carnival, and other forms of creative community-building activities. It is the exhilarating feeling of pleasure, the joy of building a more emancipatory, caring world. For Richard Schechner (2002), play involves doing something that is not exactly "real." It is "double edged, ambiguous, moving in several directions simultaneously" (79).

While there are any number of ways to conceptualize play, most studies begin with Johan Huizinga's *Homo Ludens: a Study of the Play Element in Culture*, a work which has inspired social movement players for decades. His definition encompasses many of the threads established in this opening discussion. These include the conception of play as "a free activity standing quite consciously outside the ordinary life as being 'not serious,' but at the same time absorbing the player intensely and utterly." He continues that play "promises the formation of social groupings which tend to surround themselves with secrecy and to stress their difference from the common world by disguise or other means." For Huizinga, play is anything but serious (5). It is a space for "free activity." When play takes place in public space, it often takes on a subversive character. Afterall, play offers the possibility for improvisation and imagination.

Overview

As Margaret Kohn suggests, the value of public spaces is twofold (Kohn 2004). Lively, varied public space is vital to society—not only for its democratic value as an incubator of tolerance for difference and as a stage for organized political action, but in its everyday role as a site for the kind of social interaction that permits individuals to conceive of their participation in a society. Activists have already recognized that for space to continue to serve these vital functions, its pubic quality must be recognized and defended.

To that end, we recognize that the concept of public space is actually made up of many types of space of varying degrees of publicness and inclusivity (or, as we stress, "privateness and exclusivity"), and identify those different types. By doing so, we can better understand the changes that have taken place in public spaces of the city in tandem with the economic restructuring of New York, recognize how certain types of spaces are of value to communities and activists, and consider how activists' strategies that make use of public space are unique.

The book is organized in two parts to consider two elements of a spatial dialectic of *repression* and *resistance*. The first part examines repression in the control of public space by looking at the series of strategies elites developed to exclude people from privately owned public spaces. We see that the transition from one strategy to another is closely tied to changes in the political economy, particularly the landmarks of the 1975 financial crisis and the reorganization of public space under Giuliani. The advance of these elite approaches to controlling public space help explain the growing attention by activists to defending spaces. The second part of the book explores resistance in public space—using case studies to explore the rationale, strategies, and value of mobilizations that are both located in public space and address public space issues. From the attention elites give to restrictive control of public space and that activists give to liberating those spaces, it is clear that actors from a range of perspectives recognize the power of public spaces to shape the lives, behavior, and the social organization of people who use them. As Harvey suggests, there is both a reality and awareness of the influential social role of space: "Spatial and temporal practices are never neutral in social affairs. They always express some kind of class or other social content, and are more often than not the focus of intense social struggle" (Harvey 1990, 239). Our book seeks to make that struggle apparent and offer examples of ways people have joined it. Afterall, the flip side of control is a form of ludic activity designed to resist control mechanisms.

The first chapter presents the typology of public spaces we use to understand the relationship between repression and resistance. In particular, we distinguish among privately controlled spaces the following three types: *privatized, filtered, and suburban* spaces. In response to efforts at social control, activists fashion and defend what we describe as *community* space and spaces of "temporary autonomous zones," or *TAZ* spaces, and embrace the ideal public space, *popular spaces*. Each subsequent chapter examines in terms of repression and resistance these types to understand how New York's public spaces have developed and evolved. Contrary to earlier accounts—which suggested that space takes shape incidental to other objectives, shaped more by aesthetic fashion, budget constraints, or whimsy rather than as part of a spatial strategy of social control (Frampton 1980; Wolf 1981)—we argue public space is an important location politically in part because it is so highly contested.

Chapters 2 and 3 examine the city's public/private office plazas (called "bonus plazas") to demonstrate how these barren, unusable examples of *private* and *filtered* space are not unintended failures but the very goal of elite developers who took a close interest in their design. Here, influential city decision makers seek to control and influence space for their own social ends just as earnestly as activists seek to open up and liberate space for more public purposes. Chapter 3 explores the implications of elites' interest in public space. As structural speculators, major developers model in their plazas not the city as it is, but the city as they expect it to become. As a result, public space of the past is a clear indicator of the shapes cities would take. At present, they reflect the *suburban* spaces of the present and near future. Having established the progression of repressive public space design, we go on to examine the strategies of play and resistance in public space.

Chapter 4 examines one kind of space foreclosed by shifts in the organization of public space. This ethnographic account considers the Hudson River piers, which served for decades as a *community* space for queer communities. This story details the plight of those struggling to find a place to call home, as public space shifts and evolves (Davey 1995). Through effective organizing by FIERCE! (Fabulous Individuals for Education, Radical, Community Empowerment), homeless queer youth have countered the hypercontrol of their space and have become a constituency, while democratizing access to public space itself. Chapter 5 presents another ethnographic account of a distinct event in the history of struggles for public space: the first action in New York by international public-space group Reclaim the Streets. Building on this movement, the sixth chapter highlights ways struggles for public space are intricately involved with struggles to support convivial spaces such as gardens. This chapter involves stories of campaigns by groups, such as the More Gardens! coalition, Time's Up!, and the Radical Homosexual Agenda and their campaigns to preserve public space for those at the margins.

Chapter 7 highlights innovative uses of play among users to redefine terms of debate about access to a contested public space: the bike lanes running throughout the city. The community narratives highlighted in Chapters 6 and 7 offer images of ways regular people can stake a claim and successfully build the components necessary to oppose privatizing, filtered, suburban spaces and instead create healthy communities—with Critical Mass bike rides, neighborhood meeting spaces, bike advocacy, community gardens, and community centers. The book concludes with a question posed by Woody Guthrie, which winds its way throughout the volume: is this land really made for you and me, or someone else?

Building on this question, the study of public space can properly embrace the dialectic relationship between the series of assaults on public space by private interests, and the resistance that these maneuvers stimulate, by which community activists build community spaces, use TAZ spaces, and celebrate the capacity of popular spaces to create alternatives to privately controlled space. The energy of urban public space is so great as to make physically palpable the gut-wrenching threat of private interests' dominance in the creation, gentrification, and management of public spaces. But that energy communicates just as viscerally the thrilling potential of user- and publicly-controlled spaces. By understanding the relationship of both the forces of private and public control, advocates and defenders of public space can more readily specify the threats their communities have faced from private control of spaces in the past forty years, and better define the varied kinds of public spaces they need.

As the studies demonstrate, honest and engaged examinations of public space hold the dual promises of identifying the latest threats to democratic freedom through authoritarian control of public space, and identifying the most dynamic strategies to reclaim that liberty.

It is clear that something is happening in the streets and plazas of modern America. And this reflects how we think about citizenship. Without public spaces, many would argue that talk about democracy goes out the window (Ferrell 2001). Yet, access to public space is increasingly restricted. What are the meanings of barriers to access to public space? And what will become of movements for social change if they are excluded from physical access to public spaces, and by extension, a public commons for debate? After all, if you can't walk in the street, can you be considered a citizen? (Ribey 1998). Understanding the social actors who install such barriers, and identifying movements that challenge them, are important steps to nurturing the social component at the core of the democratic potential of a city like New York.

CHAPTER ONE

Seeing Space Through Exclusion and Control

Public space is firmly on the map for activists and academics alike. After a long period when attention to space flagged in the social sciences, researchers now increasingly consider how spaces shape the social relations that take place in them, while community groups both use space as a forum to enact their politics, and set battles over space at the top of their agenda.

Theorists in the last thirty years have built on the insights of Marxist geographers, from the work of Henri Lefebvre to its elaboration by David Harvey and Edward Soja, to construct a critical understanding of the role of space (Lefebvre 1974; Harvey 1990; Soja 1989). Increasingly, urban social science research requires consideration of how space shapes the social phenomena being studied (Gans 2002; Gieryn 2000). These developments accompany the burgeoning interest in public space that developed in the work of Jane Jacobs (1961) and William H. Whyte (1988). Critics of corporatization and global capital unified these two long-running threads of attention to the social role of space and the importance of public space in their warnings about the encroaching privatization of public space (Klein 2002).

This attention has been matched recently by activists' orientation towards questions of space in their work. Community groups strategize both about how to use public space as a setting for their actions and about how achieving changes to public space is a central goal (Duncombe 2002). Issues that were formerly described in terms of other "durable inequalities" (Tilly 1999) such as race or class are strategically framed in terms of space. In this vein, activists at the World Social Forum have drafted a World Charter for the Right to the City that recognizes access to urban space as a fundamental requirement for democracy, equity, and social justice (World Urban Forum 2004). Already existing issues are being reconceptualized in spatial terms. Thus, activists recently heralded the broadcast of a documentary called "Unnatural Causes—Is Inequality Making us Sick?" that showed "where you live affects how you live" (Thompson 2008). The topic, health care disparities, has already been framed in race, class, and gender terms, but to these, the group added a spatial framing. Nationally, the Right to the City Alliance has framed the fight for "housing, education, health, racial justice and democracy" in the language used by defenders of democratic public space (Mitchell 2003). Meanwhile, attention to public space has generated new political claims—as groups such as Reclaim the Streets use their analysis of space and repression both to fashion resistance and create and preserve community in the face of global, corporate disruption and predation. In these ways and more, academics and activists have increasingly recognized the importance of public space and claimed such spaces as the cradle of democratic ideals, the victim of capitalist conquest and backlash, and the stage on which popular forces resist elite conquest of public space and democratic society.

Interest in public space has focused on two critical social processes that go on there: *repression* and *resistance*. Studies of the repressive trends in public space identify increasingly restrictive policing practices, privatization and corporatization of public spaces, and the replacement of more diverse, public spaces with narrowly tailored spaces of consumptions (Vitale 2008; Zukin 1995; Berman 2006). Documentation of resistance in public space has looked at urban activists' creative, if temporary, reclamation of increasingly privatized space through street actions, dance parties, bike events, squatting, raves, and more (McKay 1998).

Given the growth in attention to public space, there is considerable need for a conceptualization of public space multifaceted enough to encompass and relate patterns of repression to strategies of resistance. This chapter presents a typology of different kinds of public space that provides a means for understanding both the process of controlling public spaces, and the purpose of resistance.

The typology of public space presented here and developed throughout the rest of the book aims to achieve three things. First, organizing such a typology of public space allows us to situate and relate the diverse work already done on public space, from the privatization and loss of space to the radical seizure and reclaiming of space. It replaces a binary distinction between only public and private space with a much more variegated typology of public space that, while recognizing the dangers of privatization, simultaneously recognizes that co-opted public spaces can take many forms, and that people and communities need a more diverse range of types of space than a single, ideal public form.

Second, identifying the predominance of different types of public space in different periods of the last forty years of the city's history presents a narrative about the evolution of the threats to public space, replacing a single-directional "privatization" narrative with an account of consecutive spatial regimes. Elite efforts to control public space have shifted from efforts to privatize it and exclude everyone, to designs that filter space to facilitate gentrification, to more subtle exercises of power today that segregate spaces. The recognition of different types of privately controlled space rectifies, for instance, claims that public space was being utterly eliminated with studies of how it is more subtly being "mallified," commercialized, and filtered (Davis 1990; Kohn 2004, Sennett 1992, Flusty 1995). This allows more accurate identification of the challenges to public space.

Third, these typologies identify the terrain on which activists challenge elite claims on space. In studying this resistance, we highlight the importance of ludic responses to the control of public spaces. Precisely because of the spatial orientation of much activism today and the centrality of play to strategies that challenge repressive reorganizations of space, we find that play has become a valuable part of activist strategies.

Articulating Problems and Types of Public Space

Space is best analyzed in terms of two aspects often considered in studies of public space. The problem with public space, authors like Edward Soja, David Harvey, Mike Davis, Sharon Zukin, Michael Sorkin and others argue is that it is increasingly *privately controlled*, and that its use is increasingly restricted, or *exclusive* (Davis 1990; Harvey 1990; Soja 1996; Sorkin 1992; Zukin 1995). As Fran Tonkiss notes, the centrality of these categories is at odds with the idealistic presentation of public space: "The primary *ideal* of public space . . . is based on equality of access. The real life of public spaces, though, suggests that these are not constituted purely in terms of access but also are organized through forms of *control* and *exclusion*" (Tonkiss 2005, 72). These two concerns function as the two axes of a continuum that organizes different kinds of public space in a way that clarifies much of the contemporary discussion, and allows better analysis of actual kinds of public space.

Private Control

Control is a necessary component of public space—without it, a space is an unpredictable no-person's land, clearly unsafe and thus unused. Control can be asserted by public authority, private authority, or by the users of a space. Control is public when it is maintained by some reasonably responsive representative of the people. Public control is fairly represented by the everyday practice of the New York City Parks Department (although they also have treated public parks as private spaces for elite users and funders). Private control, seen in the office plazas studied in Chapter 2, is most often by a private corporation that owns the land on which the space is located, or a public-private authority that operates like a private corporation and is not democratically accountable either formally (its members are not elected), or culturally—the organization, unlike the Parks Department, does not have an established history of considering, representing, and legitimizing the interests of a broad range of the public. Control of a space by the users of that space can take shape as a celebration of grassroots organizing, or a means of parochial exclusion. The source of control is often suggested by, but in practice not synonymous with, ownership or control of the space.

Private or public control is never absolute, but a space is weighted, often quite clearly, in one direction or another. Thus, a generally public space like Central Park is now run by the Central Park Conservancy, which is less public than a city agency. On a day-to-day basis, control of the park remains generally public, so that a maximum of uses are legitimized. For instance, one user had initially been ticketed for eating plants in the park. Today, this use has been legitimized, and he leads tours of the edible plants in Central Park (Kharakh 2007). However, the Conservancy has been criticized for being biased towards the interests of its well-heeled donors, forbidding demonstrations in the park (Hauser and Cardwell 2004a); closing parts of the park for expensive private parties; preferring a reconstruction along the Olmstead plan rather than, say, the equally legitimate but more populist parks renovations by Moses; or maintaining Fifth Avenue flower gardens and all-American baseball diamonds, but deciding not to provide any soccer fields particularly popular with the city's immigrants. Public control and government control are not synonymous. Police control of a space, particularly during an enforcement "blitz" intended to reassert control from a particular category of users, is government control, but is often too restrictive and top-down to be democratic. Police departments do not embody democratic control structurally or culturally (Levitt 2009, McArdle and Erzen 2001). In fact, private control relies on state power to enforce its claim on space, so that different branches of the same government may work to support public or private control of different spaces.

Though discussions of control often focus on public or private control, it is important to recognize that most of the regulation of a space lies in the hands of its users. Though the police can enforce prohibitions against any range of behaviors, most of what we don't do in public space is determined by the social norms and authority of our fellow users. To a critical degree, private owners, state authority, and the police do not keep order in a public space (though the state's threat of violence always lurks in the background). The fact that on any sunny weekend in New York, tens of thousands of nearly naked strangers spend a hot day at the beach together in relative peace, leaving their towels unattended, swimming through the water together, throwing balls, running races, and building empires of sand castles in harmony is testimony to their collective social control, and not the effect of a few dozen lifeguards' whistles.[1] In situations where access to the space is essentially determined by the people who use the space, it becomes user controlled. A block party is controlled by the block, a street corner may be controlled by a tough-looking group of teenagers, the keys to a community garden may be shared amongst the gardeners. In all these cases, users effectively control the space, sometimes making it more accessible, other times using their power to keep others out.

Exclusion

After control, the second axis along which to categorize public space is exclusion. Exclusion occurs when decision makers (that is, people with decision-making control over a space, such as those who plan the form it will initially take, or those who make decisions about its day-to-day management) actively seek to keep people out of a space. Exclusive spaces may unambiguously keep people out, or block "symbolic access" so that use is limited to an entitled few (Carr 1992). Designers have become increasingly sophisticated at developing subtle means of achieving their clients' exclusionary desires. Steven Flusty, for instance, identifies a range of "interdictory" strategies to exclude disenfranchised people from nominally public space. Interdictory strategies are found in public spaces from which decision makers wish to exclude people, including hiding the space from view (stealthy space), or making it accessible only by concealed entrances (slippery space). Designers may exclude with physical gates (crusty space), install railings on walls to prevent seating (prickly space), or litter a plaza with video cameras that make potential users anxious about constant surveillance by authorities (jittery space) (Flusty 1995). Exclusion may be explicit or implicit, including symbols that indicate an indoor mall like Trump Towers or Citigroup Center is for upscale shoppers only, or those advocated by Oscar Newman to identify spaces as resident-controlled and hostile to outsiders. Recognizing exclusion as a fundamental ingredient in the construction of space produces a different concept of the city, which becomes "a site of constant processes of social inclusion and exclusion," in which "unequal power and resources are being translated at a material level" (White 1996, 83). Exclusion shapes public space, and can help define what public space does.

As Tonkiss points out, while the public space ideal celebrates inclusivity, public space is fundamentally organized around control and exclusion. To evaluate public space, writers critical of globalization's effects on the city and others critical of postmodern developments in urban design have both focused on the degree of exclusion in a public space. Such an approach is not only useful to criticize a space's shortcomings. To more broadly understand public spaces and the design of urban space—just as the planning and construction of elite neighborhoods sheds light on residential segregation—the study of exclusion proves to be a valuable approach to understanding public spaces. As the subsequent chapters show, beginning with the study of bonus plazas, exclusion is not an anomaly in public space, but is often one of its defining and constitutive elements. Excluding others can even be the purpose in creating public space.

Despite the concern public space writers have with accessibility, exclusion has not been considered systematically. Writing on public space typically asks that space be "accessible to all."[2] But this expectation disregards one of the things that makes public space distinctive and that requires it be studied on its own in the first place: its distinctly spatial component. Other social structures may be theoretically aspatially accessible, like the justice system, the electoral process, or family structures. But an urban neighborhood park, even a crown jewel of a park, is only practically accessible to people twenty minutes from it. This is no minor point; it means that a park in a homogeneously wealthy county is by its nature not accessible to poor people, and is class segregated. Users of the parks in New York City's downtown Battery Park City neighborhood are more racially and class-homogenous than those of Central Park, simply because of the surrounding neighborhoods. Spaces cannot actually be "accessible to all." Studying the ways in which exclusion is and is not practiced in a space illuminates the space's important social roles.

Types of Public Space

It is therefore more useful to consider different types of exclusion than to define public space as an unattainable ideal. In particular, several questions need to be asked of any set of related spaces: *who* is to be excluded, *how* are they being excluded, and *who* wants to exclude them? Since, even in a single space, there will be divergent answers for each of these questions, this approach demands attention to the different interests of an array of different user groups, while also bringing into consideration those who are prevented or discouraged from using the space. Finally, it identifies the actions that lead to exclusion so that these may be altered if desired. (Regarding who excludes, as the discussion of control suggests, this investigation into exclusion identifies two different sources of exclusion: exclusion by decision makers—those who create, design, own, manage, and control a public space—and exclusion by users.)

Three points along the continuum of exclusion stand out. At opposite ends, there is *total* exclusion (which makes a space usable by almost no one) and *no* exclusion, in which case the barriers to entry have been minimized as much as possible, and the space is presented in a way that symbolically communicates that it is public and all are welcome. In between is *selective* exclusion, in which some people feel welcome and others are either denied entry, discouraged from entering, harassed if they do enter, or feel distinctly uncomfortable while they're there.

Public space can be categorized effectively using the questions of who controls the space, and who is excluded. The result is the typology of public space seen in Figure 1.1. In this way, public spaces studied in this book are distinguished as *privatized, filtered, suburban, community, TAZ, policed, and popular* spaces. These types are located on two continua: of whether *exclusion* is total, partial or minimal, and whether *control* is private, governmental, or by users.[3]

Figure 1.1. Typology of Public Space.

Types of Public Space	Control is by...		
	Private Owners	Current Users	Government
2000 / None	**Suburban** No local exclusion needed in an exclusive neighborhood. (Millennial plazas)	**TAZ** (Temporary Autonomous Zone) Users control space and access. (Very large protests)	**Popular** Users not restricted; diverse uses accommodated. (City parks)
Exclusion Is ... 1975 / Selective	**Filtered** Who uses the space or what activities are permitted is restricted. (Shopping malls)	**Community** Users control who uses the space (Community gardens)	**Policed** Public authorities selectively exclude users or uses (Neighborhood stop and frisks.)
1961 / Total	**Privatized** Goal of decision-maker is to minimize people using the space. (Empty plazas)	**Abandoned** People who could use the space don't. (Beach in winter)	**Utility** Publicly owned but not legally accessible. (Train tracks, highway medians)

The types can be used to illustrate two key processes in New York City. The historical development of bonus plazas from 1961-2000 moved up the left column. In the period of greatest white flight, spaces were initially *privatized*, with the expectation that there would be no users of the spaces whatsoever. By the 1970s, gentrification and re-colonization of the city was foreshadowed by *filtered* spaces that welcomed urban professionals but used design techniques to exclude others. More recently, *suburban* spaces reflected a belief that the core of the city is securely in the hands of corporate professionals, and barriers that formerly kept out those not part of this new economy no longer need to be as pervasive. Instead, exclusion is achieved, as it is in the suburbs, by keeping other social classes at great distance and through stricter police controls.

Under the next two columns, communities and activists have mobilized to defend community space, TAZ space, and popular space, and used them to counter privatizing trends. An outer ring of *policed* space is currently used to insulate lush suburban space from the consequences of contemporary inequality.

Popular Space

Popular space is the ideal advocated by most writers on public space. It mirrors closely the expectations of writers like Carr et al. (1992) and Dijkstra (2000) that the space be, like Hannah Arendt's public realm, "accessible by all." In terms of exclusion and control, popular space is not exclusive (as much as a geographically bounded space can be accessible to a wide range of groups), and it is controlled by public, democratic institutions. Popular spaces include the most usable public parks, places that accommodate a wide variety of users and uses. The most frequently cited popular spaces in New York include Central Park, Prospect Park, and Washington Square among others. Popular spaces represent the ideal type of public space. It is against this type that other kinds of public space are inevitably compared.

Privatized Space

A privatized space is one in which control of the space tends to be more private—that is, managed by an individual or group that does not have an institutional tendency to consider the needs of the broadest range of potential users. The exclusion sought by managers of such spaces is total: the goal is to keep people away from the space, with no distinction as to who those people might be. This union, in one space, of the managers' concern with a narrow group of interests (say, those of building management and tenants only) that leads to a limited number of *uses* in the space, plus simultaneous efforts to minimize the number of *users*, leads to probably the most empty and uninviting category of public space. In fact, privatized spaces would not be public

Privatized Spaces. From left, a plaza is rendered unusable by bags of garbage, spiked rails, and a sunken location. 55 Water Street's vast plaza two stories above ground is accessible via an obscure escalator.

space at all (after all, the description of restricted users and uses would describe the interiors of private buildings, too) if the space were not presented in some way that suggests that the public is supposed to have some claim to the space, but in practical terms does not. For instance, the bonus plaza program used in New York and other cities gives developers economic incentives to provide public plazas. Though they may try to minimize use of the space, such plazas—as unfenced, paved, outdoor spaces, for instance— still appear to the public, correctly, as sites to which they have some legitimate claim. Privatized space generates a palpable resentment with the sense that the space should be more generally accessible. The built form of privately controlled spaces hints at more public uses strongly enough to make public space advocates wish for the broader possibilities of the real thing.

As detailed in Chapter 3, privatized space is closely associated with the 1960s and early 1970s, when the earliest bonus plazas were being built by developers who wanted the incentives offered by the city in exchange for privately owned public spaces, but could see no advantage to providing spaces that were actually usable. The voids of privatized spaces reflected widespread flight from the city.

Filtered Space

By the 1980s, both among the bonus plazas and public spaces in US cities generally, *filtered* spaces became more common. Private developers, sometimes with local government support, had decided it would be profitable or desirable to attract middle- and upper-income whites back to urban areas. To do so, they built more attractive (yet still private) plazas and downtown "festival marketplaces" like Boston's Faneuil Hall. Filtered spaces overtook privatized spaces as the norm for new projects, as developers and other elites began to reverse years of urban flight and decreasing levels of downtown investment (and often disinvestments). During that preceding period, elites expected cities to be little used, abandoned by the upper and middle classes either because of the pull of the suburbs, the push of urban unrest, or unsuitability of the city for modern life. But as Harvey and others show, urban reinvestment began as early as the 1970s and became a significant trend in many cities through the 1980s and 1990s (Harvey 1990). As part of such investment, developers needed public space that was more usable, if selectively so. Thus, architects and planners working for such developers created filtered spaces, designed for certain purposes and certain users.

David Harvey found in Baltimore a clear example of how the ebb and flow of social unrest drove elite financial disengagement and reinvestment, which in turn produced particular forms of public space. First, unrest drove disinvestment. "In US cities, urban spectacle in the 1960s was constituted out of the mass oppositional movements of the time. Civil rights demonstrations, street riots, and inner city uprisings, vast anti-war demonstrations, and countercultural events (rock concerts in particular) were grist for the seething mill of urban discontent that whirled around the base of modernist urban renewal and housing projects" (Harvey 1990, 88). Those modernist urban renewal projects and housing towers reflected that discontent in their plazas, which constituted some of the earliest privatized spaces in the postwar period. But the elite class known as "city builders" (Fainstein 2001) was not satisfied with the defensive posture of privatized space. Shocked by riots, after the 1968 assassination of Martin Luther King, that threatened the investments made in the modernist downtown, a small group of Baltimore politicians and business people sought what Harvey characterized as a "bread and circuses" strategy, replacing strife with a festival atmosphere. Harvey quoted a Department of Housing and Urban Development report that promoted a festival form of public space to encourage a return to the city. "Spawned by the necessity to arrest the fear and disuse of downtown areas caused by the civic unrest of the late 1960s, the Baltimore City Fair was originated . . . as a way to promote urban redevelopment." From the annual fairs, it was a short step to institutionalize the effects of the festival year-round in Harborplace, one of many Rouse Company malls built in the 1980s explicitly designed to provide space for the return of certain groups to the city (whites, middle and upper classes, those who had fled to the suburbs). This social program required a new design program, replacing modernism with a postmodern facade of historicist surfaces and the deceptive festival: "Judged by many an outstanding success (though the impact upon city poverty, homelessness, health care, education provision, has been negligible and perhaps even negative), such a form of development required a wholly different architecture from the austere modernism of the downtown renewal that had dominated in the 1960s. An architecture of spectacle, with its sense of surface glitter and transitory participatory pleasure, of display and ephemerality, of *jouissance*, became essential to the success of a project of this sort" (Harvey 1900, 90–91). Just as changing social objectives for the city required a new aesthetic approach, they required public space that functioned differently. Rather than keeping everyone out of a potentially public space as privatized ones had done, these new spaces were *filtered*. Filtered spaces were designed to welcome the new "pioneers," as they were sometimes called, while excluding people (who were poorer and darker skinned) from whom they had fled in the first place. *Popular* public spaces were unlikely to be created because decision makers were private, and thus were strongly predisposed to create one of the kinds of privately controlled space. Furthermore, according to Graham and Aurugi's paradigm of fear and mallification, people returning to the city were unlikely to feel comfortable in more public urban space (1997).

Planners recognize several techniques by which filtering can be achieved. Filtered spaces often create unequal ease of access. In downtown Manhattan's

Winter Garden Mall, for instance (before the destruction of the World Trade Center), entry by the thirteen thousand suburban commuters who took ferries to the Financial District was almost unavoidable; likewise, those who worked in the World Trade Center had an enclosed pedestrian bridge directly from their complex to the inviting crystal atrium mall they could see below.[4] But entry from street level was almost impossible because standing across the street from the mall, there was no access to the pedestrian bridge, and the single, tiny entrance into the mall was virtually unmarked and invisible. Similar differential levels of access are built into bonus spaces like New York's Citigroup Market, which can serve as a welcoming lobby for workers in the large office tower above, but was recognized by the City Planning Commission as seeming like part of a private office tower to those passing by, deterring use by people who do not feel, for reasons of class or other status, entitled to enter office buildings.

Such spaces, from the Rouse Company's malls forward, sought to filter space in another way, by creating space that was useful almost exclusively to a relatively privileged class. Though Rouse, in projects including Harborplace, Boston's Faneuil Hall, and New York's South Street Seaport made reference to the working-class city, sometimes even appropriating industrial buildings or working-class markets, the renovated space in each of the projects was leased to tenants who would cater to and encourage a clientele of upper–middle-class shoppers looking for novelty food, entertainment, and leisure items, not necessities or more affordable fare. If the retail mix was useful only to either middle- or upper-income shoppers, the space was effectively segregated, or filtered, since poor or working-class people had little reason to go there. Less subtly, retailers filtered by actively making people feel uncomfortable—wealthy whites could feel pampered in Tiffany's jewelry store, but African American and Latino customers were followed, insulted, verbally harassed, and asked to leave, filtering a public accommodation by race (Zukin 2004, 151–57).

Filtered Space. South Street Seaport, like many urban malls by James Rouse and Company in the 1980s, sought to draw the middle class back to the city with novelty shopping experiences, historical architectural references, and entertainment.

Furthermore, filtering strategies could create two parallel environments: one private and exclusive, one public but abandoned by those allowed in the new space. Thus, historian Lizabeth Cohen found that at the same time exclusive suburban malls were being built in New Jersey, shrinking traditional downtown shopping areas continued to cater to the less fortunate clientele left out of mall-builders' target demographic (Cohen 2003). Similarly, Jack Byers found that cities with extensive networks of privately owned elevated walkways (with stores and services available throughout them) did not lose their public street-level retailing; rather this continued to cater to those who felt unwelcome in the walkways above (Byers 1998, 200). Add to such a space the status message conveyed by decor and the careful selection of geographic location, and the effect was to filter out some groups and welcome others nearly as neatly as posting a sign.

Elite city builders stopped relying on privatized spaces, as filtered space proved an effective way to profitably recolonize the city. By the early years of the twenty-first century, their success in using filtered space to resecure a white collar beachhead in the city led developers to enlarge their holdings, building more expansive suburban space encircled by policed space.

Suburban Space

Suburban spaces are lushly appointed, well-maintained spaces. They are often artfully designed by architects, landscape architects, and interior designers who can make the best of these urban spaces seem startlingly chic, rich, clean, and

stylish. By 2007, urban plazas that had been privatized or filtered were being renovated as far more suburban spaces, rich with amenities like moveable seating, dense plantings, and abundant cleaning staff.

Suburban Space. Representative of the trend to retrofit privatized spaces as suburban spaces, between 2001 (above) and 2007 (below) managers of the Alliance Capital added more seating, longer benches, and a flower bed. Usage by white collar workers from the area increased commensurably.

New plazas lacked the filtering mechanisms of earlier projects—dispensing with gates, stairs, and obscuring walls to open more easily onto the street. Filtered spaces can be luxurious as well, but whereas filtered spaces are hidden behind some real or symbolic barrier, suburban spaces seem to be open to all. Whereas filtered spaces were in isolated citadels, firebases of luxury consumption, suburban spaces were part of a more complete recolonization of center-city urban space that sought to transform New York into an imperial city. The Imperial City is analog to the Forbidden City for the early twenty-first century empire of global capitalism. Such a city deigns to accommodate working-class people, immigrants, artists, and others only to the extent that they serve the needs and consumption habits of international finance capital and its managers.

In the first decade of the twenty-first century, reductions in crime and a regentrification of most of Manhattan led developers and architects to conclude that filtering, at the level of the design of individual spaces, was no longer necessary there. (However, the *practice* of filtering continued in other spaces.) Largely unremarked upon, new plans for plazas created suburban space rather than filtered space. Some suburban spaces were new, others were existing spaces renovated during the real estate bubble that gave owners access to additional capital with which to renovate their buildings and plazas.

One such suburban space is the plaza at 1166 Avenue of the Americas in Midtown. Built in 1972 but renovated in 2005, the space is relatively accessible, filled with trees and abundant seating. At lunch, its comfortable seating areas are very popular. Comparable spaces were built in the filtered era, such as the Citigroup Mall, or the fenced-in park behind San Francisco's Transamerica Tower, but they included much more obvious barriers to access. The space at 1166 is remarkable for not having the structural barricades earlier spaces did, but retaining the same seemingly filtered clientele. Not only is the space without the drug dealers and homeless that earlier architects

Suburban Space. The renovated plaza at 1166 Avenue of the Americas. Suburban space lacks the obvious barriers that filtered space has, but in practice is no less filtered, due to aggressive police action beyond the boundaries of the space.

feared and used design to exclude, the space is also lacking people that would represent the full diversity of the city and its public activities.

The exclusivity of suburban spaces indicates the completion of large portions of the urban gentrification project, and is more effective than the exclusion achieved by individual "citadels" or filtered spaces. Calling these spaces "suburban" is not meant to be the cultural slight that urbanists sometimes imply by the term *suburban*. Our purpose in describing "suburban space" is not to slander suburbs or venerate cities—both harbor inequality, and in both we find strategies used to maintain that inequality. "Suburban space" describes the strategy, developed in suburban housing developments and suburban single-use zoning, of using geographic distance to rigidly segregate communities and create large residential neighborhoods that are relatively homogenous by class and race. In such a stratified spatial regime, spaces in affluent communities can appear relatively open and unguarded, a hallmark of suburban spaces built in downtowns today. The block-by-block diversity urbanists celebrate is, at present, a relic that is being systematically dismantled. It is not included in current development plans by private developers or public agencies like the Battery Park City Authority. Such fine-grained diversity was necessary in the pedestrian city of more than a century ago. It was given an unintentional boost during urban disinvestments in the postwar period, when people with less money could gain entry to space in formerly more exclusive areas. But today there are no serious efforts to produce or preserve it in development efforts in New York, though there could be. Diversity falls victim to the suburban land-use model that is hegemonic, as space is developed in large, economically homogenous zones.

The people who use suburban space are much like those who use filtered space: upper-middle class people who have abundant disposable income, and dress and act in ways that attract others with abundant disposal income. But whereas in filtered space it is quickly discernable how people who don't fit this description are kept out, suburban space (such as 1166 Avenue of the Americas) relies less on barriers between the street and the space, like a mall entrance or the lobby of an office building that would clearly discourage more people from using the space. Suburban space seems to perform magic: filtering without filters. Of course, guards are always nearby if "undesirables" such as homeless people or protesters do make an appearance. The illusion of tranquility achieved by suburban space (despite the persistence in New York and the United States of rampant inequality and disenfranchisement that might otherwise lead to periodic conflict) is only possible because very aggressive filtering is taking place beyond the borders of suburban space, in policed spaces.

Policed Space

Suburban space is so closely connected to its dialectical antithesis, policed space, that the discussion of suburban space is only complete with a consideration of the policed space at the fringes of the contemporary Imperial City that makes suburban space possible. Policed space is under governmental control, but excludes or closely controls selected users (Johnson 2003; Levitt 2009).

An individual suburban space such as a verdant plaza could dispense with filtering design elements because a set of middle-level filters had been instituted largely outside its boundaries. Poor people, homeless people, queer people, people of color, and many others who might democratize the tone of spaces that felt like open-air luxury malls could not access them for three reasons. First, as regular people were increasingly pushed to the periphery of re-gentrified cities, filtering in the city took place more and more as it did in the suburbs—by geographic distance—and by mass incarceration (Herbert 2009). Ever-larger working-class communities have been overturned and gentrified, as most of the Southern two-thirds of Manhattan was converted to luxury-rate housing. Non-elites are often too far away to reach suburban spaces, just as most homeless are too far away to sleep on suburban front yards. Second, New York took the lead in the United States in implementing increasingly harsh police tactics outside the boundaries of the Imperial City. Policed space is implemented in African American and Latino neighborhoods throughout the city. In policed space, the state implements extreme levels of control and denies residents the right to the city in order to create a more homogenously privileged enclave in suburban spaces. Thus, the suburban space of affluent New York could seem increasingly sedate. But in the policed spaces of Black and Latino neighborhoods beyond the luxury core, over five hundred thousand civilians are subject to "stop and frisk" encounters by police each year. The vast majority were African American and Latino residents, and were innocent people the police had no legitimate reason to suspect of wrongdoing. These same communities had already been outraged by the shootings of Amadou Diallo, Patrick Dorismond, Sean Bell, and others, as police shot and killed Blacks and Latinos at the rate of approximately one per month in the ten years after Diallo's killing (October 22 Coalition 2009). The NYPD set up roving observation towers, sought to expand the use of video cameras, subjected drivers in African American neighborhoods to repeated and abusive "Terry stops," and through other means helped insure that while inequality grew in New York, the crime that was normally its telltale sign did not. Finally, a range of quality-of-life policing initiatives beginning in the 1990s sought to make New York not only safer but also more attractive for people (McArdle and Erzen 2001; Vitale 2008). Included among those initiatives were ones that reduced the visibility of marginalized people in public space, including 1995 zoning restrictions on sex shops (Shepard 2009), removal of homeless people from Midtown, and renovation of public spaces formerly used by homeless people, queer youth, or others into spaces that were more attractive to the upper middle class but less accessible to the groups that had previously claimed them.[5] In these ways, suburban space is defined not only by the design of the space itself, but by the larger stratified social and political context in which it exists, and by the policed space that is implemented in tandem with the deceptive "opening up" of suburban spaces. Policed space includes the more repressive public space tactics, practiced at the urban margins, that allow suburban space developers downtown to create places that paradoxically seem open and accessible, but remain homogenous and exclusive. In a society of dramatic inequality, the maintenance of upper-class suburban space requires a periphery of policed space simply to create the incongruously homogenous groups of users that populate suburban space.

In the contest for public space, arrests, detention, and violence are tools only available to the police. Max Weber used the term *gwealtmonopol* to describe the "monopoly on the use of force" held by the state. Weber saw governments as "a human community that (successfully) claims the *monopoly of the legitimate use of physical force* within a given territory" (Varon 2004, 273–74). An exclusive right to engage in physical force is what makes the state, in essence, a state. The continuous use of this kind of violence reflects the state's unwillingness to engage with citizens in the margins of policed space as citizens— people with whom the state might politically negotiate a resolution to the people's grievances of social inequality. Instead, policed space implements strategies that clear the way for spaces without conflict—suburban spaces—in a city very much defined by the inherent conflicts of political, economic, and racial inequality. It is in response to the experience of this inequality that activists make use of a range of other types of public space—community space, TAZ space, and popular space—to challenge and reclaim the suburban space, policed space, and privatized spaces that enable the stratified organization of the Imperial City.

Community Space

Shifting from privately controlled spaces, we consider user-controlled spaces. Those that are controlled by the same group that uses them are *community spaces*. A dead-end street in a tight-knit neighborhood may be the perfect place for residents to play, but not a place that would be comfortable for outsiders to use. The union of inclusion and exclusion in a single place epitomizes community space. A community space of a different kind would be a secluded section of a park used by men cruising for sex: it is not vacant, but claimed by a particular community. Chapter 4 explores the importance of Hudson River piers to queer communities that claimed them as their own. The piers were not publicly welcoming spaces, but were central to the construction and maintenance of a community that was itself excluded from other spaces. A community space is one of selective exclusion, because only a certain group, or community, are comfortable using, or permitted to use, the space. It is different than filtered space because the predominant form of control is not private and top down, but public, grassroots control by the users themselves. Community space embodies both positive and negative social implications.

The difference between a "community" space and a more public one is generally overlooked in the literature. "While we use the word 'community' interchangeably with the word 'public,'" Kridger notes, "community involves selection; a distinguishing of those who belong from outsiders. The public, on the other hand, is—or should—encompass everyone. This is not a subtle distinction, yet difficult for Americans whose ideals waver between demands for equality of access and territoriality" (Kridger 1995, 76–77). Typically we think of community in terms of residential neighborhoods. Often, community has a positive connotation. But community is also represented by parochial and even violent practices of exclusion and discrimination. For instance, in his study of white reaction to Black integration, Jonathan Rieder described white residents' assaults on Black people who entered their racially transitioning Brooklyn neighborhood (1985). The white residents believed they were defending community. For our book, the distinction provided by Kridger is central: community spaces are those where a distinction is made by users between those who belong and those who don't. Community spaces can also strongly resemble that holy grail: *popular* public spaces enjoyed by all. A lively park, a neighborhood street busy with activity on a warm evening, or a community garden can all be community spaces.

There are limitations to community space. Community spaces can be the preserve of exclusive communities, the spaces where outsiders of any kind feel that status most acutely. This also makes them potentially dangerous to outsiders who enter places from which other users seek to exclude them. At the same time, it is important not to disregard other, potentially positive roles of community spaces. At times, people benefit from the comfort of a community space. Equally important, these are places where community identity and membership is defined, represented, and made meaningful. An individual feels a part of a community by spending time in the company of that group, and by developing ties that connect them to others in the group. Community space can also create a safe space for a threatened community, or strengthen an existing one. The recovery of communities near the World Trade Center after September 11 relied heavily on connecting with people in public space, in particular, with other residents who had shared their experiences, in the community space of the isolated neighborhood (Kasinitz et al. 2005). Without diminishing public space advocates' efforts to make privately controlled space more inclusive, for both everyday and exceptional uses, community spaces need to be included in the fabric of the city as well as popular spaces. Only by appreciating the differences among kinds of public space is it possible to consider what different types are needed.

The role of community space is evident in the battle over the State Office Building in Harlem, one of the few cases in which plans for a privatized office plaza were challenged by residents with an alternate plan. The Adam Clayton Powell State Office Building on 125th Street in Harlem is a classic tower-in-the-plaza design, with an expansive unused and unusable plaza to match. Community residents ultimately opposed plans for the State Office Building (or SOB, as it came to be known locally), and participated in drawing up alternative plans that illustrate the difference between privatized space and community space.

The initial plan to build the SOB in Harlem was the state's response to African American leaders' demands for economic development in Harlem. In 1966, Whitney Young, director of the National Urban League, publicly challenged Governor Nelson Rockefeller to locate the World Trade Center, then planned for lower Manhattan, in Harlem. Rockefeller, looking for ways to demonstrate his

After it was finally constructed, the State Office Building in Harlem loomed over 125th Street (upper). Its public plaza took up a city block but beyond a single row of benches, remained a vacant expanse (lower).

commitment to Harlem (particularly in an election year) announced that a portion of the state offices originally scheduled for the Trade Center would be located in Harlem. At the time, the governor said that his decision was in accordance with the wishes of the Harlem community. But by the time construction began in 1969, opposition was extended and spirited. The change, according to Pearl Robinson, then at Columbia University, occurred because the goals of New York's Black community had shifted from integration to community control. The question was whether the complex was to be built "in" Harlem or "for" Harlem (Long and Robinson 1971; Siskind 2001). In June 1969, the building site was occupied by up to four hundred protesters, whose numbers sometimes swelled to six thousand—filling the space with rallies, nightly bonfires, drummers, political education classes, and red, black, and green flags. The new residents renamed the site "Reclamation Site #1," declaring it "the first piece of land reclaimed by Black people for the use of Black people." Activists demanded that construction be halted, and that local residents decide what the community needed on the site. To determine Harlem residents' preferences, the Architects' Renewal Committee in Harlem (ARCH) surveyed people about what they wanted built on the space.

In October 1969, ARCH published three plans that reflected the priorities voiced by community members in the protest. The plans include low-income housing, a public school, a medical center, a day care center, a cultural center, and a shopping center. The plans ARCH drew up with the input of that survey are a fascinating alternative to privatized space.

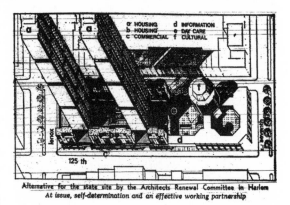

Alternative for the state site by the Architects Renewal Committee in Harlem
At issue, self-determination and an effective working partnership

A typical office plaza sits unadorned like a landing pad for its sky-bound office tower. ARCH's plans made maximum use of the space for a community with many unmet needs. The public spaces were trans-

Plans for community space in Harlem. One of three alternative plans drawn up by the Architects Renewal Committee in Harlem shows alternative uses, and physical plans, for the State Office Building site on 125th Street. In each one, buildings come all the way to the sidewalk's edge, and the plaza space is marked off from the street as courtyards of community space.

The other ARCH plans included space for science and computer technology, "Academic Houses," retail, theatre in the round, and a cultural museum.

formed from barren plazas into a playground, performance spaces, and an auditorium. Buildings maintained the continuity of the street wall, with interior courtyards. The plans promised to achieve much more with the space than the state planned to.

All three plans share important differences with popular space. These differences match the "community-control" ethos of the protesters and of ARCH. First, the spaces are designed so that there is a strong distinction between the public sidewalk and the space. As seen in the illustrations for the plan, for instance, the entrance to the plaza is not wide open, but covered by a gateway, labeled "d," which would signal to users that they are entering an enclosed, controlled space. The spaces are paved differently than the surrounding sidewalk. Developers of bonus plazas often alter the paving in the same way to signify that the space is private and that the public at large is not welcome, to discourage users who are uncertain of their entitlement to use the space. (In fact, the Department of City Planning now requires that bonus plazas be paved in the same material as the adjoining sidewalk, and be as free from barriers between the plaza and the sidewalk as possible, in recognition of City Planning's observation that such distinctions make a space less public.) Second, both of the open spaces in plan A are designated for specific uses by particular groups. In fact, both are closely associated with an organization located in the complex. The first is "an open community space, which is used by the cultural center for outdoor festivals. This space is entered through an opening on 125th Street which is bridged over by an information center." The second is "an outdoor community space next to it [the daycare center] which could be used as a play area for the center." (Alternatives to the SOB 1969). In another plan (not shown), a school of performing arts has an auditorium "available for community meetings." None of these spaces are expected to be used at will by the public at large, but are associated with particular institutions expected by designers to have meaning to the community.

The protesters were eventually cleared from the building site, and conventional plans that lacked community services were implemented. As built, the plaza of the SOB is vast and unusable. On a recent site visit at lunchtime on a sunny, seventy-degree weekday (typically the time such space is most heavily used), the plaza was almost completely empty. The design of the space made it difficult to use. The central part of the plaza in front of the building is bereft of amenities, and is thus almost inevitably empty except for people cutting across it on their way out of the building. The few users of the space are concentrated in two areas: smokers immediately outside the building, and people sitting at the very edge of the plaza near the sidewalk—near recently installed planters that are both raised and surrounded by fences so that no one can sit or lean on the planters, or even get an unobstructed view of the flowers.

The space is unused, but the vitality of the surrounding neighborhood demonstrates that this need not be so. The sidewalks are crowded. Chains like H&M and Verizon jockey for position with local stores along 125th Street, and stores even occupy the second floor of buildings, evidence of unusually high retail demand (Whyte 1988). As ARCH pointed out, their plans sought to maintain street-front retail and the street wall—two goals that receive universal endorsement today, but which were unheard of in the earlier period of privatized office plazas. As ARCH explained, "On all three proposals, commercial retail shops line the ground floor the entire length of 125th Street. This feature reinforced pedestrian activity along the street, while large public plazas occupy space away from this prime commercial area. In contrast, compare these proposals to the State Office Building proposal, where 600 linear feet of prime commercial frontage on Seventh Avenue and 125th Street is wasted on a pretentious lobby and plaza" (Alternatives to the SOB 1969). The ARCH proposals were drawn up after the architect members of the group studied how Harlem residents used public space. As then-director of ARCH Arthur Symes explained in an interview for this book:

> One of the things that we focused on was how do . . . black folks, particularly in Harlem . . . use their spaces. We talked about, for instance, people would use the street as their living room. In effect. Or their front stoop. The connection between the front stoop and the second floor. . . . So a person has a pillow on the window of the second floor and is having a conversation with two people—who are not just passing by, but a conversation that's going on and on with two people down on the street. That gave vent to the idea of making sure that when you develop the housing, that the exterior is well planned for usage. Not just as a space outside the building. And the state office building, I know that's not used. It's just a means for getting from the sidewalk into the building.

As a result, housing in the alternative plans often connected to courtyards or was close to other public spaces.

The alternative plans demonstrate the importance of recognizing what distinguishes community space. The plans for space "for" the community were consistent with the movement's focus at that time on local control, and also reflected one of the sources of residents' opposition to the state office building: activists argued that it was just the first step in the gentrification of Harlem's main street, ahead of further displacement of the Black community to make room for whites and their corporate interests. The state office building was a tactic to bring white workers into the neighborhood (though Symes says there were originally plans to include a subway exit on the site so that workers would never actually have to go through the public spaces of Black Harlem), and residents saw that plan as an affront to their community and a disruption to the fabric of the neighborhood. In response, ARCH's alternate plans did not seek to create universalistic, popular public space for outsiders as well. Instead, they concentrated on community needs, and how community space could serve the neighborhood and secure the claim of locals to the space that they feared they would lose. In this case, planners proposed community space for two purposes: to meet community needs, and to firmly establish, in concrete, a community's claim to the space.

Because of community space's dual roles of reinforcing community and enabling exclusion, community claims to such space inherently carry the risk of dangerous exclusion. But community space can also be strategic and useful. This kind of duality is an inherent feature of much public space. After all, public space itself always simultaneously embodies the promise of freedom, new experiences, and opportunity along with risk. Community space may be the most ambiguous of all the types of public space; it is one that is used to create communities that have real meaning for people, but can at the same time exclude others in ways that are damaging, discriminatory, or unfair.

Members of the groups occupying Reclamation Site #1 met in September with a representative of Governor Rockefeller, who promised no action would be taken until the governor responded to the residents' request for a meeting with him. At dawn three days later, two hundred police in riot gear arrived and evicted the squatters, arresting eight who refused to leave. Protesters recounted that police met their efforts to march later in the day with billy clubs (Harlem News 1969b). The governor promised jobs on the site to Black construction workers, but state plans to include community services in the project fell apart (Kihss 1969; Hunter 1970). The campaign for community space in Harlem had transformed the construction site into an autonomous zone that protesters controlled for twelve weeks before police reasserted state control. Activists employ autonomous spaces strategically in struggles like the one over community space and the Harlem SOB, and it is to such temporary autonomous zones that we now turn.

TAZ Space

Temporary Autonomous Zones, or TAZ spaces, are spaces groups have claimed to the temporary exclusion of state control. They are controlled instead by users, but remain open to all. Hakim Bey's descriptions of TAZs make reference to pirate hideaways and Quilombo-like communities of escaped slaves, fleeing whites, and Native Americans. TAZs are temporary constructions that exist under the radar of state surveillance. According to Bey:

> The TAZ is like an uprising which does not engage directly with the State, a guerilla operation which liberates an area (of land, of time, of imagination) and then dissolves itself to re-form elsewhere/elsewhen, before the State can crush it . . . the TAZ can "occupy" these areas clandestinely and carry on its festal purposes for quite a while in relative peace. Perhaps certain small TAZs have lasted whole lifetimes because they went unnoticed, like hillbilly enclaves (Bey, 1991).

Thus TAZs are political, they "must be *for* something." They seek to catalyze social change by giving participants just a small a bite of the forbidden fruit of liberation. And because they thrive to the degree that participants can find areas of confusion and white noise in the organization of state power, play is foundational to the creation of TAZ spaces.

 Classic examples of a TAZ (see Bey 1991) are the street party (described in Chapter 5) and the monthly Critical Mass bike rides, which started in San Francisco and spread to other cities including New York. (See Chapter 6.) Coincidentally, both authors lived in San Francisco when the bike events began in the early 1990s. A fabulous example of San Francisco political culture, the rides highlighted the possibilities of community members coming together to build a space for people to connect and create social relations outside of capitalist means of control, however temporarily. A brief description of the development of a TAZ in 1997 (based on Smithsimon's observations) is useful in elucidating the challenge of creating TAZ spaces.

Critical Mass was the coming together of several groups and traditions in San Francisco. The rides happened the last Friday of every month. The gathering place was at the far end of Market Street in a plaza near where a lot of the bike messengers hung out in the Financial District while they waited for delivery jobs. The rides always had plenty of messengers as well as politicized cyclists and other commuters who opted for alternatives to overcrowded trains and buses.

On a typical Friday evening as work let out, people would mill about. A handful of flyers might circulate proposing a route. Eventually, there would be a general drift down Market Street, and two thousand or so cyclists would completely occupy the major downtown street right in the middle of rush hour. Critical Mass at that time in San Francisco was a leisurely paced, solid parade of cyclists occupying the entire street for several blocks. Particularly if cars seemed impatient or were trying to edge into a crowd of cyclists, individual cyclists might "cork" an intersection by blocking the front car with their own bike so everyone else could go through, but most of the drivers understood what was going on, or even if they didn't, accepted it as part of San Francisco's political and street culture. Most drivers waited in good humor, some applauded, or pointed to bike racks on their roof to show they were cyclists, too. Some were exasperated and wanted to get where they were going, but they knew there wasn't much they could do about it.

CRITICAL MASS

Artwork inspired by Critical Mass in San Francisco captured the anti-corporate, anti–auto industry cast the event had for many riders.

Not that the police hadn't tried to control Critical Mass before. But as one long-term attendee (who denied, as everyone else did, that he was an organizer of the event) explained to me, people in Critical Mass had done an effective job of having leaderless events. The police initially wanted to know who the leaders were, and why those leaders hadn't gotten a permit, and wanted to let those leaders know that they would be responsible if people didn't stop for red lights and follow traffic laws and police instructions. But there were no leaders for officials to talk to, and so the police quietly gave up. They'd ride along with Critical Mass on bikes, mopeds, and motorcycles, but rarely intervened. The bikes would follow a different path every month, sometimes split up and regroup, and end up at a park, from which people would drift off to a bar or some other event once the dark, damp, fog, and wind of a San Francisco night spread from the ocean over the city.

The police's concession to Critical Mass events was broken when Willie Brown became mayor. While a veteran California politician, Brown had been in Sacramento, away from local San Francisco politics. In the summer of 1997, Brown began a rhetorical escalation against Critical Mass, comparing them to "Hell's Angels" and saying that they needed to be arrested, disciplined, and get permits (Dorn 1998). The police immediately began to backpedal Brown's comments, suggesting that he didn't really mean that Critical Mass participants were thugs. The police had already tried to confront Critical Mass and failed. But Brown insisted: Critical Mass would be stopped, and police force and state power would do the job. The weeks leading up to the July 1997 ride were ones of increasingly incendiary demonization by the mayor, along with the city's efforts first to identify and designate "representatives" of Critical Mass and then require them to negotiate with the city and file for permits. (Williams 2002, 132). Shortly before the ride, the city announced that it had met with Critical Mass leaders and agreed upon an approved route, and required that all cyclists follow police rules during the ride. Regular riders were mystified, since such an agreement would require a single leader, which Critical Mass had intentionally avoided. Normally, different route options were considered just before departure, after which bikers departed from the plaza and made collective decisions about the route. Participants were likewise nonplussed by the police requirement that riders pay careful attention to the very traffic laws that marginalized bikes, since one purpose of amassing a critical mass of cyclists was to show riders' power and demand fuller, safer access to the streets that were otherwise dominated by automobiles.

So as people gathered on July 25, 1997, the mood was tense, nervous, and anticipatory. This, in many ways, is characteristic of a TAZ: as people gathered, they knew the unstoppable power they collectively held, and were eager to see it exercised. The cops couldn't stop *all these people* from going where they wanted! At the same time, there were pre-ride jitters: The police know a thing or two about crowd control, and forcing people to do what they want. Such a confrontation can also bring violence. With enough cops and enough coercive power, perhaps the independent spirit of Critical Mass *would* be broken. Adding to the tension was the unprecedented size of the event. Where a regular ride might have two thousand people, there appeared to be twenty thousand participants. Brown's comments had incited many more people to show up than ever before, angry that he was trying to shut down a beloved institution.

The police distributed flyers saying that Critical Mass was an illegal event, that anyone violating traffic rules or police instructions would be arrested. The flyers included a map of an approved route everyone would have to follow. Rather than going down Market Street, the route turned left down a side street and stayed away from rush-hour traffic.

The cyclists began to gradually turn their gears. As people started out from the plaza, the first group obediently turned left off of Market Street. Some riders were crestfallen: they had been broken. But then, just behind them, others did not turn off. They continued up Market Street. More followed and found themselves, exhilarated, beyond the police, with Market Street theirs once again. The riders paused, unsure what to do or what would happen next. Was it really that easy? Had they really claimed Market Street? Or was the other shoe about to drop: what were the cops going to do in response?

Soon it became obvious that there was nothing they could do. More people streamed up Market Street, and despite a heavy police attendance, there were far too many people. The police had made a claim on space, and Critical Mass riders had defied and dismissed that claim: "they didn't control Market Street, or Critical Mass," cyclists' actions said, "we did." The mood was ecstatic and defiant rolling up Market Street.

Just a couple of vignettes remind me of what made the event a TAZ. Just a few blocks beyond the starting point, we rolled across an intersection. At some point, the light changed. No one paid it any mind, but a police officer stopped a cyclist, and told him he had run a red light. The officer took the man's bike and put it in the trunk of his cruiser. He started writing a ticket, and the crowd circled in. The cop was arguing about why he was writing the ticket, and people responded. They began chanting "Give it back! Give it back!" about the bike. The crowd got angry, and the police officer, who knew he was outnumbered, called for backup. People got nervous for a minute, knowing that backup in this kind of situation could mean brute force and a lot of head knocking. We heard the wail of sirens. People stopped and looked down the street. The squad cars were four blocks away but couldn't move through the crowd. They were stuck. Reinforcements *weren't* coming. We ruled the street. As we rode on, people related different bits and pieces of what had happened. One man said that someone had removed the bike from the trunk of the squad car. Certainly no one stopped for red lights.

Now, cyclists knew that police control had been suspended. On a normal Critical Mass ride, people could ride through a red light, but that was about it. This time cyclists knew that with police cars stopped in traffic, everyone had several long minutes during which they could do whatever they wanted, enjoy it, and then disperse without repercussion before the police could possibly reach the scene.

In a TAZ, users are responsible for regulating behavior when necessary. Cyclists engaged with, even argued with, angry motorists. In one case, a tow truck driver who had been stopped at an intersection by Critical Mass angrily drove his truck into the crowd, almost hitting people. When cyclists yelled at him for endangering people, he jumped from his truck and chased them, swinging a chain in his hand. His targets quickly scattered. After a moment of horror at his behavior, people recognized the police were not going to discipline him. Cyclists could act on their own behalf to insure he would not try to drive into anyone else when he returned. There was mention of damaging the truck, or driving it away, but others in the crowd rejected that idea. Instead a quick-thinking cyclist reached inside the tow truck's open door, pulled out the ignition key, and dropped it in a storm drain.

The group kept biking.

There's a feeling that accompanies the knowledge that typical authority has been suspended that has always been how I recognize I'm in a TAZ. Some designations are intellectual, others visceral: When economists declare that there was, officially, a recession two years after the fact because there were two or more consecutive quarters of declining GDP, that's a technical definition. When someone gets fired, is broke, and is desperate, they know economic times are tough viscerally. The technical definition of a TAZ is a moment when control of the space and appropriate behaviors are determined by the *users*, and not by the state, property owners, or corporate power, and access is not restricted. But beyond the formal definition, you know you're in a TAZ when you have butterflies in your stomach, unleashed by twin emotions of great potential and uncertainty. This tension accompanied by release characterizes much of the subversive nature of play (Huizinga 1950). There is an inherent subversive quality to the pleasure enjoyed in these kinds of moments. TAZs are viscerally thrilling because they remove restraints we don't even normally recognize we bear. There's a thrill to realizing one is not answerable to authority that is at other times taken for granted and all-pervasive. This doesn't mean people in a TAZ can do anything: after all, there were twenty thousand cyclists in the Critical Mass ride, and their behavior had to be acceptable to their comrades. A TAZ is a space where temporarily, the people there use their collective norms to decide what is acceptable and what is not. There's excitement in realizing people can do things they can't normally do: in TAZs, people are more likely to smoke marijuana outdoors, run naked into the sea, or paint slogans on the window of a Starbucks. But in a TAZ, the companion to the sense of great possibility (Liberation! Freedom!) is the sense of great risk: the end of the TAZ comes with the repression the state will exercise to reassert its control. State authority appears at the borders, and participants recognize that it is time to decide whether to abandon the TAZ (if they can) or suffer unusually serious consequences.

Indeed, the end became apparent for that Critical Mass TAZ. A group on the move has a momentum that keeps it powerful and free: for cyclists or marchers, moving feels like winning, and the most the state can do in response is try to keep up. But eventually the participants run out of momentum, or energy, or ideas. The event slows, or reaches its destination, or stops in front of a big state building that's the symbol of their dissatisfaction. The police circle round, and the stage is set for a static confrontation—between baton-wielding police and cyclists—that citizens can't win (Besser 2002). Some people are more defiant than I, and won't leave till the very end. I had had an exhilarating, liberating time, but knew that the TAZ wasn't going to last forever. Afterwards, thousands of people got on their bikes and dispersed across the city, carrying unauthorized knowledge of the TAZ, and the in-your-gut experience of sudden liberation from state power.

Utility Space and Abandoned Space

Two types of space on the typology that merit brief attention here are utility space and abandoned space. Utility space is that which is publicly controlled but cannot be used as public space. Train tracks are utility spaces (although the trains that pass above them may be more public), as are paths for high-tension power lines that prohibit trespassing, urban tunnels, and remote National Forest Service land. *Utility spaces* can provide the seclusion graffiti artists require to do large, elaborate pieces—if they break in and use the walls. Parks and community gardens that have been shut down and encircled by construction fences by the local authorities so that the government can use the space for another purpose become utility spaces. Such space may later be claimed by public or private interests. *Abandoned space* is paradoxically controlled by users, but used by no one. That is, those who were formerly in control of the space have left and abdicated responsibility for it, like a once crowded beach long after Labor Day has passed and an icy wind thunders across untouched sand. Such spaces can become socially significant again if they are regenerated by users. Without denying their potential to become meaningful to people again, utility and abandoned spaces are peripheral to this discussion because by definition they are rarely used and offer little social potential to anyone.

Shifting Spaces

By categorizing public spaces within this framework, several trends emerge that are central to the rest of the book. First, privately owned public spaces in the last forty years have transitioned from privatized spaces, to filtered ones, to suburban spaces—reflecting political and economic changes and the evolution of elite developers' plans for the city. Recognition of this development clarifies the evolving nature of the risks posed by privately controlled public spaces. Second, in the context of ongoing social and economic polarization, the blossoming of enticing suburban space is one part of the story. Beyond suburban space is often a much harsher policed space. The renaissance celebrated in downtown suburban spaces must also take account of the renaissance in intrusive, often abusive, policing methods in neighborhoods farther from the affluent downtown. Third, activists create community space and TAZ spaces to catalyze changes in the regimes of control of public space, and to build alternative publics counter to those represented by privately controlled and policed spaces. The chapters that follow elaborate these three narratives in public space.

CHAPTER TWO

Dispersing the Crowd

Bonus Plazas and the Creation of Public Space

As icons of modern architecture, urban plazas encapsulate some of the key contradictions of contemporary urban public space. Why is some of the most expensive real estate in North America virtually empty, occupied by plazas that are supposed to be public but are used by almost no one?

Urban plazas offer a case study with which to examine the impact and evolution of public space outlined in the previous chapter. In this chapter, we make use of field observations of New York urban plazas, interviews with key architects and planners, archival data, and a quantitative assessment of plazas.[1] This chapter establishes several foundational facts about public space. First, we show that most such plazas built in the twentieth century were indeed unwelcoming, harsh environments. Second, we demonstrate that the design of these barren spaces, and the antisocial impact those spaces have are

While occasional plazas in front of office buildings are well used, barren, unusable places are more common. While construction workers sit to eat lunch at one plaza (left), at another planters are sloped, polished, and raised to prevent sitting.

not incidental, but intentional products of social actors. Third, we challenge conventional aesthetic-focused examinations of public space, which hold architects solely responsible for the shape and function of a plaza, recognizing instead that architects' work reflects the desires of their developer clients. Fourth, we see how urban plazas reflect the social objectives of their developer-owners, and that most often, New York office plazas reflect developers' desire that the public not use these nominally public spaces.

Most mid-twentieth-century plazas are harsh and unwelcoming. In a survey of Manhattan's plazas, the majority were found either to not attract users, or to actually repel them (Kayden et al. 2000). For decades, observers have blamed the architects for the failures of these plazas. Wanting to be the next Mies van der Rohe, the conventional wisdom goes, architects drafted wide, flat plazas consistent with the aesthetics of the International Style but inconsistent with the way people actually use city space. Such was the critique by everyone from renegade urbanist Jane Jacobs to new urbanist Andres Duany to elitist dandy Tom Wolfe (Jacobs 1961; Wolfe 1981, Duany and Plater-Zyberk 1994). The white elephant towers of the urban renewal era seemed to offer abundant evidence that modernism was ill-suited for building practical, usable, pedestrian-friendly public spaces. Barren plazas, in this view, are nothing more than the unintended consequences of a moment in architectural fashion. No one wanted them that way, they just happened as architects forced their designs on their developer-clients. "Has there ever been another place on earth where so many people of wealth and power have paid for and put up with so much architecture they detested?" asked Tom Wolfe (1981, 1).

But Wolfe's stock in trade, of course, is to giddily invert the power relations of the subjects he writes about. A careful investigation of plazas reveals that architects don't dictate design; developers do. Indeed, the players in the city building game are unambiguous on this point, and show that it was developers who determined the shape of these public spaces. General Motors Plaza, catty corner from Central Park, had been notorious for its private quality since it was built in 1968. Most of the plaza was sunken far below street level and empty. William H. Whyte observed that sitting on the ledges was uncomfortable because "there is a fussy little railing that catches you right in the small of your back. . . . Another two inches of clearance for the railing and you would be comfortable (Whyte 1988, 129)."[2] The building's architect was Edward Durell Stone. Wolfe had praised Stone for his rejection of modernist conventions. But contrary to Wolfe's claims about modernism being at fault for bad design, Stone's more classical aesthetic style did not change the fact that his plaza was a dead zone. "The owner didn't want people loitering and thus the railings were not designed for comfort," Stone explained. (Whyte 1972a).

Indeed, contrary to the notion that architects didn't know what they were doing, analysis of Manhattan plazas showed that the same firms designed the best and worst plazas: what mattered was who the developer was.

Bonus Plazas

Bonus spaces are the public spaces included in many high-rise building projects in New York and other cities. They include outdoor plazas as well as indoor arcades, sidewalk widenings, public passageways, and a host of other spatial forms. The term *bonus* derives from incentive-zoning regulations that give builders additional floor area ratio (FAR), allowing them to build larger, taller buildings, in exchange for providing public plaza space at street level. Thus, the bonus FAR and the plaza represent a contract between a developer and the city (and its citizens), in which public access is provided in exchange for private benefits. Unlike other privatized spaces, the city recognizes the public's rights to the space, such as the right of anyone to use the space as long as they're not disruptive. Specifically, the City mandates that "Public plazas are . . . intended for public use and enjoyment. The standards . . . are intended to . . . serve a variety of users of the public plaza area; [and] to provide spaces for solitary users while at the same time providing opportunities for social interaction for small groups." (New York City 2009).[3] Because of such requirements and the way spaces are used, bonus plazas meet common standards for a public space, namely that people can access it, use it, claim it, and (modestly) modify it (Lynch 1981; Carr et al. 1992; Dijkstra 2000), even though the plazas are not publicly owned.

The bonus plaza period formally began in 1961 when New York's zoning revision included bonus FAR in exchange for plazas in high-rise districts. Though it was modeled after the landmark tower-in-a-plaza that Mies van der Rohe designed for Seagram in 1958, the new zoning law was more than the institutionalization of modernist aesthetics. The towers offered floor plans that were easier to design, build, and rent than the "wedding cake" buildings dictated by the earlier codes, whose floor plans were set farther back from the street every few stories. Thus, the bonus plaza regime, in theory at least, provided something for everyone: plazas for the public, the latest styles for architects, additional FAR for developers, and simpler floor plans for tenants.

Incentive zoning produced particular relationships among actors in the construction of a building. Initiating the process was a developer. In the high-density, high-value, high-FAR areas of midtown and downtown New York, where zoning allowed a plaza bonus, real estate development was led since World War II by fewer than a dozen family-controlled development groups.[4] In the development process, a developer acquired a property. An architect worked with the developer to design a building for the property, but the goals were very different from those suggested in most architectural history accounts, which give the impression architecture is largely an aesthetic process (Frampton 1980). This may be true for brand-name architects when they design vacation houses. But even in the rare cases when a famous architect designed a New York office building, they were basically decorating the facade. With or without them, the entirety of the building took shape under the direction of the "architect of record."[5] As described by New York City planners, the job of the architect of record is to fit as much rentable space on the property as possible. In addition to an understanding of building, therefore, successful architects have an intimate knowledge of the complex building code (which governs the size of the building and defines what kinds of spaces count against the FAR and which, like structural elements, do not), and excel at organizing space efficiently. As a result of this specialized knowledge, local firms worked on the buildings, and a small number were hired repeatedly, often developing relationships with developers (though architects worked with more than one developer, and vice versa). It was through the architect's interaction with the building code that city planners would first become involved in the process. Until 1975, all bonus plazas were "as-of-right," meaning the building received the FAR bonus and the developer could build it as long as the plan conformed to the zoning regulations. After 1975, increasing numbers of buildings needed to be approved by the Department of City Planning (formerly the City Planning Commission), which allowed planners to evaluate plans. In addition to being able to assess compliance with the code (seeing that a plaza had the mandated number of trees or seats, for instance) the City's planners could make other recommendations on the road towards approval.

Developers also introduced another player into relations between themselves and the city: the real estate lawyer. A real estate lawyer can lobby for zoning exceptions for a project, to get more rentable space in a building. While there were other actors in the process—a major tenant, financial backers, the Department of Buildings—the relationship relevant to the construction of bonus plazas was among the developer, the architect of record, and, through the building code, City Planning.

The bonus plazas that have resulted are significant for several reasons. Not only do they capture the ideal of urban design in the mid-twentieth century, they were the first experiment with private developers building public space to meet planning and zoning objectives. The privatization process that created privately owned public spaces is now widespread. New York's bonus plazas and incentive zoning regulations have become models for cities across the country. (Kayden et al. 2000; Whyte 1988). The process of privatization demonstrated so clearly in bonus plazas is representative of larger efforts to privately control public space.

Evidence of Empty Bonus Plazas

While there has not been substantial examination of the possible motives of actors involved in the creation of bonus plazas, extensive evidence has documented that the vast majority of the bonus spaces are indeed barren, unusable, and exclusive. In fact, bonus plazas are at times so maligned that they have become, like public housing towers and urban renewal, a symbol of what is wrong with cities and modern urban planning. Three separate bodies of research established bonus plazas as dead space.

First, Whyte's extensive fieldwork in these plazas compellingly documented that most such spaces are not public, and "were awful: sterile, empty spaces not used for much of anything" in what were otherwise crowded, busy central business districts (Whyte 1988, 234). Whyte sought to discover the features that would make spaces usable, but his research also identifies numerous spaces

The developers of 299 Park Avenue received a bonus for space that was barred and used as a driveway. Lest there be any uncertainty, signs underscored that the owners considered the space private property.

that were not. "The evidence was overwhelming. Most of the spaces were not working well—certainly not well enough to warrant the very generous subsidies given for them" (245). Whyte's work, in association with the Department of City Planning, first established that the products of incentive zoning discouraged public use, and framed that shortcoming as a breach of the contract between developers and the public.

The second assessment of bonus plazas is *Privately Owned Public Space* (Kayden et al. 2000). This was the first systematic study of all New York City bonus plazas—prior to its publication, not even the Department of City Planning, a coauthor of the study, knew which spaces in the city were covered by bonus plaza regulations. Full of examples of private encroachments such as restaurants' seating areas overtaking public plazas, the study presented a telling pattern of private control of public space. *Privately Owned Public Space* provides a valuable quantitative assessment of bonus plazas. After assembling an archival record of the spaces from City Planning and Department of Buildings records, with the cooperation of the Municipal Art Society, researchers led by Jerold Kayden evaluated the use and public quality of the spaces. Each space was evaluated and then graded. To assign a grade, every one of the 503 spaces in the study was visited several times.[6] Grading "relied on extensive empirical observation and users interviews, culminating in the exercise of judgment about use or potential use" (Kayden et al., 51). Each bonus plaza received a grade from "1" (meaning the space was virtually unusable) to "5" (indicating it was a destination space). Researchers focused on how people used the space (including how many people used it, what they did there, which of the provided amenities they used, and who they were demographically), and on design and operation of the space, "with particular attention paid to how it supported or discouraged potential use"—including design, actions by the current owner and manager, and compliance with legal requirements governing the space (Kayden et al., 52). In Midtown and the Financial District, over half such spaces were found either to fail to attract people to the space, or to actively repel them. This actually understates the original scope of the problem, since in the intervening decades some owners significantly upgraded their spaces, under direction from City Planning, in exchange for permission to make other changes the owner wanted, such as the introduction of retail uses to a space or the closure of a space at night. Furthermore, the grades given by the *Privately Owned Public Space* researchers were particularly generous, because they graded the space primarily on assessments of potential use, not on actual use. Still, the unmatched rigor and thoroughness of the study establishes the survey as an invaluable source against which to compare other findings.

Third, the archives of New York City's Department of City Planning show the agency regularly reached similar conclusions during the forty years it has been encouraging bonus plazas and rewriting regulations in an effort to produce more popular spaces. The Commission wrote in 1975 that "too many have merely been unadorned and sterile strips of cement. These 'left-over' spaces are merely dividers of buildings, windy, lonely areas, without sun or life."[7] The records are also a valuable guide to exclusionary design elements, since as soon as one was identified, the Commission sought to prohibit it from future buildings. Paving treatment was eventually required to be the same on the plaza as on the adjoining sidewalk, since a granite courtyard next to a concrete sidewalk reads to passersby as a separate, private entity. Other changes were required that would make the plazas more publicly accessible.

Because bonus plazas were intended to be public amenities created in exchange for permission to build a larger building (which benefited the developer), New York City's Department of Planning required spaces that were too well hidden from public view to announce that they were public.

Throughout the forty years of the bonus plaza program, these three sources have consistently found that the spaces are often not public at all, and that the city has failed to obtain the types of spaces they hoped to gain in exchange for FAR bonuses.

Exclusion Through Design

How is a physical space used to achieve the social process of exclusion? The idea of security guards escorting scruffy patrons out of an elite establishment is not hard to imagine. The idea of actors transferring their agency and goals to inanimate objects is somewhat harder to accept. But the use of actual people, like guards, to exclude can be a sign of vulnerability, like a state's use of violence rather than more subtle means to achieve obedience. Design, unlike guards, can silently do its job year after year. Before discussing the intentionality of exclusion in bonus plazas—*why* it happens—it is worthwhile to describe the well-established means by which space excludes—*how*, in concrete terms, spaces have the effect of keeping people out. Whyte's research on the mechanics of exclusion is already well known. The New York Department of City Planning's archives, coupled with the first-hand experience of its planners, are the most detailed accounts of which design elements exclude, so we will use these to describe how exclusion is achieved through design.

Philip Schneider, in the thirty years he worked at the Department of City Planning, saw many design elements that deterred use of a public plaza.[8] First, "any barrier to entry" like walls, fences, or steps kept people away. Some plazas had locked gates. People also tended not to use a place if there was nowhere to sit. Covering the space with plantings, like ivy, made the space attractive, but thoroughly unusable. Other studies of public space have enumerated similar design technologies in New York and elsewhere (Jacobs 1961; Whyte 1988; Flusty 1995).

One reason it has yet to be established whether exclusion from plazas was intentional and, if so, who was responsible is that for most buildings there is no existing record of the intentions of different players or their distinct contributions to the design process. Instead, we compared four primary sources of data to develop a consistent explanation of how plazas became exclusive and to determine the motives and relative influence of each actor. These sources include interviews with actors who created and regulated bonus plazas, quantitative analysis of bonus plaza data, archival material from the Department of Planning, and field observations of the plazas themselves.

We tried to interview developers—approaching ten who had worked on more than two buildings in the bonus plaza survey. (Other developers with more than two buildings were either deceased or, identified in public documents as shell companies, difficult to identify or contact.) We also pursued references provided by architects. However, most New York developers are notoriously averse to publicity, and none consented to an interview. That outcome is not entirely surprising, in the context of a study of elite behavior at odds with public policy. Such interviews may have shed more light on *why* developers acted the way they did, but as we will see, the consistency of data from diverse sources—the architect and planner interviews, the analysis of the *Privately Owned Public Spaces* quantitative data, the Planning Department archives, and field observation—provided a high degree of confidence in the conclusions reached about the role, behaviors, and involvement of developers in the bonus plaza process.

Intentional Exclusion by Developers

Most bonus plazas were empty and unused by design. Developers did not want them to be used. More influential than architects and city planners, developers play the decisive role in creating highly exclusive public spaces. These actions were not simply an effect of the financial motivation to "do the minimum" to get a square footage bonus, as observers of the bonus plaza program have often suggested (Whyte 1988). Nor were they the result of architects blinded by the glitter of architectural modernism, as others believed (Wolfe 1981). Instead, *exclusion* was a goal of its own.

City planners with extensive, first-hand knowledge of the process of creating bonus plazas identified developers as the actors responsible for exclusionary spaces. Jonathan Barnett, who was director of urban design for the New York City Planning Department from 1967 to 1971, took this position: "spaces are often inhospitable, not because their designers were stupid but because the owners of the buildings . . . deliberately sought an environment that encouraged people to admire the building briefly and then be on their way" (Barnett 1982, 179). One current City Planning staffer concurred: "Well, everything pointed in that direction, which is why we changed the regulations so many times. The client [i.e., the developer] wanted the space to be private, as private looking as possible, as private feeling as possible."

City planners often explicitly see themselves as advocates for more usable spaces and recognize that this role can put them in opposition to developers and architects. Philip Schneider, who had worked for the Department of City Planning since the 1970s, called his office's emphasis on public accessibility "a general tension" in the development process. Architects who worked closely in cooperation with developers actually paint a more critical picture than city planners, and assign responsibility with less reservation. Richard Roth, whose firm Emery Roth & Sons designed a quarter of the bonus plaza buildings in Midtown and Downtown, gave this explanation in an interview with me:[9] "The plazas got bleaker and bleaker and bleaker—less people-oriented," explained Roth. "The owners of the buildings didn't want a lot of people sitting in those spaces. Why do you never have seats in a lobby of an office building? Because they didn't want people sitting there." When asked how the plazas were made bleaker, Roth elaborated, "They kept putting less and less in. The client kept saying 'No, I want it as minimal as possible.'" Roth also provided specific examples of developers' instructions. For instance, Paramount Plaza, at 50th Street and Broadway, is notorious for having two unused sunken sections, even though sinking plazas below street level is known to keep people out of them. In the 2000 catalog of bonus plazas, Jerold Kayden wrote:

> Successor owners to the original developer of this Broadway office tower have faced an inherently problematic site condition at their full blockfront special permit plaza. . . . Sunken spaces have always presented difficulties and their pathology is not hard to discern. Compared with street-level spaces, sunken spaces require greater effort on the part of the public to reach them. They are frequently dark and cold, lacking sunlight more available at street level. Without the eyes and ears of pedestrians, they can be downright scary. Without usable amenities and supportive retail uses, they can be dead. . . . The empirical record of sunken spaces in the city is not a happy one (Kayden et al. 2000, 148).

While he succinctly describes the well-known problems of this and other sunken plazas, Kayden restricts himself to discussing the space passively, as if it were a natural feature. The sunken plazas are "an inherently problematic site condition," but why would the plaza be in this condition? Roth explained much more actively why that space was built as it was. "When we designed Paramount Building. I mean, again, it was Uris, and they didn't want anybody on the plaza." (Brothers Percy and Harold Uris were the site's developers.) "That's why we had the two sunken areas on either side. It took them forever to rent those sunken areas. One side was a restaurant, the north corner was a restaurant. On the south corner, it was a perfect thing because it was connected to subways, but Percy and Harold didn't want people." I asked what the developers said to him about their desires for the plaza. "We want something that people walk across and not stay there. You know what your parameters are."

Did the Uris's, who developed the site, understand that their goals of excluding people from this privately owned public space could be achieved through design? Roth makes clear they did, and that they were committed to that goal. "I remember when we were doing 55 Water Street. I got Larry Halprin from the West Coast to do the plaza for the building. And Larry Halprin was very people-oriented, to the point where his plazas became 'people' places. And when Percy and Harold Uris saw this people place that Halprin had created, he was fired! Now Larry Halprin happened to be a first cousin of the Uris's." The fact that the Uris's fired their own cousin suggests the importance of building exclusive spaces.

Saky Yakas, an architect from a younger generation than Roth, strongly agreed that spaces would be designed to be unusable by people on the developer's instruction. He suggested that the goal, in more recent plazas, was not total, but *filtered* exclusion.

> Although the intent of these is to be public, a lot of the design is geared towards making people think before they use them. A lot of people don't know that these are public spaces. I think a lot of developers like them to not know they're public spaces. And one of the ways is how you do your fencing or how you change the grade, how you situate them in relationship to the buildings, how you use your cameras. They want them to be used, but you want a feel of exclusivity.

From the early period Roth discussed to the more recent buildings Yakas designed, the influence of developers remained constant.

It is possible, of course, that architects are simply creating this explanation after the fact to assign blame to developers rather than themselves. But while this role of developers has not been established in public discussions, it is consistent in the accounts of different architects. In addition, the influence of developers can be felt in Department of Planning meetings. Further, Roth remains on good personal terms with developers he worked with, and it is unlikely he would inaccurately slight them to make himself look better.[10]

Finally, comments by developers themselves are consistent with those of planners and architects, and support the finding that exclusion was the developers' goal. "Building plazas usually have few if any seating accommodations," explained a sympathetic profile in the real estate section of the *New York Times* about Edward Sulzberger, president of the Sulzberger-Rolfe real estate firm.[11] "One of the biggest problems of buildings' security, Mr. Sulzberger points out, is loitering on the premises. . . . Builders therefore do not seek to make their plazas more comfortable to encourage passers-by to spend time resting there." (New York Times 1969, 8) This developer thus redefined the prerequisite to using public space—spending time there—as a "security problem," and responded with design choices to prevent people from sitting down, and he would have been quite disturbed to find anyone actually using the space he provided for the public. Unusable, barren, empty public space devoid of seating or other basic amenities was not an accident of design, it was *by* design.

The case of developer Melvyn Kaufman, though exceptional in the types of buildings he produced, illustrates the centrality of the developer. Kaufman is recognized for his distinctively whimsical plazas, which encourage public engagement and rely on lively street life for their impact. Rather than shirking from the public, Kaufman's designs invite people in and entertain them with large swinging benches, human-size chess pieces, *Wizard of Oz*-reminiscent winding brick paths, abstract twenty-foot high clocks, and unconventional lobbies in a 1970s science-fiction aesthetic. His spaces are also, by the grades of *Privately Owned Public Spaces*, exceptionally *public* places. In a survey where 56 percent of plazas received grades of only 1 or 2 for their usability by the public (5 being the highest on the scale), and where, even counting only a building's best space (some have more than one), the average grade was 2.52, Kaufman's average of 3.50 was the highest for any developer who had more than one building. Not only was his average high, but his scores were more consistent than almost any other developer.

Roth took credit for getting Kaufman interested in plazas, but not intentionally. According to Roth, he invited Kaufman to visit an architecture class he was teaching in the 1960s, and Kaufman became interested in the ideas and energy of the students. From then on, he wanted to reflect this energy and enthusiasm in his plazas. But Roth makes clear these spaces were different than those he designed for clients like the Uris's or the Fisher's because of the explicit instructions and social goals of each developer for their plazas.

Architect Peter Claman agrees that developers influenced the quality of a plaza. "It's a question of basic attitude [on the part of a developer]. . . . The plaza was not made for the developers' benefit, it was made for the public's benefit: that was a tough sell to certain developers." Unlike city planners, who, records show, advocated consistently for public space, or architects, who designed more or less accessible spaces depending on their client, developers decided whether their plaza would be usable or not.

Analysis Of Privately Owned Public Space Data

Comparing the bonus plaza scores of developers and of architects provides quantitative evidence that developers had more influence over the quality of a plaza than did the architect. To do so, we gathered information on the architects and, with more difficulty, on developers of bonus plaza buildings. While architects are listed for the buildings in *Privately Owned Public Space,* shifting ownership and the use of holding companies made identifying developers more difficult. We gathered this information from Department of City Planning Records, the interviews with architects and planners, and occasionally from field sources. Correlating plaza grades to architects and developers for the first time provided a means to use the *Privately Owned Public Space* data to critically assess not just the spaces, but the actors.

What is significant here is not the score of particular developers or architects; there were high and low grades among both. But, if developers had more influence over spaces, then there should be *less deviation* in the grades their spaces received. If developers had more influence, then architects' grades would show more deviation because their grades changed as their clients changed. Whoever called the shots would have more consistent grades. We compared the grades of plazas by developers and architects who had both done more than one building. This included 80 buildings by a developer who had done multiple buildings, and 110 done by architects who had worked on multiple buildings. Among these, 64 spaces appeared in both lists. The size of this overlap is likely to mute any difference in deviation between developers and architects: if only those 64 spaces had been used, for instance, the average of standard deviations for developers and for architects would have been the same. Even with that much overlap in the two sets of buildings, the results demonstrate the influence of developers. The median standard deviation for architects who worked on multiple buildings was 1.03. For developers, it was only .84. (See Figure 2.1.) Developers were more consistent than architects. Architects might build an accessible space for one project, only to design an exclusive project for the next.

The case of Melvyn Kaufman is again instructive. Roth was the architect on most of Kaufman's buildings. But even with substantial overlap, Kaufman's standard deviation was only .84, one of the lowest among developers of three or more spaces, while Roth's was 1.21. Roth's plazas garnered both some of the best and worst grades. Substantively, the explanation is clear: the

Figure 2.1. Mean Grade and Standard Deviation for bonus plazas by architect and by developer.

Architect	Mean	N	Std. Deviation	Developer	Mean	N	Std. Deviation
Emery Roth & Sons	2.62	37	1.21	Cohen	2.83	6	1.17
Skidmore, Owings & Merrill	3.31	13	1.03	Kaufman	3.50	6	0.84
Kahn and Jacobs	2.71	7	1.25	Fisher	3.20	5	1.48
Schuman, Lichtenstein,	2.67	6	1.03	Helmsley	2.60	5	1.14
Claman & Efron				Uris	2.00	5	1.00
Shreve, Lamb & Harmon	2.00	6	0.89	Durst	2.00	4	0.82
Philip Birnbaum	2.00	5	1.41	Macklowe	2.75	4	1.26
Fox & Fowle Architects	2.25	4	1.26	Rudin	2.25	4	0.96
Johnson/Burgee	3.33	3	1.53	Tishman	2.75	4	1.50
Kohn Pedersen Fox	3.33	3	1.15	Kalikow	3.00	3	0.00
Murphy/Jahn	3.00	3	1.00	Minskoff	1.33	3	0.58
Kevin Roche John Dinkeloo	4.33	3	0.58	Park Tower	4.00	3	1.00
& Assoc				Zeckendorf	2.33	3	1.53
Swanke Hayden Connell	4.50	2	0.71	Atlas McGrath	2.00	2	1.41
Eli Attia	3.00	2	0.00	Eichner	2.00	2	0.00
The Eggers Group	2.50	2	0.71	Hines	3.00	2	1.41
Frank Williams & Assocs.	3.00	2	1.41	NY Telephone	3.50	2	0.71
Harrison & Abramovitz	3.00	2	0.00	Resnick	2.50	2	0.71
Edward Larrabee Barnes	3.00	2	1.41	Rockefeller	3.00	2	0.00
Raymond & Rado and Partners	1.00	2	0.00	Ronson	2.50	2	0.71
Pelli/Vinoly	2.00	2	0.00	Rose	1.00	2	0.00
Median			**1.03**	Sharp	3.00	2	0.00
				Solomon	3.00	2	0.00
				Median			**0.84**

Developers' grades are more consistent, demonstrating that they exercised more influence over plaza quality than architects.

Sources: Privately Owned Public Space: The New York City Experience, New York City Department of Planning, Richard Roth, Jr.

architecture firm of Emery Roth & Sons knew how to design popular plazas that drew people to them, and when demanded by a developer, that is what they produced. When developers made clear that they didn't want the space used, the firm provided exclusionary spaces. While the design of a building is most often considered in light of the architect, this evidence points to another way in which, as David Brain (1991) argues, architects are constrained in their work. Students of design should look more closely at who makes decisions about a space rather than at who designs it. In an important sense, developers, the patrons, create the space—not architects.

Common Rationalizations for Exclusion in Public Space

Given the regularity over the last forty years with which developers built plazas that didn't attract people, it is surprising how often this outcome is considered accidental. Contrary to the evidence presented above, previous studies have treated barren public plazas as the unintended consequence of unrelated priorities. They are thought to be the products of developers' drive to save money (and miscalculations regarding the returns on investing in public spaces), or architects' romance with modernism, or building managers' urge to lighten their workload by keeping plazas empty. Some (though not all) of these play roles, but none are as influential as suggested by the literature. While these explanations dominate the discussion of unusable public spaces, few of these arguments hold great merit. In most cases, the exclusivity of public space is more often intentional than incidental, the desired outcome and not the side effect of other choices.

Doing The Minimum, And Minding The Bottom Line

A common assumption is that developers' actions were simply motivated by their drive to maximize profits. By this logic, developers "do the minimum" required to get the square footage bonus. But consideration of the actual expenses of a plaza actually casts doubt on whether developers were "doing the minimum," whether economic considerations alone would have driven them to do so, and whether this would have led inevitably to unusable spaces.

Philip Schneider voices a common conclusion when he says that they "were interested primarily in getting the bonus and doing whatever they had to do to get past City Planning. They would look to do the minimum." Whyte (1988) similarly believed developers did the "minimum" to gain the bonus. Jonathan Barnett of City Planning took this position and pointed out two specific costs developers attended to: insurance and maintenance.

Barnett's experience with builders of public plazas and his firsthand observation of their work allowed him to distinguish the priorities of building owners more finely than most. He explained that the actual priorities for a privately owned public space depended on what kind of organization owned the building. Buildings owned by corporations are run by "facilities managers," who run them much as they do shopping malls. They're hired to keep the place clean, and are therefore interested in keeping maintenance easy and inexpensive. The fewer people to clean up after, the fewer plants to water, the better. Entrepreneurs operating their own building want to squeeze as much money out of it as possible, so if they can find a retail tenant or a cafe interested in paying for the privilege of spreading their chairs into the plaza, so much the better. Only if they "get it," concluded Barnett, would an owner try to make their plaza a lively, public place. Thus, while for Barnett the financial concerns dictate the quality of plazas, who's minding the bottom line determines the specific effect it will have on the space.

There is some evidence for this "cheap developer" argument. Consistent with Whyte's findings, when given free reign, from 1961 to 1975, developers failed to build a single space of even decent quality. After the passage of regulations specifying what amenities must be provided in 1975, the record has been much better (Kayden et al. 2000). (The new regulations were a direct result of Whyte's efforts to improve the spaces by specifying what developers must provide in the plazas.) But other changes occurred in the city during those periods. And while earlier spaces were poor, that is not to say that they were cheaply built, or that keeping building costs low was the primary consideration.

After all, "doing the minimum" may in some cases have been more costly. Richard Roth provided the example of the banal pay phone. Telephone booths paid the highest rent per square foot of any use an office building could have. They were, said Roth, "a *very* big source of income." But booths in the lobby also brought outsiders into the building and might create nuisances if the space was damaged, vandalized, or misused. By the beginning of the bonus plaza period, developers stopped putting booths in their lobbies.

Furthermore, plaza costs were not generally significant. Yakas observed that "it's not a lot of money when you think of what he's spending on each tower, it's really a very small percentage of each project." David West, a partner at the architectural firm Costas Kondylis, said that though he had worked with a wide range of clients over the past ten years, he had never been on a project that couldn't afford to hire a landscape architect for the plaza. Peter Claman estimated the cost of a good versus barren plaza at ten dollars per square foot, which would be forty thousand dollars for an average-size plaza on a building worth many hundreds of millions of dollars.

A more significant challenge to the economic sense of "doing the minimum" comes from comments by developer Mel Kaufman. Kaufman suggested that popular plazas could actually be an asset to a building. Whyte reported that in a 1972 conversation, Kaufman "confided, as if top secret, that the fun plaza [is] a big selling point. Rented out 77 Water St. much faster than next building. At 747 3rd Avenue, doing better than the competition" Whyte 1972b). The accuracy and generalizability of this statement still needs to be determined. Richard Roth recalls Kaufman's buildings having been very difficult to rent (though it's not clear plazas were the cause). Others have suggested that Kaufman was successful in his niche, but that the approach would not have worked for all kinds of tenants. Still, his example shows that hewing to the profit motive would not in all cases have led developers not to invest money in their plazas.

Interviews with architects of more recent buildings add further support for this argument. David West took it for granted that in the buildings he designed from 1995 to the present, the developer wanted a plaza to "succeed," he said, because an attractive, well-used, well-maintained plaza added to the appeal of the building.

A more detailed consideration of one bonus plaza helps demonstrate that while cost was something developers always attended to, it is too simplistic to think this would lead only to unadorned and therefore unused spaces.

Consider the Alliance Capital Building at 1345 Sixth Avenue. The space was notable for the effectiveness of its exclusion. Built in 1969, before stricter design requirements were imposed, it did a remarkably good job of keeping people off the public space. In observations in 2001, at lunch hour the sidewalks abutting the space were so packed with people that it was difficult to get through. Yet the plaza was empty—only a half-dozen people were seated on its ten thousand square feet to eat lunch. A closer examination suggested why. Though the plaza stretched a full city block from West 54th to West 55th Streets, there were only three benches; even on a calm day, two of them were intermittently sprinkled by a fine mist from one of the two fountains. The fountains themselves were remarkable: while the fountain ledges that ran along the public sidewalks were crowded with people sitting, eating and talking, the fountains had been designed such that within the plaza, they actually had no ledges, preventing even that improvised, but popular, seating option. The immense fountains also effectively put half of the plaza's area off limits by putting it under water. And unlike other, similar front plazas which used some of their space for a park-like cubby of trees and benches, the remaining

Contrast the lunchtime crowds just north of the plaza (left) and east of the plaza's edge (center) with the emptiness of the public plaza itself (right).

half of the plaza space was a barren, dark, stone-paved expanse leading to the entrance. Considering that the entrance only consists of three revolving doors, it seemed unlikely that the entire two-hundred-foot-wide granite plane needed to serve only as an entrance.

But as clear as Alliance Capital's plaza was as a demonstration of antipublic space, it also serves as evidence against "doing the minimum." For as Jerold Kayden explained, water features, like fountains, are notoriously costly and troublesome to maintain, which is why he found that several of those mandated in post-1975 spaces had been surreptitiously decommissioned (Kayden et al. 2000). They need to be constantly cleaned, they have mechanical features that break and require maintenance, and some are further complicated by water heaters to allow year-round operation. The property manager of an East Midtown tower estimated the annual costs of a much smaller fountain on his plaza at seventy-five hundred dollars per year. This is not a large sum of money when compared to the annual costs of maintaining a large New York City building, but it is considerably more than the cost of people-friendly amenities like benches.

Fountains have other ongoing costs. They're a liability twenty-four hours a day that can cause people to slip on wet stone pavement or even drown. If

The "dandelion" fountain at the Alliance Capital building was custom-built for the space (top). Such fountains have the effect of pushing people off the plaza to the sidewalk's edge (bottom).

they're operated year-round, they have to be heated. And since Manhattan plazas are almost never built over solid ground but rather above several basement floors, leakage is a costly risk (New York Times 1969). With each of these characteristics, fountains add to the leading developers' worries identified by Barnett—maintenance and insurance, which owners have paid throughout the building's thirty-year existence. But they also achieve the developers' goal Barnett identified: encouraging people to admire the space briefly and then be on their way.

Richard Roth, whose firm designed the Alliance Capital Building for the Fisher Brothers, described a design process that incurred still greater costs. Roth had admired a fountain shown in a photograph from Australia. "I loved it," he said, "And I presented it to Larry Fisher, who also loved it." But efforts to locate the designer in Australia turned up nothing. Ultimately, he commissioned a fountain consultant to recreate the dandelion-shaped fountain for the Alliance Capital Building. The fountain was popular enough, said Roth, that the consultant made and sold smaller copies of it.

To call such developers too cheap to invest in their plaza is unfair. To attribute the emptiness of the plaza to capitalists' penny-pinching rationality would be just as inaccurate. Most plazas are empty, but not because making them useful was too costly.

Architects And Modernism

Arguing that developers, not architects, have a decisive influence on design contradicts the conventional aesthetic presentation of architecture fostered by articles about landmark buildings in glossy architecture magazines that suggest the form is an expression of the architect's artistic vision. Blame for architects came from other sources as well. Herbert Gans (2006) points out, for instance, that Jane Jacobs blamed empty public spaces on "unknown architects (she called them planners) who were designing International Style public housing projects."

David Brain's examination of the profession of architecture stresses that architects have far less autonomy than imagined. "The autonomy of the architect is hemmed in on all sides: The client controls the budget; building technology is controlled by builders, engineers, and industries that produce materials and equipment; the construction industry is an intersection of several markets" (Brain 1991, 263). Design is hardly in the architect's hands alone.

Regarding the influence of modernism itself, it is unlikely that the style or conventions of modernism affected the public quality of the spaces. While architects did admire the Seagram Building, the inspiration for New York's bonus plazas program, the absence of amenities was explained clearly enough by developers' expectations. Nor were all plazas' architects conventional modernists: Tom Wolfe celebrated the work of Edward Durell Stone as a departure from barren modernism. But Stone's plazas were as barren and unusable as any (Hales 2004). Developers played a much greater role than architectural style. Little of our data suggests that architects had a decisive role.

Building Management

Discussions of plazas' shortcomings sometimes also focus on the role that building managers play. While some developers own and operate the buildings they constructed, most buildings are sold. Often, the current owner will hire a building management company to run and maintain the building. While initial design decisions were made by the developer, the current building manager can alter the space and make day-to-day decisions about its operation and accessibility that are just as important as the developer's original design decisions.

Planner Jonathan Barnett's identification of different management goals—whether the cost minimizing of contracted corporate facilities managers, or the profit maximizing of the entrepreneur—makes clear the effect building managers can have on a space. Schneider cited examples of spaces that had

changed: Philip Morris' space (at Park Avenue and 42nd Street) had become "just deadly" once, under the guise of security, doors were locked, bags searched, and movable chairs removed. Other changes made after the fact have been significant enough to require City Planning approval; the IBM plaza and Sony Plaza (formerly the AT&T Building) were the best known among spaces that had changes of use, and tenants that significantly altered the original design and intent of the spaces. An image of homeless people in the IBM plaza from several decades ago illustrates the users managers wanted to remove from the plazas. As Roth said, "I think it mattered very much who was running it. There were people who didn't want the problems

Homeless people in the IBM plaza, late 1980s. (Photo by Caroline Shepard.)

. . . who wanted the people to go away." Even everyday decisions and alterations, like the permissiveness of guards, the locking of a gate, and the quality of maintenance, can collectively have dramatic effects on the public quality of a bonus plaza.

The plaza at 330 East 39th Street offers a hopeful example. The plaza there was identified in *Privately Owned Public Space* as one in a serious state of neglect; the most blatant violation of the expectations for bonus plazas being a gate across the entrance that remained locked most days. As a result, its public quality was severely compromised. Peter Claman, whose firm designed the building, conceded "no, that was not a successful plaza," even saying that a plaza like that, six feet above street level, "never should have been approved"[12] by City Planning. When asked why it had been built as it was, Claman pointed out that it was built on top of a parking garage, and the elevation of the garage had to be raised because there was a lot of water in the soil.

In 2004, the space was in an awkward state of transition. On a field visit, a homeless person sleeping in a rear corner stairwell was joined across the expanse by two businessmen holding an extended conversation near the entrance. Some of the lamp posts were clearly broken, but others had been replaced. Most of the plaza was dreary and empty, but a dense, geometric array of tulips bloomed in what had been an unused fountain. At the entrance, another long-empty fountain had been filled with new plantings of hydrangea, climbing roses, and wisteria.

After publication of the *Privately Owned Public Space* survey, City Planning contacted the manager of the building and instructed him to remove the gate. (Before the book was published, such enforcement was virtually impossible, because there was no record of what bonus plazas existed, and what requirements had been placed on them as a condition of a building's construction.)

Joseph Flanagan, the building's manager, explained his response to city pressure. Flanagan had initially resisted the city's order to remove the gate, fearing the plaza would be filled with homeless people. But rather than seek a variance from the City, he removed the gate and then went on to make improvements not required by the City. Thus, the tulips and other flowers were planted, and he planned to install a Japanese-style trellis. He had also been working with a Seventeenth Precinct detective, who offered technical assistance to plaza managers, essentially disseminating means of selectively filtering a space (like posting a list of rules and prohibitions prominently near the entrance). Flanagan hoped that these alterations would attract more users, perhaps from the small office building next door.

When asked why he was improving it, he laughed and said, "Because my apartment overlooks it?" Though he objected to being forced to remove the gate, he was also upset when he visited Madison Square Garden to find that the sitting ledges had been intentionally obstructed with rails and planters. As a result, he came to appreciate the City's demands regarding his plaza. "If I'm going to complain about Madison Square Garden, somebody should come and make me take it [the locked gate] off when I'm not opening it," he reflected. In addition, he appeared to have a tolerant and respectful attitude towards the homeless. He knew several details about the homeless man who regularly slept in the stairwell, and described his stack of cardboard (which a fire inspector had called a hazard) not as junk but as the man's "private property." The fountains had been urinated in, and the plaza still had human excrement in it, but he blamed both not on homeless people staying there (who, he said, carted out their own waste in buckets) but on drunken revelers passing by on their way home from bars. Thus, despite actual experience with some of the most disagreeable possibilities of a public space, he retained a fundamentally tolerant attitude that seemed to motivate cleaning up the plaza and seeking more users. Flanagan's plaza demonstrates that while the original disposition of a space by the developer is significant (in this case, it is a serious handicap, since few people can see it or pass by it), current decision makers can also try to influence how accessible a bonus plaza is.

Space Contested From Above

Understanding the decisive role developers play in shaping bonus plazas provides insight into this persistent failure of urban design and the source of one
of urbanists' and planners' longstanding frustrations. It also demonstrates one
way in which public space is a contested site—both for elites, as this chapter
demonstrates, and for grassroots activists, as is seen in the second part of the
book. A more accurate account of barren plazas could help activists improve
plazas, and help urbanists improve public-private programs, preventing more
unusable space from being built.

Developers' privatizing intentions have had significant effects on public
spaces. Since the bonus plaza program, cities seeking more public space have
increasingly turned to public-private partnerships. The problem with such an
approach is that spaces are public to the degree that they meet the needs of a
broad array of users. Private developers build spaces that meet their own
needs, or at most the needs of their tenants. They are therefore almost
inevitably not equal to the task of welcoming a diverse public. Popular public
spaces are most often developed and maintained by public organizations that
are connected more closely to the democratic process, and have a long institutional commitment to public access. This study suggests that incentives to
build privately owned public spaces are not enough: even with regulations and
interventions, developers often create a public realm that is unusable and
undesirable.

The design of plazas to exclude users identifies one of the key mechanisms by which changes in the social, economic, and political order of the city
were translated into changes in the physical and spatial organization of the
city. By establishing this relationship we can, in the next chapter, examine how
such spaces reflect—or in some cases foreshadow—social changes in the city,
and link shifts in economic relations to shifts in the disposition of public
space. The result of the most recent spatial and economic shifts are not just
privatized and filtered spaces, but policed and suburban spaces.

CHAPTER THREE

The City as Seen from the Plaza

Changing Regimes of Private Control

As the previous chapter demonstrated, developers of high rise offices and urban plazas in New York shaped those plazas to render them exclusive. Developers' imprint on their plazas allows us, in this chapter, to track the changing vision elite developers had of New York over the last forty years, by identifying the evolution of designs they chose for bonus plazas and other public spaces. We have used field observations of plazas and interviews to identify three historical periods in plaza design, which correlate to the privatized, filtered, and suburbanized spaces identified in Chapter 1.

The actions of developers and the changes in who they sought to exclude show how elites' vision shifted over the second half of the twentieth century from a city that was privatized, to one which was filtered, to one that was suburban. (See the table on page 29.) The concrete representation of those periods in different types of bonus plazas helps us delineate those distinct periods in an urban political-economic history of US global cities. In the earliest period of the "as-of-right" plazas (1961–1975), developers' goal was *privatized* space that excluded everyone not going into the building. Such spaces reflected elites' negative conception of the city as a place of disorder and chaos. During the middle period (beginning in 1975), designs reflected efforts to *filter* users, and architects identified designs to exclude the homeless, drug dealers, and others engaged in behavior deemed unacceptable. Such filtered designs reflected developers' new belief that parts of the city could be gentrified and reclaimed (or recolonized) by professionals and the upper- and upper-middle classes. In the last period, since 2000, plaza designs have been used that do much less filtering at the level of the individual plaza, but have retained the class, occupational, and racial bias of filtered spaces. These spaces represent the third development, *suburban* space, in which filtering is implemented on a citywide level (through policies such as ongoing residential segregation, rigid quality-of-life policing, and harassment of homeless people, young people, and others who might transgress the boundaries of the privileged Imperial City). Across these three periods, bonus plazas become historical markers that tell the tale of capital's serial abandonment, recolonization, and overconfident claiming of urban spaces.

Efforts to exclude people from public space have been identified before, from the militant policing and bum-proof benches of Mike Davis' Los Angeles, across the malling of American public space, to the Disneyfication of Times Square, and the citadel exclusivity of New York's Battery Park City (Davis 1990; Kowinski 1985; Kohn 2004; Berman 2006; Sorkin 1992). But it can be challenging to reconcile these narratives. Is public space being eliminated, or privatized, or reduced to space for retail consumption? Is everyone being evicted from the commons, or only the homeless, or everyone save wealthy consumers and elite global businesspeople? Students of public space can make sense of these disparate accounts by recognizing that elite decision makers have shaped public space to achieve goals that shifted over time. Public space has not been on a unilinear trajectory (towards privatization, or elimination, or elitism), but has been a tool in the pursuit of evolving social objectives by elites.

The final implication of developers' involvement in bonus plazas is that these spaces don't simply reflect current elite attitudes about the city, but offer glimpses of what the most powerful and influential real estate speculators expect the city to become. Because these developers are what Logan and Molotch term "structural speculators," bonus plazas become leading indicators of contemporary capitalism's plans for the city, and therefore merit particular attention for those who would challenge the plans of corporate capital.

Shutting out the City with Privatized Plazas: 1961–1975

Most plazas built from 1961 (when the bonus plaza program first allowed developers to build taller office towers in exchange for providing the public with plaza space at ground level) until 1975 were privatized spaces.

The plazas could have been more usable—and in fact later, in the filtered and suburbanized periods, they were. In Kayden et al.'s assessment of the bonus plazas, the majority of spaces built in the privatized period received an "F" grade, for failing to attract—or actively repelling users. (See Figure 3.1.) No spaces from the period received an "A" and only 4 percent received a "B." During the era of filtered spaces, in the 1980s, the pattern was nearly reversed, with only 3 percent of plazas getting an "F," and 54 percent receiving an A or B. Developers could orchestrate the construction of usable or unusable plazas.

Figure 3.1. Plaza Grades by Decade

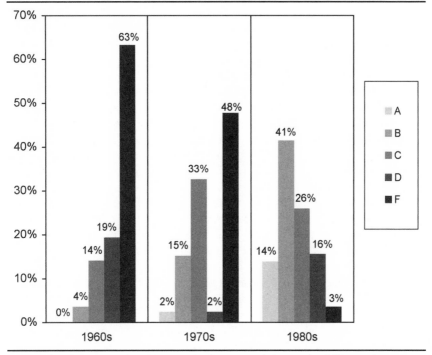

In three decades, the grades plazas received were nearly inverted: a failing grade went from the most common to the least common grade, as A and B grades became more prominent.

Developers hoped that the unwelcoming design of these spaces would minimize their use by anyone. The predominance of this kind of space, with its assumption that urban public space can only bring trouble and is best minimized, reflects the sharply negative reevaluation of New York by elites and the middle class in this period.

By the early 1960s, alarm about crime and security had become a common rhetorical trope. City streets were suddenly seen as dangerous, uncontrollable, and unpredictable. Then as now, fear in public spaces like Central Park had a distinctly racial quality to it. In 1961, the police sought to "abolish the myth that the parks are 'jungles'" (Illson 1963, 21). During his 1961 run for mayor, Attorney General Louis J. Lefkowitz used similar language, promising he would end the "terror in the streets" that had turned the city into a "jungle" during the previous administration. "You know the fact it's not safe to walk the streets, in the parks," he intoned, arguing for a return of "law and order"

(Grutzner 1961). Richard J. Whalen, in his book *A City Destroying Itself: An Angry View of New York,* asked rhetorically, "Is the world's greatest city no safer than a jungle?" (Whalen 1965, 22). Eric M. Javits' equally overheated *SOS New York: A City in Distress* claimed "New York City's tenement under-brush has become a paved jungle where muggers, rapists and gangs roam poorly lit streets, assaults, beatings and sex crimes sweep the city" (Javits 1961, 124). Throughout both books, the authors readily associated race with crime and crime with a "jungle," drawing from the culture's store of racist imagery.[1] The city was in a desperate state of siege, not simply by opportunistic crimi-nals, but by a wave of racialized and sexualized assaults and panics (Chambliss 1995). After the riots, wrote Whalen, "Whether or not the city suffers further racial explosions, it will remain frightened by its inner turmoil and capacity for violence" (Whalen 1965, 21).

The earliest bonus plazas—overwhelmingly unfriendly—were built in the context of this climate of increasing anxiety. The architect Richard Roth, whose career began before the bonus plaza era at the firm run by his father and grandfather, was involved in many of the earliest plazas.[2] To Roth, the goal of privatized plazas was to keep away people he (and others who have studied public space) called "undesirables." But he denied that the aversion to such "undesirables" was concretely related to crime or security. "I never heard security." he explained. "Security was an issue used for fighting something, but I don't think it was a real issue." Rather, developers "didn't want a bunch of people out there disturbing their tenants who were coming through in suits."[3] When asked later who those people might be, Roth said that "They were the messengers, they were the crazies, they were anybody who didn't have a suit on."[4] Thus, the design and management of such spaces sought to close the space to everyone but those entering and leaving the building. Privatized spaces reflect that conclusion, foreclosing any use of the spaces either by the public, retail tenants, or employees from inside the building.

In the privatized period of 1961–1975, US cities were losing population in the midst of white flight, and white collar workers were increasingly uncertain of their control of public space in the face of demands for equal public rep-resentation by people of color. In this context, public spaces around office buildings were no longer the preserve of middle-class workers, and as those workers retreated, the spaces were rolled up, gated, and eliminated in their wake. In many respects, the public sphere of urban public spaces was aban-doned by the classes of people who populated brand-new office buildings, and designs for buildings reflected widespread consensus, not just among elites but among whites more broadly, that whatever uses the city might retain, control of its public spaces by the old guard was no longer assured, and thus those spaces would no longer be used.

Fear and Control as Motivation for Privatized Space

The public spaces around central business districts like Midtown Manhattan were never very dangerous places. Instead, exclusionary decisions were driven by anxiety in what Stephen Graham and Alessandro Aurigi (1997) call the "city of fear." Fear, they suggest, has an exaggerated effect on urban space beyond the actual frequency of the events that are feared.

Mike Davis saw the privatization of public space specifically shaped by racial fears. The civil rights contest "that began in the long hot summers of the 1960s has been institutionalized into the very structure of urban space," wrote Davis. The privatization of public space represented "a continuation of the race war of the 1960s . . . at the level of the built environment" (Davis 1990, 224, 228). Sharon Zukin similarly saw racial fear as a strong explanatory variable in understanding shifts in public space since the end of legal segregation in the 1960s "when—not surprisingly—perceptions of danger among whites increased." The result was public space design based on exclusion. "Reacting to previous failures of public space—due to crime, a perceived lower-class and minority group presence, and disrepair—the new parks use design as an implicit code of inclusion and exclusion" (Zukin 1995, 41, 25).

William Whyte, who was not typically critical of corporations, dismissed CEOs' claims that they relocated their headquarters to the suburbs because of high taxes in the city. Instead, he concluded that the real motivation was executives' belief that "the center city is a bad place: crime, dirt, noise, blacks, Puerto Ricans, and so on" (Whyte 1988, 297). Finally, historian Lizabeth Cohen's research on retail areas in the New York metro area concluded that developers "did not exclude inadvertently." Instead, "not by accident, public space was restructured and segmented by class and race . . . just as African Americans gained new protections for their right of equal access to public accommodations" (Cohen, 2003, 179). Setha Low (2003), who researched gated communities across the country, found gated community residents' fears of crime, racial minorities, "others," and economic decline provided significant explanation of residents' decision to move to gated, privatized, carefully controlled spaces like malls.

Crime was not as common in spaces such as bonus plazas as is sometimes assumed. In a study of reported crimes at Paley Park in Midtown Manhattan, Whyte found that in almost twenty years (1967–1986) none of the movable chairs had been stolen. During that period, the only reports were of minor vandalism and a break in at the snack bar (Whyte 1988). The actual incidence of crime was quite low. However, talk about security was still prevalent (Vitale 2008).

In the record of the City Planning Commission, crime problems are actually rarely mentioned in discussion of bonus plazas, and then only in reference to particular spaces, not as a general problem. Those same archives also indicate that City Planning and local community boards often felt that claims made about security problems, in the spaces where they did arise, were sometimes opportunistically made, and could often be dealt with through better management of the spaces.[5] Spaces with security problems, both groups argued, often had been permitted to become particularly dirty, poorly maintained, or poorly lit. Community boards typically insisted, and City Planning agreed, that managers seeking to restrict usage or hours of a bonus plaza for security reasons first make improvements to lighting, cleaning, and programming. Both groups also apparently believed that some managers of bonus plazas were making claims about security as an excuse to close down, shrink, lease out, gate, or reduce the hours of operation of their plazas. Fear of crime was real, but crime in plazas was rare.

Architects acknowledged that events in a period "do influence and do carry over" in plaza design. Some discussed plaza design in terms of crime, drugs, or homelessness—all of which can be superficially nonracial terms by which to express racialized conceptions of public space (Bonilla-Silva 2003). But those tenants and developers who were most fearful of a new, more racially diverse city could have left.

When asked why developers wanted to exclude people from their plazas, Richard Roth argued the problem with a plaza for developers was that "they couldn't control it."[6] In research on elevated pedestrian walkways in three US cities, Jack Byers (1998, 204) came to the same conclusion. "For property owners and managers, control of the publicly used spaces within their jurisdiction is paramount." In both cases, private management means that individuals representing only a certain set of private interests make all significant decisions for the operation of the public space. In contrast, spaces run by public agencies (like a parks department) or controlled ad hoc by users are governed by groups that by definition, and in practice, consider the interests of a broader array of users. Thus, establishing bonus plazas as entities to be privately managed (instead of, for instance, having private development fund publicly owned spaces, as in Battery Park City) left control in the hands of people with a mandate to defend the interests of only a narrow group. Based on observations of a wide range of New York public spaces, we found that spaces that were created under more inclusive planning procedures (with public meetings, input from a wide range of potentially interested parties, and influence from one of the more publicly minded municipal agencies), led to more diverse users, a wider range of uses, and more truly "public" space. The more narrow and private the design process is permitted to be, the more privately exclusive the resulting space is likely to be.

Recolonizing the City with Filtered Plazas: 1975–2000

Filtered designs began appearing in bonus plazas around 1975. Whereas most plazas built in the 1960s scored very low in the survey by Kayden et al., the first space to earn an "A" for usability opened in 1975—the shopping mall of the slope-roofed Citigroup Tower in Midtown (Kayden et al. 2000). The Citigroup Tower heralded a new direction in public space design. The space was still exclusive, but the objective had clearly changed. The mall needed to attract people to retain retail tenants. To the extent that it attracted users with more disposable income, it was better positioned to survive. Planners expected that affluent users were attracted to a space to the extent that poorer users were kept out. Thus, such bonus spaces had the same motivation shopping malls did to filter potential users. Whereas the earliest plazas had been designed to bluntly keep everyone out, later accounts describe efforts to remain exclusive, but to selectively welcome more elite users. This is reflective of the second, filtered period of bonus plaza design, and correlates to the earliest efforts to gentrify the city and reclaim public space for the upper and upper-middle class.

Architect Peter Claman worked in the filtered period. He began working at Schuman Lichtenstein in 1952, but did not become a partner until the 1970s. He suggested that developers were not explicit in their desire to keep people out, and were interested in "curb appeal," or the attractiveness of the plaza to potential tenants.

Claman described the people to be excluded as criminals. Developers' concern was "securing the plazas. I have some plazas on the West Side that put people in business. [*Q: What kind of business?*] Dope, crack, white cloud!" But for Claman, "security" was inseparable from a process of exclusion, not just of criminals, but of those not desired by shopping mall managers. He continued, "the problem was securing it. How do you keep homeless people out of it? How do you keep evil people out of it? It was a problem. It is a problem."

Saky Yakas, who began working at the same firm as Claman in 1985, referred to security in terms of homelessness in the 1980s and similarly conflated homelessness with crime. "One of the problems in the eighties was you still had quite a lot of homeless people and quite a lot of crime, one of the initial problems you had with the initial plazas was how are you going to police these and not have people hanging out at all hours of the day and night. So part of the design of them had to include some sort of security." (Yakas did concur, however, with Roth's characterization of "security" as a rhetorical device, saying developers obliquely expressed their desire to keep out classes of people who would "lower the tone" of a plaza: "They wouldn't say it like that, they'd put it more in security-type concerns.") Yakas elaborated on who was to be excluded, and why:

> Exclusivity is . . . well, it's human nature and snobbery . . . people for whatever reason perceive that certain dress or certain habits or certain ways of doing things lowers the tone of their investment. And if you can figure out ways of reducing the number of people who might come in, they like you to do it. And that's unwritten. Because this is supposed to be public, it's supposed to be open to whoever wants to have a sandwich or whatever, you know, within reason.[7]

This description of the objectives of exclusion distinguishes it from both privatized and popular public space. Whereas earlier privatized spaces sought to keep out everyone who was not an employee in the building, filtered spaces sought to keep out those who would lower the tone. Outsiders who were "high tone" were welcome.

Among the plazas, the most barren period parallels that of maximum white flight and disinvestments from the city. With the beginning of white reinvestment and gentrification in the mid-1970s (Zukin's analysis, for instance, identifies this as the period when manufacturing lofts-turned-residences began frequently renting for luxury rates [1982, 142]), plazas became less privatized and more filtered. "Cafe creep," described by Kayden et al., took hold, in which old bonus plazas were used for profitable retail purposes (sometimes with city permission, often without). In this way, the filtered period witnessed *selective* exclusion in newer privately owned public spaces. "Most importantly, they [developers] consciously organize the way their space is used by the general public in order to influence who is considered a welcome guest, who is tolerated, and who is discouraged from entry at all" (Byers 1998, 202). The affluent were made to feel welcome, while others were made to feel uncomfortable, as if they were in an expensive jewelry store (Zukin 2004). While this filtering suggests a significant shift in public space during this period, filtering also foreshadowed a more ominous form of exclusion.

The Shopping Mall Paradigm

The shopping mall paradigm is relevant to the filtered period. Here, space is privately developed and controlled, the product of "corporate and state planners, [who] have created environments that are based on desires for security rather than interaction, for entertainment rather than (perhaps divisive) politics" (Mitchell 1995, 119). In the case of bonus plazas and privately owned public space more generally, the goal may not be maximizing retail income, but the creation of space with a similarly narrow range of possibilities and stricter private regulation than would be achieved through public ownership and management.

Indeed, the influence of suburban shopping malls on bonus plazas is particularly evident because architectural firms developed shopping malls and then brought that experience back to the city to design mall-like bonus spaces. Mall designers created exclusive places through their use of luxury finishes, enclosed access, expensive stores, private security guards, limits on permissible activities, and separation from the street, among other methods. The firm Emery Roth & Sons had designed shopping malls in the New York metro area and elsewhere before turning to the brand new category of *indoor* bonus space in New York. The results, including 575 Fifth Avenue and Citigroup Market (completed in 1975), represent the introduction of a shopping-mall aesthetic to the city. (It is worth noting, however, that making shopping malls successful in Manhattan continues to be a considerable challenge. Many have been perennially empty.)

In the wake of the fiscal crisis of 1975, developers unveiled filtered spaces that would profit from a white collar return to the city. At the same time, elites forcibly reshaped New York into a place that was far more hostile to the working class and organized labor, and oriented more singularly towards white collar business and elites. Just as the economic stagnation of profit growth of the early 1970s led, at the national and international level, to the abandonment of the old economic system and the aggressive restructuring of the economy in the interests of capital and at the expense of the general public, so the economic crisis in New York was an opportunity for elites to restructure the city to renew opportunities to extract surplus value. The "global city" that resulted was one unabashedly oriented towards the needs of white collar corporate headquarters, real estate investors, and the upper-middle class that served as the managerial elite in the new global city. It was unclear at the outset of that political, social, and economic transformation that the result would be the global city now so widely recognized and critiqued. But the filtered spaces built at the time were an early indication of whom the city was being rebuilt to serve.

Though developers did use shopping mall technology to create filtered spaces, at the time, at least some of the most important techniques suburban shopping malls use to create exclusive public space—geographic distance and isolation in a homogenous suburb, and access by automobile—were unavailable to designers of New York bonus plazas (Friedan and Sagalayn 1989). Filtered spaces adopt some of the exclusive technology used by shopping malls, but did not turn Manhattan into a car-oriented zone. Yet, over time, the spaces diminished New York's local culture. When those techniques of neighborhood-level homogeneity and isolation were finally introduced to the city in the luxury projects of the turn of the twenty-first century, it ushered in a very different, still more suburban period.

Designing the Imperial City with the Suburban Strategy: 2000 and Beyond

By the mid- to late-nineties, the exclusion that had been a constant, if shifting, preoccupation of plaza design began to recede in the priorities of architects and their developer clients. Design elements that selectively filtered out potential users were no longer necessary because the people architects most wanted to keep out were already pushed out, not from individual properties, but from the city center more broadly. As Chapter 6 explains in greater detail, the administration of Mayor Rudolph Giuliani undertook an aggressive, unapologetic, and unprecedented campaign to cleanse the city of homeless people, sidewalk entrepreneurs, prostitutes, drug dealers, the poor, people of color, and anyone the police considered undesirable or suspicious. The problems of homelessness were not addressed, but homeless people were banished from locations like the Port Authority and Pennsylvania Station, often to shelters or jail. Men of color were subjected to pat down searches en masse. Protesters were barred from the streets with an endless barrage of requirements for permits. Youth were driven from downtown parks. The result of this relentless campaign to remove anyone who didn't look like they belonged in a suburban shopping mall was to render redundant designs that kept those people out of individual bonus spaces. The era of the suburban space had arrived (Goldberger 2001; Hammett and Hammett 2007).

David West, who began working for a firm frequently involved in bonus plazas in 1995, saw security and homelessness as less of a problem. (He believed they were more significant in the 1980s, in the filtered era). As an architect working in the period of suburban spaces, West believed everyone, including developers, wanted a "successful" plaza—though he acknowledged that could mean different things to different people:

> I don't think it's as much of a problem as it used to be. I think there are two main factors in that. One is that, they used to have to be open twenty-four hours a day. Now, I don't remember the exact regulations, but you're allowed to close them [bonus plazas] off at night. . . . The other factor that I think is even more significant is that the nature of the city has changed. A lot . . . Twenty years ago, the streets were completely different. You know, there was crime, there was a lot more riff-raff on the streets, the streets were dirtier, it was just, it was a different culture, and a lot of these plazas became not very inviting spaces as much as anything because of the environments they were in. Didn't even necessarily matter whether they were in a, quote, good neighborhood or a bad neighborhood, it had to do as much as anything I think with the culture on the streets. That's changed really radically in the last ten years. And, for better and worse, you know, there was sort of an interest to it. New York City was a little more bohemian twenty years ago than it is today, but the public spaces suffered.

The city had changed along with its architecture. West was aware of some of the ambiguity of displacing people from public space, just as opponents to the mayor's drives were aware of the gains to personal safety the city attributed to its intolerant (or so called "zero-tolerance") policing. But the significance of these changes for his role as an architect was that designs no longer needed to filter themselves; the state provided that service for a sizeable, affluent zone of the center city. Though creative design professionals like West may have regretted some of the loss of "bohemian" flavor, their work for developer clients by necessity adapted to the change in state policy to create a new, paradoxically more open but more exclusive form of privately owned public space.

The suburban period has been characterized not only by the construction of new, suburban spaces, but by the retrofitting of older, privatized spaces. Selectively filtered public spaces had become so successful that in the past few years, property owners substantially retrofitted the old, barren concrete plazas. In some cases the introduction of seating, plants, and other amenities had come at the behest of the Department of City Planning in exchange for some other zoning variance the developer had sought. In other cases, plazas which had been good for little but hurrying across towards the revolving doors were now filled with decoration, places to sit, and people having lunch, a cigarette, or a conversation. The wasteland plazas that were so abundant even five years earlier, when this fieldwork began, became far more rare. This should be unqualified good news. Given that the original barren plazas were built concurrent with the era of white flight, it is tempting to believe that the more welcoming design of plazas today means that the United States' long convulsive reaction to the Black Great Migration of the early twentieth century is over. Racial hysteria has cooled at least enough to disabuse gentrifying white Americans of their anti-urban prejudices and bring us all together in the public spaces of the city.

This conclusion is tempting, but evidence elsewhere suggests this would be too optimistic. The assumptions of homogeneous land use of the suburban strategy are still dominant. Corporate priorities go unquestioned. And while the spaces are no longer hostile, there is still little accommodation in them for less wealthy New Yorkers. Instead, that hostility has moved to the borders of the gentrified, Imperial City, directed at those who would cross the boundaries into suburban space. Police harassment takes place on a massive, systematic scale in the boroughs with large populations of Black and Latino young men, where police conduct warrantless "stop-and-frisk" searches without probable cause. The police searches, which violate a consent decree, take place at a rate of one per minute in New York City, over five hundred thousand per year, virtually all of law abiding people of color.[8] The searches find very little evidence of illegal activity, but discipline residents outside the Imperial City's boundaries—out of sight of the new, seemingly more open suburban public spaces of the center of the city. Likewise, "quality of life" legislation and policing, which seeks to cite, arrest, and discourage once-common public activities by queer youth, transgendered people, customers at adult bookstores, and others, clears still more public space of activities that would be inconsistent with the apparent new openness of suburban space. In this way, policing the boundaries of the gentrified Imperial City and the transgressions of the norms of the Imperial City help maintain the illusion that suburban spaces are only modestly surveilled, because more aggressive policies of control are implemented just beyond.

Instead, the more usable bonus plazas at best reflect the confidence of developers and building managers that their public spaces can today be physically opened to the public and remain nonetheless quite exclusive. There are no walls, but the imperial personnel and the peasants are still separated. The difference today is the confidence of structural speculators that outsiders will not disrupt the workings of the Imperial City. The Imperial City and its suburban spaces are not unlike Versailles, which was insulated from Paris less by walls than by distance, and was filled with beautiful gardens.

The successful implementation of the suburban strategy has failed US cities—despite its creation of attractive spaces and despite the return of upper-income whites. City segregation has remained or even increased. Displacement of lower-income residents and working-class employers from the center city went fundamentally unquestioned. And even when the state had center city land to plan for, homogenous and high-end development were seen as the only natural use for such space. Mixed-income, multi-racial affordable housing projects that were for a time the setting for proud ribbon cutting ceremonies have since been pushed to the side, and in the case of New York, been bought out and replaced with luxury-rate tenants.[9] Critics of a more culturalist bent criticized the suburbanization of urban culture in this period, but our identification of the suburban strategy does not refer to that critique of the arrival of large, nationwide retail stores in Manhattan (Hammett and Hammett 2007). The rise of suburban space speaks not to niche consumer preferences but to the norms by which space and classes are organized in the city. The hegemonic adoption of the assumptions of suburban space made it nearly impossible to propose land uses that would produce economically diverse neighborhoods (as opposed to homogenously upper- or lower-income projects like Battery Park City or the occasional affordable housing project), or counter a century of extreme racial residential segregation (Massey and Denton 1993).

Saying that the city is characterized by the suburban strategy does not mean that the city will become like the suburbs in every way. It will not. In particular, US suburbs have a middle-class orientation, and its residents are relatively more concentrated in a narrow economic band than are residents of the city. The polarization of incomes characteristic of a global city augurs against the blossoming of a comparable middle-class core in New York. Quite to the contrary, New York has become increasingly unaffordable, and real estate bubble or no real estate bubble, shows no signs of becoming more affordable to most of the people who live here and try to establish lives here (America's Most Expensive Cities 2009). Rather than become like contemporary suburbs, the polarization of incomes under contemporary globalization is likely to lead to a bifurcation of American cities—between a small number of cities that have seen the size of their global managerial elite class grow, and the rest of urban America. Just as polarization has spelled two very different futures for the classes at the top and the bottom of individual cities, so city-by-city differences explain why whole cities will absorb different impacts from globalization. The era of suburban space has introduced the spatial and land-use homogeneity of the suburbs but also the polarization of the global city.

The Contradiction of the Suburban Strategy

A spatial strategy is a virtually inevitable element of any effort to keep a city so polarized between rich and poor. Beyond the suburban spaces of the Imperial City are large areas of policed space that closely control people who are not fully vested members of the Imperial City, and help insure that they make little direct impact on those in the elite spaces in the city's center. As well, the strategies of policed space are sometimes used in suburban spaces, whenever a group threatens the climate-controlled serenity of suburban spaces.

Intensive policing of the most powerless is a hallmark of policed space. Throughout the early 2000s, one of us (Shepard) worked in a syringe exchange program in the South Bronx. Most weeks, program members returned 90–95 percent of the syringes they received from the program. While the program was funded and monitored by city and state agencies, the police made a habit of arresting members of our syringe exchange program going to and from the program. While New York Department of Health regulations superceded laws related to possession of drug paraphernalia such as the syringes, this did not stop the members of the NYPD from picking off those going to and from the program. Program organizers held meetings with the Department of Health and talked with the police. The police said it was a matter of training and that they would work to make sure police understood the laws regarding syringe exchange programs. But little changed.[10]

The tactics of policed space result in frequent police intrusions into the lives of people of color (McArdle and Erzen 2001). In 2007, a group of thirty-two African American and Latino young people in Bushwick were arrested while going to attend the funeral of a friend. Initially, Police Commissioner Ray Kelly claimed the teens were blocking traffic, damaging property and were part of an "unlawful assembly" as they walked from a park to the subway station to attend the funeral, which was of an alleged gang member. The Brooklyn district attorney claimed "they were not just walking on one car; they were trampling on all sorts of cars. It was almost as if they were inviting their arrest" (quoted in Herbert 2009). Yet, no evidence supported the police claim that the students were blocking traffic or jumping on cars. "Witnesses who saw the kids, including one man who used his cellphone to take photos of some of them who were handcuffed on the sidewalk, said they had been orderly, quiet and well behaved," reported Bob Herbert (2009). Greer Martin, a witness to the arrests outside her front window, spoke on the record, despite her fear of repercussions from the NYPD. "[S]he felt the police officers had abused their power," noted Herbert. "I was shocked beyond shock," she explained. "My windows were open, and it didn't look like the kids had done anything wrong." In the wake of the event, citizens started mobilizing. Make the Road by Walking, one of the members of New York's Right to the City Alliance, helped the students in Bushwick get organized. The students formed a group called Student Coalition Against Racial Profiling (SCARP), which was able to get the charges thrown out for its members and procure a legal settlement, with several thousand dollars being paid to minors who were held by police for a day and a half. (Herbert 2009; Lee 2007). The prolonged detention for minor infractions that the teens suffered is a regular part of the control exerted in policed spaces (New York Civil Liberties Union 2006). While SCARP, Make the Road by Walking, and others highlighted throughout this book have fought for a right to the city, their experiences suggest that structural violence continues to be a common experience for social outsiders.

The intensity of surveillance is markedly different for people of color in policed space than for people in the more privileged communities that are home to suburban spaces. Michael Scolnick, a lawyer for those arrested in Bushwick, said, "what I have been told by my clients is that their being stopped on the street merely for being on the street is about as common an occurrence in their lives as me getting up in the morning and brushing my teeth, and that's pretty outrageous" (Herbert 2009). These arrests reflect a larger pattern of hyper-regulation of public space and preemptive action against any behavior deemed deviant by the NYPD (McArdle and Erzen 2001). Aggressive policing came to characterize the control of public spaces in communities of color during the suburban period. Public space is a uniquely useful site in which to discern such shifts in strategies of control. But public space not only reflects such changes, it foreshadows strategic shifts by the urban growth machine before they can be recognized in other areas.

Leading Indicator

We used bonus plazas to discern the ways in which urban elites changed their orientation to the city from the privatized period to the eras of filtered and suburban spaces. Bonus plazas are *leading indicators* of developments in the capitalist city.

Bonus plazas, permitted in the highest-density sections of New York, were components of building projects in an especially competitive real estate environment, and were built by a particular type of developer. Logan and Molotch identify three different types of real estate speculators. The first are serendipitous entrepreneurs, small time landlords who simply profit from a single property they happen to own. The second are active entrepreneurs, who make some effort to strategically buy property that will increase in value due to external factors like growth or other large development. Third are the structural speculators. As Logan and Molotch explain, structural speculators do not simply "estimate future locational trends; they supplement such intelligence by intervening in that future. . . . [They] seek to alter the conditions that structure the market. Their strategy is to *create* differential rents by influencing the larger arena of decision making" (Logan and Molotch 1987, 30). The small group of successful Midtown Manhattan real estate developers are successful in that highly competitive environment not by building what is expected (since the property they buy is already priced to reflect that value) but by building something more profitable than others had thought possible. This may mean gaining zoning variances, creatively interpreting zoning regulations, secretly assembling a large property out of many small lots, or inducing state investment in a project that will increase the value of their property. Being unapologetic and ruthless are job requirements—as those in the field repeatedly pointed out in our interviews, "it's not a genteel business." Succeeding as a structural speculator, more specifically, requires the ability to predict the future and *make* the future: Structural speculators decide that New York's far West Side rail yards can become a densely developed business and entertainment center. They propose that the state expand a convention center next to their own development project. Or they encourage the local government to displace poor people to make room for ambitious corporate projects. Structural speculators seek to make the city, and know the shape of the future city in advance of everyone else.

Thus, to the extent that major real estate developers are successful (and most Midtown developers are family dynasties that have been central players in the game since the end of the Second World War), the public spaces built by such speculators are not a response to the current moment in the city, but self-fulfilling prophecies about what the city will become. Generations of urban writers have looked at the built form and architecture of the city to understand what it was, or what it has become. Careful examination of structural speculators' bonus plazas reveal such developers' plans for what the city will become in their hands.

Each of the periods we identified—privatized, filtered, and suburban— preceded by several years popular recognition of the trends with which it was associated. Privatized spaces, characterized by a flight from public space, preceded popular recognition of widespread flight from the city. For many, the 1950s were still the economically promising and socially stifling years of Eisenhower-era postwar America. The plazas of the era are stark. The office buildings took a step back from the city—leaving a concrete expanse like a free fire zone between the building and the public, or levitated above the city entirely, elevated above private plazas. Though census data only begins to show population declines for cities in 1960, by then plans for public spaces that retreated from the city had been in the works for years. The public still embraced the city, but structural speculators, even those who stayed in the city, backed away.

An even more dramatic contradiction emerged in New York City around 1975, as filtered spaces became more typical. In the spotlight, the *Daily News* was proclaiming "Ford to City: Drop Dead." President Gerald Ford claimed (inaccurately, it turned out) that he wouldn't bail out the nearly bankrupt city, and pundits and the public alike prepared for the utter collapse of New York. Yet, at the same time, reinvestment in New York had already begun. In public plazas, developers stopped instructing architects to design office plazas as barren no-man's lands, as they had for decades. Instead, architects and planners introduced amenities to bring white-collar workers to the spaces: bright artwork, playful chairs, and planting arrangements all appeared where years earlier there would have been only flat concrete.[11] Just as the public confirmed their fear that New York was a sinking ship they needed to abandon, developers were laying the foundations for the gentrifiers' return on a scale few would have believed.

The era of filtered spaces offers a particularly striking example of bonus plazas as leading indicators. In 1975, the same year the city nearly defaulted on its debts, the Citigroup Center opened. In fact, the New York fiscal crisis was itself precipitated when Citibank led a group of investment banks that refused to roll over the city's debt (Harvey 2005, 45). Yet, Citibank apparently had the foresight to see New York would be restructured in the interests of corporate priorities, and opened the filtered Citigroup Mall at the base of their new landmark office tower. The same actors who prompted the crisis that so frightened the public were confident that the crisis would be resolved in their favor. The return to the city during the filtered period was initially cautious, undertaken through carefully enclosed and defended spaces. In addition to filtered shopping malls like Citicorp, designs were drawn up for what planner Oscar Newman christened "defensible spaces," huge complexes for thousands of residents, with privately owned plazas in the middle and only one way in or out (Newman 1972).[12]

But the impact of defensible spaces was only noticed a decade later, so that by the time popular culture had recognized the filtered city, structural speculators were employing the suburban strategy. *Citadels* is Friedmann and Wolff's (1982) term to describe the filtered, heavily fortified "towers of steel and glass and . . . fanciful shopping malls" that were capital's "most vulnerable symbol." While citadels were first designed in the early 1970s, Friedmann and Wolff described the "citadel and the ghetto" in 1982, the same year the movie *Bladerunner* presented pop culture's comparable vision of elite segregation from dystopian urban chaos. As public recognition of citadels grew, developers began to move on, embracing less defensive structures. Critical urbanists used "citadel" to make sense of projects like New York's Battery Park City (similar to London's Canary Wharf, and a few blocks from the festival market-place of New York's South Street Seaport). Battery Park City as citadel became the most criticized neighborhood in New York City, but there were unacknowledged inconsistencies with describing Battery Park City as a citadel. For one, there was no ghetto surrounding it, only the high-rent financial district and increasingly chic Tribeca. Second, there were minimal walls. Battery Park City was hard to get to, to be sure, but the master plan that was actually implemented was far less exclusive than the five that had preceded it (Smithsimon 2011). Battery Park City was problematic, but the citadel label was out of date. As it neared completion at the turn of the century, the neighborhood had become one of the first suburban spaces in New York. Critics correctly intuited that the public spaces of major development projects articulate a larger vision of what the city should be. But the spaces are generally seized upon as evidence of what the city already is—not cutting-edge predictions, by those who have the power to make those predictions come true, of what the city will become.

Post-Suburban Spaces for the Post-Imperial City

The latest projects of structural speculators offer insight into the direction the city is headed. The defensible spaces designed since the 1970s to draw professionals have been a success on the terms set by their developers. Likewise, the verdant parks of the suburban strategy have attracted and retained an elite demographic in this new urban form.

Manhattan's recently opened High Line Park presents the ambiguous promise and peril of the city's most recent public spaces. The High Line is a promenade built on the remains of the last standing mile and a half of a steel-frame elevated freight train line which operated from 1930 to 1980. In the 1990s, developers enlisted Mayor Giuliani to help them tear down the High Line for redevelopment. In response, a group of supporters of the High Line called on the city to make this piece of history accessible as a public park (Loew 2009). With much effort by an alliance of residents, activists, and developers, the High Line opened to the public in 2009 and drew widespread praise (Filler 2009). The park's views suggested that the city could be a work of art. Karen Loew, a supporter of the park

The elevated High Line Park cuts a romantic path across the gentrified West Side of Manhattan.

proposal, wrote, "Saving the High Line and opening it for everyone promised not only personal pleasure, but the opportunity to build something together. You could get on the ground floor of a community playground for the world" (Loew 2009).

The park was undeniably beautiful. Yet, the construction of the space in the core of a rapidly suburbanizing and gentrifying part of the city compromised the vision of some of the people who supported the High Line's conversion into a public park. Because space is local, public space in a community that had become less open, affordable, or accessible to most city residents reflected not the promise of popular space as much as the ambiguity of the Imperial City's selective, luxurious beauty. The park became a centerpiece in the process of renovating its industrial west side neighborhood into a battery of luxury buildings.

High Line Park. Countering claims that the park was built with sustainable materials, activists from Rainforests of New York unfurled a banner from the elevated park in 2009 protesting the use of rain forest wood.

As a new public space, the High Line provided a glimpse of the assumptions that reshaped the Imperial City. At least before the financial crisis of 2008, suburbanized spaces exhibited growing confidence on the part of elites. This confidence began to outstrip itself, to curdle into hubris. The High Line, for instance, violated important lessons learned over the last forty years about usable space—in particular City Planning and William H. Whyte's (1988) observation that people don't climb stairs to get to open space, and Jane Jacobs' (1961) dictum that good public spaces need visibility, "eyes on the street," and constant traffic. The park was rightfully celebrated for its innovative design and perspective-altering views of the city. Nonetheless, as an elevated walkway, it joined the ranks of the skybridges of Atlanta's Peachtree Center and the elevated walkways of San Francisco's Embarcadero. Such passages are attractive, but soon become dated, under-used white elephants. If anything, the High Line at present has even less utility as a passageway. The hubris of the city's latest public space is reflected in the assumption that the High Line couldn't fail to be a popular success.

In contrast to the last decade of suburban spaces that were built with care to make sure they would be usable, safe, and exclusive, the latest round of signature public space designs express hubris. While one may not be the product of the other, it's roughly analogous to the economic booms and bubbles of the same period that were predicated on the belief that success was the only outcome—that technology stocks could only go up, that real estate prices could only go up, that homeowners couldn't fail to make their payments. After years of caution, and years before that of concern that no public space would succeed, the most recent moment was one in which builders assumed that they couldn't fail. Much like the overconfident foreign policy of that period, developers believed that in the Imperial City, every new plaza would be greeted with flowers.

Pointing out the imprudence of such projects has echoes of a tradition of gleeful pessimism among some, in which each downturn is a sign of the terminal crisis of capitalism, each uptick requires a reminder that the cycles will reverse, and the end is still near. An aversion to the irresponsibility of that *politique du pire*—hoping for the worst to bring about the downfall of the powerful—makes us reluctant to use New York's imperial boom to sound an alarm. Nonetheless it's not surprising that these recent examples suggest something for the next decade less certain than the moment in which they were built.

Forgetting the past was nearly inevitable in the imperial boom, and was central to the overconfidence that built the Imperial City. This is striking given how recently New York seemed in very different straits. In December 2006, the mayor's office unveiled a massive, comprehensive master plan, PlaNYC 2030, that assumed in important respects that everything would continue as it was. Most critical were the assumptions that the city, which not many years before had been losing population and floundering in extended recession, would continue to grow indefinitely in size, wealth, and employment at the rate it had most recently.

Economic and population growth are important and linked assumptions. In recent decades, population growth filled once-abandoned neighborhoods, and economic growth (though accompanied by growth in inequality as well) provided resources that have at least given the city financial options if not equality. But not only is economic growth never to be taken for granted (nor assumed an unqualified good), the cycles of New York are likely to be sharper than elsewhere. The economy of a global city like New York, so dependent on the financial markets, is especially volatile (Gladstone and Fainstein 2003). Population growth is likewise variable.

Our purpose is not to predict one specific failure or another. The point is that New York has had good times and bad times, and in the long march out of the twentieth century, designers found once again the principles of public space design that made for a pedestrian city that worked well in booms and busts. The most recent wave of building, however, ignored those rules, and it's not hard to see that such spaces will be ill suited for anything but fair weather.

What happens in those inevitable stormy days, however, is not a question of just the weather, but of social organization. The Post-Imperial city calls for strong, creative, and dynamic social movements that can make the best of the city's Post-Imperial Age.[13] Many of the activists whose work is explored in the second half of this book have worked for just such a future. (Perhaps this Post-Imperial Age, like others, will muster the political wherewithal to establish long-needed social protections.)

Increasingly, social movements have organized their demands and their strategies spatially. Groups like FIERCE, Right to the City, Reclaim the Streets, and the Lower East Side Collective have framed their demands in terms of the right to space and towards spatially framed injustices. Oppositional social movements have long included contests over space, but the strategies they employ, the demands they make, and the spaces they claim depend on the historical moment. As the chapters that follow show, the suburban strategy opens certain kinds of terrain for engagement. In doing so, spatially oriented activism has invoked the liberatory potential of play. The presence of accessible, well-appointed suburban spaces provides a new and promising stage on which such politics can play out. A cordon of policed space notwithstanding, suburban spaces remain fundamentally more accessible than the physically barricaded spaces of the privatized era. By anticipating the direction of the city through investigation of leading-indicator spaces, spatial activists have the potential to reorient both the spaces and the social realities that exist within them.

In 1975, everything seemed to be pointed downward, yet the city was on its way up. Today the options do not have to be so stark. Rather than the image of the citadel, which evoked a rage of impotence at the financial masters of the universe, the hubris of the public spaces of the moment is evidence instead of the city's vulnerability. The belief that nothing can go wrong speaks of a regime of overconfident elites unprepared for challenges of any kind. They are beautiful gardens built with expectations of an endless summer. This time around structural speculators are likely to be surprised when seasons change in the city, but we need not be. In public space we see more entrances, openings, and opportunities as well as filters and fences. Those openings don't yet provide genuine popular access to these public spaces, but suggests how we can remake formerly suburban spaces in the Post-Imperial City.

With an eye to the leading indicator of public space, instead of reacting to the past we can organize and plan for the future. Change this time around will not be a repeat of disinvestment, white flight, and the genocide of "planned shrinkage" (Wallace and Wallace 1998). The Imperial City contains vulnerabilities to people-powered social movements that will no longer need to scale the citadel's walls to get noticed, but will reach the airy, accessible, well-appointed plazas in order to claim space and be heard. Even in times of financial crisis, activists have fashioned activism focused on public space and used play to help reimagine the city's meaning.

RESISTANCE

Introductory Notes to Part 2

Though elites had initiated privatization of public space as early as the 1960s, by the 1990s, the pattern of erosion was broadly recognized. The private was overtaking the public. In the larger political field, "privatization" was ingesting everything from health, to water, to basic services, to public space itself (Brechner et al. 2000; Klein 2003, Warner 2002). In New York, the results were showing in the streets, plazas, and treatment of public spaces around the city.

City agencies and private developers renovated areas that had for years served as community spaces for a range of distinct groups, and transformed them into suburban spaces. Queer direct action groups SexPanic! and FIERCE! recognized that spaces where queers had converged for generations—the Ramble in Central Park, the piers off the West Side Highway—were being squeezed and regulated in unprecedented ways. When the city attempted to sell off community gardens, environmental groups such as the More Gardens! Coalition, Lower East Collective, and Time's Up! organized their own defense of public space. As means of defense, these groups utilized elements of play, including bike riding, agitprop, and creative direct action to defend public space from gardens to streets to parks, while demonstrating ways to make use of it.

Archival flyer of early public space movement. By the 1990's, street activists were expressing their demands in terms of public space.

One striking transformation in the period was activist groups' reframing of their movements in terms of public space, challenging this encroachment of the private into the public. "A central goal of American social movements involves redefining norms of public and private space," wrote Michael Warner (2002,

31), who worked with SexPanic! to fight the attack on a queer public commons (see Shepard 2009; Warner 1999).

I (Shepard) remember October 4, 1998. walking with members of Sex-Panic! over to the West Side Highway, to the Christopher Street piers, where SexPanic! hoped to convince the city to leave one "Queer Pier" for those who had long hung out at the space. There we passed out flyers. "Demand a Queer Pier," the flyer read, "Supporters of the plan to develop the piers on Manhattan's west side promise something for everyone—soccer fields for kids, movie theatres and stores, even a habitat for bird watchers." Yet something was amiss. "[W]hat's there for the people who are already using the piers—queers who want to cruise, sunbathers showing a little flesh, people shut out of bars and clubs because they aren't old enough or just can't afford the cover charge?" The group called supporters to: "Fight the plan to make the piers PG-rated and sold to the highest bidders. Demand that at least one pier stay queer and stay free . . . We won't be chased out of the village." To defend the space, the group echoed William H. Whyte's adage that the best public spaces are well used public spaces, calling for users to demonstrate what was unique about this space by using it. "Not a protest, not a demonstration. No picket signs, no slogans. Just a queer day on the pier—now and forever."[1] The piers seemed to embody an ideal of community space. Such public spaces could be easily contrasted with private spaces. Michael Warner distinguished between the two kinds of spaces:

Public	Private
open to all	restricted to some
accessible for a fee[2]	closed to even those who would pay
state-related, public sector	non-state, often described as private sector
political	nonpolitical
in physical view of others	concealed
outside the home	domestic (Warner, 2002, 29)

Throughout that fall of 1998, members of SexPanic! had been organizing to defend spaces where communities of difference could converge. Reports of anti-queer violence had been on the upsurge throughout the fall (Sweeny 1998). The Matthew Shepard Political Funeral that October included arrests of some hundred-plus queer activists when police sought to restrict the movement of over five thousand people as they attempted to march without a permit in memory of the Wyoming college student who had been killed that fall. "GAY RIOT" and "Chaos in Midtown: 120 Arrested in Rally Against Anti-Gay Violence" read the headlines of the *New York Post* and *Daily News* on October 20, 1998. At one of the rallies proceeding the action, a friend from SexPanic! who wore a black bandana passed out a flyer for an action by a group called Reclaim the Streets (RTS). The protest was planned for the afternoon the same day of the "Demand a Queer Pier" event described at the beginning of this introduction. After the picnic, members of SexPanic! walked over to Astor Place for the first Reclaim the Streets (RTS) action in New York. Arriving at the action at the Astor Place Cube, where Smithsimon was conducting fieldwork, a horn blared and several hundred people ran out onto Broadway. A few people anxiously hoisted one of the activists up into the air atop a thirty foot high tripod, where he sat looking down as the sound system started pumping rave music. Instead of the image of traffic, he witnessed an image of, "gyrating bodies" as a dance party filled the once sterile space, blocking traffic for three hours.

Watching these events, we became aware of a broad movement around public space. The first two reports in Part 2 of this book consider these early flashpoints in the burgeoning public space movement in New York. The first in Chapter 4 addresses the struggle for a queer public presence along the west-side piers. The second Chapter 5 considers the early Reclaim the Streets group, which helped organize the street party described above.

If the types of public space we have articulated in the first part of the book, served to describe the arc of privatizing developers' serial embrace of privatized space, filtered space, and suburban space—in the second half, the typology tells a different, less chronological story.

In the case of the piers, the community space was an end in itself, a place where community could be experienced and strengthened. The piers present a strong sense of the promise and perils of community space. Reclaim the Streets demonstrated through its actions the means by which a TAZ space can be established, and the way in which it both creates a liberated space for participants (if only for a moment) and presents a point against which to contrast tightly controlled, state-regulated space.

The last two reports build on the work on RTS and FIERCE to consider the struggle for a place to ride a bike, plant gardens, rally and enjoy public space—each representing different kinds of community spaces and temporary autonomous zones. The means these movements would employ to hold space included a joyous brand of play. Over the years after the RTS and FIERCE campaigns, these movements would overlap with global movements aimed at reclaiming a public commons (Klein 2002; Klein 2003).

Chapter 6 follows community garden activists' response to the aggressive privatization campaign by the Giuliani Administration. "Mayor Giuliani consistently uses police force to stifle political expression and punish his critics," wrote garden activist Lesley Kauffman (2000a). "Going to any publicly announced demonstration nowadays means walking into an armed camp: Staggering numbers of police are mobilized for even the tamest rallies" (Kauffman 2000a). Here, the struggle for community space is part of an effort to challenge the recolonizing agenda of the Imperial City. Chapter 7 then makes clear the link between disruption in public space and the uses of play by activists—all to force the city to enforce its own laws supporting access to bike lanes.

In New York City, public space campaigns take a particular urgency. Here, it seems that everything is done in public. People sleep on the subways, connect with partners in the parks; play music on street corners, hold meetings in community gardens, and stage rallies wherever one can find a space. In 1982, nearly one million people rallied against nuclear arms in Central Park, New York's public commons. That was a time when Central Park was considered a public space for debate, discussion, music, and celebration. Recall the mood during the September 1981 Simon and Garfunkel concert in Central Park. After being introduced by New York's Mayor, Paul Simon thanked everyone who had contributed to making the event special—including the pot dealers for selling individual "joints" to the crowd. The crowd roared with laughter. Two decades later, much of this spirit of openness and conviviality had been crushed, a casualty of the "quality-of-life" crusade to eradicate difference or signs of deviance. As part of a larger campaign to recolonize the city and create a core of suburban space, an overly aggressive police force and pro-growth regime had sought to squeeze much of this spontaneity out of the city (Sites 1997; Sites 2003; Vitale 2008). Yet, the hunger for authentic public space and expression would remain.

And activists fought back. When the city denied a homeless group access to the City Hall steps for a rally on World AIDS Day just days after five thousand had stood in the same spot to celebrate a World Series victory, activists sued the city and won on First Amendment grounds. According to the New York Times (2000), a Federal judge, "declared unconstitutional the right of restrictions imposed by the mayor on the use of the steps and plaza in front of New York's city hall for public demonstrations." But for every win, another challenge lay ahead for public space activists. New York Civil Liberties Union attorney Norman Siegel pointed out that under the Giuliani Administration, more suits protesting curtailment of First Amendment rights had been filed against the city than at any other time (Sachs 1998). The city's hostility to protesters was the product both of Giuliani's vindictive personal style and a larger trend towards curtailing exercises of political and cultural dissent. The latter tendency outlived the Giuliani Administration. When anti-war activists tried to hold a march similar to the 1982 anti-nukes action in Central Park before the Republican Convention in 2004, their application of a permit was denied by the city. "The mayor, a Republican, has rolled out the red carpet for the convention," noted Bill Dobbs (2004), who after years of work with ACT UP and SexPanic!, had decided to work with the antiwar group United for Peace and Justice, the group pushing to organize the rally. "But he [Bloomberg] has thrown obstacle after obstacle in the course of protesters, including stopping us from holding a rally in Central Park, a very basic constitutional right." Activists would describe the restriction as part of an ongoing pattern of suppression of dissent through hypercontrol of public space (Bogad 2006; Boghosian 2007). "These regulations strike a serious blow against the constitutional rights of a large group of people to get across their point of view," Dobbs would note, referring to the mayor's argument that so much private money had gone into refurbishing the park that the city could not risk damage that might occur if people walked on it. "The Bloomberg administration conjured up the specter of damage to the lawn without thinking about the threat to civil liberties," Dobbs concluded. The mayor would note philanthropists had earned the money to refurbish the space and they deserved to make sure the space was clean. Those struggling for a place to rally argued that First Amendment protections were more important than clean grass (Bogad 2006; Boghosian 2007). A regime of suburban space, it turned out, threatened civil liberties. As more and more space was restrictively designated as privatized, filtered, or suburbanized, activists resisted the threat that this held for their rights to free expression. Over and over again in the second half of this book, activists' challenges to the suburban space regime are played out as a conflict between expression and repression.

Literature for the first RTS action noted that "We demand great feasts of public space. We demand our freedom to express. We demand clean air—as if the basis for democracy were not the ability to breathe!" The chapters which follow build and elaborate on this interplay of play, activism, and a hunger for public space.

CHAPTER FOUR

Fences and Piers

An Investigation of a Disappearing Queer Community Space

On October 5, 2002, two women from the AIDS Coalition to Unleash Power (ACT UP) cut a hole in a fence separating a walking path from a Hudson River pier facing towards New Jersey on Manhattan's West Side Highway "as a gesture of solidarity" with the queer youth who had used the space before the fence went up. "We could hear a bunch of my girlfriend's kids cheering us on across the street, and as soon as we started it was over—the police were there, dragging us off the fence," one of the participants explained (Fraser 2002). The police arrested both women (Amataeu 2002).

This chapter examines the importance of community space to disenfranchised groups, the colonization of such community spaces to create suburban spaces, and how activists use a *spatial* frame to demand group visibility, equality, and vitality. In this case study, we examine queer youth, many transgender, who in the 1970s and 1980s made the Hudson Street piers their community space. We use personal narratives of people who lived and "hung out" among the crumbling piers, abandoned warehouses, and industrial detritus of the Hudson River waterfront to understand the vital contributions of community space in constructing and enacting counterpublics and counterhegemonic queer identities. By the 1990s, these spaces were being razed to create more suburban space, the Hudson River Park, as part of the larger restructuring of the Imperial City.[1]

As the people who used the piers knew best, the space was never perfect. It was dangerous, sometimes horribly so, for the people who went there. But participants in the venture to construct a community out of these spaces nonetheless viewed them as safe havens, even as home. It is not necessary to sanitize these accounts of community spaces to recognize the important social functions they played for the people who used them or to appreciate what was at stake in the efforts to fence them off, destroy them, and reconstruct these areas as suburban spaces.

Why Snip a Fence?

Author Naomi Klein (2002), a journalist who has spent years covering the convergences, riots, and worldwide confabs of the new global justice activism, explains that conflicts over public and private spaces are at the center of the movement. And so is the theme of fences. For Klein, fences serve as "barriers separating people from previously public resources, locking them away from much-needed land and water, restricting their ability to move across borders, to express political dissent, to demonstrate on public streets . . . Fences have always been part of capitalism" (xviii–xix). As areas of life ranging from health care and education to intellectual property, seeds, genes, and even water and air are commodified, fences become part of the "invading of the public by the private" (Ibid., xx). Those not thought to contribute economically are fenced out as fences of social exclusion discard entire countries and peoples. Corporate globalization creates a lot of fences.

Fences also represent political barriers. After years of an often unpopular quality-of-life campaign, former New York Mayor Rudy Giuliani erected a fence separating citizens from City Hall. Activists tried to cut that fence open in 1999. Even before the elaborate antiterrorist functions of post 9/11 New York, Mayor Guiliani supported a blandification and hyper-control of public space—replete with elaborate security, racial profiling, and "stop and frisk" policing (see Wilson and Kelling, 1992/2001). Bloomberg merely extended the process. The results can be witnessed in the transformation and control of New York's physical spaces. Fences are part of a methodical process used to target "communities of difference" as urban areas are redesigned as suburban space (Goldberger 2001; Hammett and Hammett 2007). In order for these entertainment zones to thrive, the state must heavily regulate their use. Anthropologist Jeff Ferrell (2001) explained: "The caretakers of these newly segregated spaces—politicians, business leaders, community associations—contend that such closed spaces are essential to the economic vitality, interpersonal safety, and emerging identity of the city" (43). They bring down the weight of the law on those, such as pier users, who trespass on spaces once considered open to all. Yet the process has not been without opposition.

What takes shape in the story of the Hudson River piers is a flashpoint in an ongoing class war: on the one side, a pro growth urban regime favoring the suburbanization of public space, on the other a do-it yourself public space activism aimed at preserving public space for people. The struggle involved the West Side Highway in New York's historically queer West Village, where fences cut queer youth of color, sex workers, runaways, and the homeless off from the piers and the feeling of safety and place once found there (Shepard 2004). This analysis focuses on the history of access to this space, considering the phenomena of queer community space as a liberatory geography and as counterpublic, the ways users congregated there, what happened when they were fenced out of the space, and the way the group organized to fight back. Countless groups have fought the process. Their challenge—the fences they face—speaks to circumstances facing public spaces in cities around the world. In the pages which follow, we consider the struggles of those involved with FIERCE, a West Village group of queer activists who have spent the last decade fighting displacement from the piers. Much of their response was born of a carnival of protest and possibility, as individual pier users reimagined their own beach beneath the streets.

Waves of Carnival

On September 7, 2002, a gender-variant crowd of West Village street youth, drag queens, anarchists, and local vagabonds, led by FIERCE! and the Radical Faeries, pounded drums and paraded in platform shoes in support of the continued presence of young, multiracial queers in the neighborhood. Global justice and other public space activists joined jugglers, students, and hundreds of colorful people dressed in bright oranges, reds, and yellows as they "flamed through the streets," dancing in solidarity with young people who had recently been profiled by Sixth Precinct cops and harassed by other Village residents. The carnival roamed the Village in support for those most targeted by the quality-of-life campaign initiated by Giuliani and perpetuated by Bloomberg. The action was a part of a decade-old battle between those in favor of "quality of life" for the rich and those helping to preserve New York's colorful street life. In the days and weeks after Rudy Giuliani left office in 2002, fear of a return to the "rotten apple" days of the mid-1970s through the early-1990s could be felt in the regular community board meetings of the 6th Precinct, the West Village neighborhood. That year, an engineer was murdered in a manner that harkened back to that earlier era. Subway riders complained they were witnessing an increase in panhandlers, prostitutes, and homeless people. In response, a small group of village residents got together to form a group called Residents in Distress, or RID. Their goal was to regain control of the village from the runaways, the prostitutes, and transgender people who frequented their neighborhood. RID organized to get more police into the West Village. On January 19, 2002, the New York Times published an article entitled, "Tolerance in Village Wears Thin: Drug Dealing And Prostitution Are Becoming A Hazard In A Normally Quiet West Village Area." It promoted RID's calls for more police, specifically referring to quality-of-life issues related to the presence of "Gay and Black kids" as well as "transvestites" and related "public safety" issues. By February, RID sponsored a community forum with Community Board 2 and the Sixth Precinct over the problems of street youth loitering, peeing in their vestibules, and engaging in prostitution. Local politicians and the police commissioner attended the event. Abrie Lees, Chairperson of Community Board 2, led the proceedings. She outlined her legislative charge to purge the youth that gather at the piers, then closed for "renovations."

For queer activists, it looked like another chapter in a long series of battles that had taken place over street youth in the thirty-three years since the Stonewall Rebellion marked the beginning of the gay liberation movement right there on the corner of 7th Ave and Sheridan Square. It appeared as yet another morality campaign to arrest and displace transgender and queer youth of color, some homeless, and sex workers. In response, FIERCE! drew up a flyer calling for neighborhood members to stack the scheduled community board meeting. Their flyer offered the question, "Whose quality of life are we talking about when . . . block associations are organizing to 'clean their streets' (whose streets?!!)" of our presence. "Many residents are calling the police 'on' us; we have been told that we are not wanted in the neighborhood because we are 'lowering their property value.'" The flyer noted an increase in police sweeps and harassment of transgender, gay, lesbian, bisexual (GLBT), and homeless youth of color in the West Village, charging the police with profiling youth of color. Throughout the community board meeting, FIERCE! called for a "Queer Pier," designed by street youth who'd been on the street for a generation, while concerned citizens called for more policing and arrests of homeless youth. Self-proclaimed "community members" argued with "interlopers." Code terms with racial overtones such as *those people* were used as other residents suggested the street kids were bringing drugs and crime into the neighborhood. The police said they would do more to "get tough on the problem" using a classic vocabulary of punitive measures. One resident even stood up to proclaim that the neighborhood was becoming like "the Crips versus the Bloods," a reference to the Los Angeles street gang wars charged with the symbolism of racial violence. Calls to "clean their streets" read as calls for class cleansing of social outsiders. Other community residents called for increased arrests for quality-of-life crimes, such as public urination. What was the driving concern of the Residents in Distress? Perhaps it was the demographic shifts taking place throughout the country, anxiety about multiculturalism, or class animosities between land owners and the homeless Regardless, FIERCE! fought back.

"We're sick of Big Business, wealthy residents, and police using curfew laws, misdemeanor arrests and physical violence to target transpeople, queer youth of color, sex workers and the homeless," said Aries de la Cruz, a seventeen-year-old member of FIERCE!.

"Where's the quality of life, and who's it for?" Tim Doody, a Radical Faerie living in New York City, pondered before the rally, cosponsored by FIERCE! and the Radical Faeries, on September 6, 2002. "Bloomberg is continuing Giuliani's priority of profits before people. Community centers face eviction and community gardens face bulldozers. The attempted purge of queer youth of color from the West Village is an odious part of this trend."

The two groups affiliated with the protest were FIERCE! and the Radical Faeries—the latter a collection of gay men who generally share spiritual and political beliefs, striking costumes that mix and match gender, and who meet in intentional communities scattered in predominantly wooded areas around the United States. Tim Doody said, "We're here to show support to this next generation of queer youth and to make a stand for public space. Nothing says resistance like an angry six-foot drag queen in six-inch heels. And we've got at least 60 of them."

Everyone met at the fountain in Washington Square Park. A man with a beard, red face makeup, and a bright red skirt passed out green flyers proclaiming: "QUEER CARNIVAL OF RESISTANCE, STARRING FIERCE, RADICAL FAIRIES AND YOU!!!" The flyer proclaimed: "As privileged allies, we're hitting the streets today, in the spirit of Stonewall. We insist that civil liberties and OUR public space not be compromised for the benefit of the wealthy! Please help us create a just and more caring society." As usual on a Saturday night, the space was bustling. Just to the south of the Washington Square arch, a group sang from the '70s anthem "Carwash," contributing to the joviality in the air. A crowd of men in feather boas, orange headpieces, and high heels met with a "comms" (or a communications team) composed of many anarchists from global justice movement circles. The struggle against the privatization and commercialization of public space is a core task of the

 WEEK-END

Protest gentrification and police brutality in the West Village

1:00pm - Midnight Saturday
Oct 5, Sheridan Square

We are sick and tired of Watching the police, wealthy resident associations and big business take over the West Village as part of their 'Quality of Life' Campaign.

We Demand an end to the curfew laws, misdemeanor arrests and physical violence targeting transpeople, queer youth of color, sex workers and the homeless!

Revolt! Reclaim! Resist!
Come Out Protest October the 5th!

FIERCE, an organization for TLGB Youth   (646) 336-6789   Please do not post this flyer

Flyers by Radical Faeries and FIERCE (above) and FIERCE (below)

movement against corporate globalization. Activists involved with Critical Mass, then in its tenth year, from Time's Up!, Reclaim the Streets and the More Gardens! Coalition helped marshal the event. Members of ACT UP, the standard bearer for the current activist resurgence, were on hand.

The Radical Faeries began the evening's ritual, ushering the spirits of the East, West, South and North, as East Village activists joined West, creating a solidarity between queer and social justice movements. Activists ate fire and screamed. Many roared with approval as members of FIERCE spoke about the challenge of maintaining the West Village as a "community" that could include sex workers, the homeless, queer youth, transgender people, and the like. An ad hoc core of drummers, some playing trash cans, others water buckets, and one particularly effective gentleman with a real drum, formed a samba band, setting the beat. Dancers in orange, lavender, and red symbolic flames flared as the march took off into the night.

The Radical Faeries, a number of whom were sporting beards, blouses and twelve-inch high heals, led the march west out of Washington Square. "Whose Village? Our Village!" many chanted. We marched up MacDougal to West Eighth, past Seventh Avenue, gradually taking Christopher Street, occasionally contending with two or three police, but facing very little difficulty in terms of clashes. We zipped down Christopher, reenergizing the Greenwich Village night, meandering through the streets, stopping to dance on West 10th Street, before converging along the West Side Highway. Once open space, this place was lined with fences, separating us from the pier users who got past the fences and still converged there. As one of the few places in the city where someone can sit without disturbance or entrance fee, the space still draws large numbers who continue to utilize it as a place for cross-race and class contact. A speaker noted that queers have used this space for a generation, and now it was being developed into a park designed more for families and tourists than the crowds of nude sunbathers who first made use of the space. In homage to Stonewall Veteran Sylvia Rivera, who had lived in these piers and died earlier in the year, the crowd ate Hershey's Kisses and reclaimed the pier as a queer space, with a mass kiss-in, followed by much dancing. Only when the police arrived did we move again. Provoked by the police, the crowd became ever rowdier, never once stepping on the sidewalk, while retracing its steps through the Village night back to Sheridan Square. "Whose Village? Our Village!" chants and "Keep the Village Queer!" filled the night air, the drummers tapping on lamp posts, water bottles, and traffic lights, with police lights and the Stonewall Inn in the distance. A bearded man, without a shirt climbed up on a street light to gaze into the night as activists blocked the streets with their dancing bodies. For an evening at least, the West Village was queer and gay and joyous yet again. Another action was planned for October 5, 2002. With every move to control their movement,

FIERCE responded in kind. Much of the struggle began when a fence appeared at the Christopher Street Pier.

Fences and Boundaries

For as long as most can remember, queer people have made use of the piers as a public commons. Abandoned warehouses and piers off New York's West Side Highway overlooking the Hudson River, these decaying spaces became an emblem for alternate uses and possibilities of public spaces. While they have no legal claim on the space, over the years the piers have come to represent a sort of sacred space and home for queer youth, some homeless runaways, and others with nowhere else to go.[2] For many years, the piers were an unbounded space. Through such openness, boundaries between private and public were lost, as distinctions between inside and outside, us and them, disappeared. Within such spaces, conviviality often abounds and public discourse thrives (Sanders 1998). Conversely, the fences going up around the space emphasize distinctions, separating the space from its users and social connections.

"They were part of the many places to play outdoors, be cooled down on a hot summer day and watch the sunset." recalled cultural critic Douglas Crimp (2007), who hung out there in the 1970's.

Things changed at night. "During the day, I think of it as a different trip. There was one pier here where people would just go and sunbathe," recalled long-term pier user Barton Benes, who has lived near the waterfront for decades. By night time, they became a space for risk and eros. "I think of getting blow jobs as playing," Benes elaborated. "Yea, having sex was playing. What I was doing was playing." They were a place to explore, imagine, and discover new worlds.

At one point in the mid-1970s, one enthusiast actually self-published his own mimeographed *Warehouse Newsletter*, with a circulation of twenty-five hundred, which he distributed along with food and supplies at the piers. The space had long been an arena for the public imagination—appropriated in myths, stories, and poems.[3] "It was a secret place with all sorts of treasures, including file cabinets, antique chairs. . . ," Benes recalled, eluding to the beauty in the ruins witnessed there. "I knew every hole in the ground, every broken piece of wood."

Once a concept like the commons enters the hearts and minds of the people, the only way to halt its use is to shut it down completely (Sanders 1998). And this is exactly what happened. "Queer Youth of Color, Pushed off the Piers, Pushed into Jails," declared a 2002 flyer by FIERCE. On October 5, 2002, FIERCE organized a rally under the slogan, "Reclaim Our Space." The event was billed as "a public celebration of the resistance of Queer youth to the gentrification, harassment, race and gender-based profiling and brutality that have become commonplace under the pretense of 'cleaning up' the West Village." It was organized to "increase public awareness of the criminalization of marginalized people in a neighborhood that has long been a hub of their communities." The day began with a speak-out in Sheridan Square Park, followed by a march to the newly fenced-in Christopher Street Piers.

Much of the rest of this chapter draws on the testimonials and six interviews taken during the Reclaim Our Space rally. Additional interviews were conducted from among clients at a South Bronx syringe exchange who had used the pier and watched it change. Through these testimonials and life stories, we consider the perspective of a queer counterpublic and its interplay with the dominant public sphere (Harstock 1998; Warner 2002).

Social Movements and Narrative Perspectives

Countless reports have considered the relationship between contested space and democratic participation (Warner 2002). The stories witnessed here highlight a struggle for access to a particular public space, the Christopher Street Piers. In doing so, they build on an increasing recognition of the interplay between individual and group narrative and social movement mobilization (Fine 1995). Striking cultural tales often propel social movements, creating spaces that allow actors to locate and construct new identities (Somers 1994). In this case, oral histories and testimonies mark the link between the Gay Liberation Movement of the 1970s and current public space activism.[4] In recent years, this space has been a flashpoint for police crackdowns over public sex as part of the quality-of-life campaign. A flyer for a 1997 SexPanic! rally to save the piers, titled "Queer Pier Facts," announced:

> In the past we fought to claim this space -
> In the present it is under attack -
> Will we let them take it from us in the future?

For many, the narrative in question involves the legacy of the Stonewall Riots, during which homeless street youth who frequented the piers fought back against a police raid and sparked Gay Liberation. Jay Dee Melendez was one of many speakers who referred to a new generation's responsibility to build on the lessons of June 1969: "That was the moment when our veterans said 'no more, we're tired' and fought back. They started it for us." Such narratives allow movement participants to integrate their experiences within larger historic struggles. These movement stories guide participants, serving as the basis for projections, expectations, and memories (Somers 1994). Many pier users locate their lives and struggles within this story. It helps them find meaning in a difficult world.

Street Youth

If there is one activist who has witnessed the ebbs and flows of queer activism, it was eighty-one-year-old Bob Kohler. He was around the nights of the Stonewall Riots, helped organize the Gay Liberation Front in the 1970s, and worked with SexPanic! and Fed Up Queers in the 1990s. And until his death in 2007, he worked with AIDS Housing Network and ACT UP, taking busts into his seventh decade. Much of the link between today's activism around the piers and the legacy of Stonewall involves the difficult conditions of the lives of queer youth. Kohler explains how he got involved:

> By the end of the 1960s I said I was going to take two years off. I used to go in the park [Sheridan Square] all the time and that's where the street kids were. I got very friendly with them and, even though I was older and represented a father figure to them, I wasn't old enough to be the dirty old man, so they trusted me. And they'd confide in me. They lived in the park. And those were the kids who rioted. I'd gotten to know them. I kind of thought I had seen what happens to black people in Harlem; I had seen what happens to poor white people—but I had never seen this with gay teenagers. It was something I just didn't know about. Fourteen-, fifteen-year-old kids with cigarette burns all over their bodies from a father who found out they were gay—or were permanently scarred, and certainly mentally scarred forever. And thrown out and living out of bags in Sheridan Square and washing in the little fountain. I did not know that. I had never understood that there were groups like that.
>
> So I got to know them very well. I would collect clothes for them. I was doing that for months and then Stonewall happened. We were doing the same thing of listening to their bullshit. A couple of them were primping to go down to cruise at the piers where the Jersey cars came. . . . But I was there and suddenly all of the things that had been welling up inside me about these kids came to fruition. Not in any way a revolution. I still will defy anybody who tells you that . . . these kids started a riot because that was the only thing that they knew to do.

Kohler recalled that legacy during the speak-out. "Stonewall started right here in this park by some kids. Some of them were only 14, 16. They were all homeless. They lived in the park. . . . These kids were at the bottom of the heap. There was no way out for them."

Yet, even after the street youth made history, many residents in the West Village looked down on the kids who hung out in the neighborhood's public spaces. They viewed the youth who frequented the piers as "outsiders." In part, tension arose between a mainstream gay

public, of those who saw politics as a matter of changing a few laws, and a queer counterpublic, who saw the struggle for liberation in terms of larger social terms and interconnections (Shepard 2001, 2009). This conflict is expressed in a play, *Queer Pier,* written about the space in 1996 by Frank Aqueno. "That's Robert. He sorta lives here," the protagonist explains. "One of those disposable youth. Runaway throwaways. Standing on a beam under the pier. . . . Oh yeah, he lives under there. . . . This is Robert's home. We're just visitors. . . ." Implicit is a split between "visitors" who have homes and the "boyz," who "live under there" (Aqueno 1996).

Class-based trepidation about the presence of street people at the piers dates back to the 1970s. "Now that the Federal House of Detention has been closed and all the men moved to the new prison downtown, the immediate area in front of Pier 48 has become more deserted during the day hours and at night," an August 14, 1975 edition of *Warehouse Newsletter* reports. "When you go up those stairs to the second floor of Pier 48 ask yourself how you are going to get out of there when the local teenage gang invades the pier?" The *Warehouse Newsletter* was anonymously posted at piers.

Over the years, antagonism towards street youth only increased. West Village residents regularly threw water from their vestibules onto queer youth, who sat there or called the Guardian Angels to patrol spaces where they hung out. At the Save Our Space Rally, FIERCE made a point to respond, wearing signs stating, "We are not trash." Within such a context, the narratives of liberation remain compelling for these youth. Leslie Feinberg, another eyewitness to Stonewall, also spoke at the October 5 rally:

> It is an honor to be here to speak from the podium on the site of a rebellion that took place not just in that bar, the Stonewall Bar, for people who could afford to go in. But took place in this park where homeless youth, many of them African American and Latina and Asian, and youth with no homes to go home to, who had to turn tricks to share a hotel room or to share a hamburger, were in this park and helped spark that Stonewall Rebellion. There was a social chemistry that had nowhere to go but explode under the heat of police repression. The police and the authorities and the big money in this city don't think it's going to happen as they drive the youth of color [from this city]. There's gonna be an explosion they are gonna help combust!

The crowd roared throughout the ebbs and flows of Feinberg's narrative of liberation and solidarity. "We're gonna stand with you shoulder to shoulder against the big developers in this city, the big real estate magnates, the billionaire mayors, this racist police force that has not changed much," Feinberg continued. The story of the piers finds its strength as part of a legacy of resistance to social controls. "You know, after the police raided that bar, they learned a lesson—because people started pushing back. They started throwing their precious pocket change. They began looking for cobblestones." Such places resonate as spaces where their users have countered spatial exclusion through direct action and won. "They drove the police back, not just under the hail of tiny projectiles," Feinberg concluded in homage to campy resilience: "But they taught the cops this: those youth that the police had ridiculed and humiliated as being limp-wristed sissies taught them that a stiletto high heel, in the hands of a drag queen, changes repression!"

A Short History of the Piers

"The Piers is particularly a place where the LGBT [Lesbian, Gay, Bisexual, and Transgender] youth go. Programs think of the piers as a place to do outreach. If you are going to meet folks, that's where they are. The trans community is also there," explained Imani Henry, a Caribbean American outreach worker and FIERCE supporter.

Artist, AIDS activist, and hustler David Wojnarowicz hung out and worked on the piers before his death to the virus. He filled journal after journal with musings, "coded descriptions of sexuality" and evocations of the space. For Wojnarowicz, the crumbling structures of the piers were symbols of what he saw as a dying country (Carr 1993).

ON THE GAY WATERFRONT

a new slide show by Allan Bérubé
author of *Coming Out Under Fire*

Since the days of Walt Whitman, Herman Melville and Langston Hughes, the promise of a place to belong lured queers to the edge of the city. This slide show uses hundreds of old and new photos to tell the dramatic stories of how sexual outcasts fought back on the Chelsea and Greenwich Village waterfront – from the seamen's strikes of the Great Depression, and the sex piers and leather bars of the 1970s, to the police crackdown going on right now.

7 PM Friday September 5, 1997
Lesbian and Gay Community Services Center
208 West 13th Street NYC
Donation Suggested

A *Sex Panic!* Event

From the 1950s to the 1990s, queers converged there unencumbered. "It's very funny. Keeping the youth off the piers. Keeping gay people off the piers," Bob Kohler elaborated. "Back in my day, that's where they wanted us. 'Decent' people didn't go past Hudson Street. That was for us. That was our own personal Casbah. It was called 'the trucks.' . . . They didn't have to see us." For decades, trucks were parked outside warehouses along the waterfront piers. People had sex and hung out here.

Dakota, a fifty-year-old African American man, who hustled at the piers in the 1970s, recalled, "It was popular on the street. . . . You come out to Christopher Street, not Hudson, in the AM. . . ." He elaborated, "In the 1970's, there was money and everything. A big fucking party on the piers." In addition, "There was never a guy or a man walking their dog. They would never come there unless they were gay and they were making a date."

Boo-boo, a forty-three-year-old African American male-to-female transgender person, actually lived on the piers from 1978 to 1986. She recalled a colorful panorama. "It was a lot of white guys coming in from Jersey. It was half Spanish and Black, Cubans. And lots of traces of heterosexuals, drag queens, sex changers, and gay men that we call butch queens that live down there," explained Boo-boo. "This was home. These people would live in the warehouses along the piers. They were abandoned trucks and things like that.

From *Pier 48: Letters from my Evelyn* by
Barton Benes (1978, self published).
Photos by Andres Lander and David
Meyers.

That was our home.
This was where we
would do our living."

By serving as an
open space in an
often closed hostile
world, the piers came
to serve as an auton-
omous zone for
queers (Bey 1985).

Adonis Baough, a
homeless thirty-nine-
year-old man noted:
"In 1981, the piers
was a place where you can go no matter what age you were and be you. If you
were flamey or loud or you were boisterous or you couldn't be that way where
you were from." Adonis, who was from Brooklyn, found it to be a space
where he could let his hair down. "You became you, and then you transformed back when you were home. I became the way I wanted to be. But I
couldn't be that way because the norms of society didn't allow me to be that
way." And he was not the only one. "Other people were being themselves.
Drag queens, transgenders. They had androgynous people. Everybody not
considered the norm could go there and be themselves and not be looked at
any other way."

Extending beyond social, spiritual, and aesthetic limitations, this space offered queers a place to transgress their everyday lives (Dessert 1997). For some it was sex, for others, it was just to be out of the closet because you "couldn't be your real self at home," as Baough recalled. "It was a place you could go and could be you. It's a place to flame around. Oh I was in heaven. It was a place I could go." Its open, liberatory quality functioned as a welcome contrast to the restrictions found elsewhere. "You felt alive. You felt happy, then you had to transform when you got home. We were accepted there, more than other places." Queer theory views the tension between normal (culturally straight) space and queer space as heteronormativity—a series of prohibitive codes and administrative protocols that mandate behavior (Dangerous Bedfellows 1996). Baough suggested that, faced with the barriers of heteronormativity at home, pier users could, "go out there, meet somebody, have sex, go home and be 'normal.'" In this way, queer space opened up a space for a more authentic self. Movement in and out of this space could be cumbersome.

Arriving

A central plotline of the narratives collected involves what brought users there in the first place. "Since the days of Walt Whitman, Herman Melville, and Langston Hughes, the promise of a place lured queers to the edge of the city," a flyer for a lecture on the history of the piers by historian Alan Bérubé announced. (See Figure 5.) It featured a 1975 photo of an African American man clad in Chuck Taylor sneakers and white shorts performing ballet along the waterfront. For decades, queer youth have sought refuge in the West Village and Christopher Street. "This is their boulevard of broken dreams," explained Kohler, while the piers were a place where dreams came true. Despite the current restrictions, the piers remain a Mecca, with queer runaways arriving at Port Authority and making their way there nightly. Some, such as James Place and L. P., came to get away from heroin treatment and foster care homes. Others, such as Steve Rodgers, were running away from non-accepting, abusive homes. Boo-boo left Pensacola, Florida after an uncle raped her in 1978. "They did find that my rectum was torn and it was bloodied. His semen was still in me. They got his DNA and he went to jail for it." When her family told her to "hush hush it," she ran away from home and came to New York:

My family was Muslim and they didn't want me to be dressin' in drag in the house. So they kicked me out to the streets. At the time I was only 16 years old, so I was homeless. So I went to the streets, and I was living under the piers at the time I met my first pimp. He had seen that I was a nice little boy. And he said I could make a lot of money if I dressed like a girl, had sex like a woman. I heard about Christopher Street from the gay parade. I ended up down there. I used to hang out in the Crisco discos. It was from the summer of 1978 to the summer of '86 that I stayed down there on those piers—almost ten years. I lived on the West Side Highway on the piers. That was like another different world. And believe me when I say another different world. It was a whole different scenery.

For others, arrival was a far lighter affair. "Curiosity" brought Samaj. Adonis came "wanting to be popular." For others, such as Dakota, the piers were the end point of a sex migration, a place to connect with guys, free from the closet. Dennis, a FIERCE supporter presented a compelling narrative. "We lived on the Lower East Side. We were really looking for somewhere to feel comfortable. And just be accepted and feel at peace, and where we lived just wasn't the place." Exploring and arriving follow. "So one day I just started walking around and I found my way to the Village. And I just followed everybody." This was Pride weekend, Dennis explained. "It was just like this amazing thing that I have never experienced in my life. Everything was still going on and it was like one in the morning. Everything was live and everybody was out." Within this milieu, one could find a sense of self. "We'd found some place where we could be ourselves. So then we started our usual coming out here every Friday night." Themes of convergence and acceptance permeate through stories of the space, as subplots within a larger tale of liberation. It's a story reinvented by cohort after cohort.

Throughout the summer before the Save Our Space rally, "Christopher Street was in full human bloom," observed Richard Goldstein, a long time pier goer. Most every night hoards of queer teens, most Black or Latino, spilled onto the waterfront. "Here, where white gay men created a sexual carnival in the pre-AIDS '70s, one of the city's liveliest youth scenes unfolds nightly" (Goldstein 2002).

Interviewees described an ideal night there. "Most of the [activity on the] pier wasn't really sex work," Adonis explained. "It was meeting." Still, sex was part of the equation. "It would be in the back, in the old warehouse or whatever." "An ideal evening was when there were people there, but not a lot of people," L. P. recalled. Friendship and interaction were just part of a larger urban panorama of public space. "A lot of friends, you know, people who had been down there for years. And then you have an evening-type community around seven-thirty, eight o'clock. That was the best time to meet because it was just getting dark." The evening was warm. "The breeze was still coming off the water. You can sit around, down by the water, and look at Jersey. And it's like the most amazing romantic thing to sit there with your friends, smoking a blunt, talking and laughing, crying, sharing." And slowly people found some intimacy. "And you'd move on to the dark corners and pick the person you were going to be with that night." The openness and warmth described by L. P. and Adonis partly explain the close connection to the space.

"The good times for us were like in the summertime," Boo-boo recalled, describing a night after work. "After working we would find a couple of young guys and we would all get together and get some alcohol and drugs and we would just get buck naked and we would have orgies down there. And we would laugh." The play of the space involved freedom and experimentation. "The virus was not out at that time."

Certainly, this level of closeness was not possible elsewhere. Kenyon Martin, another of the organizers with FIERCE, added: "People could come here all hours of the night." For Martin, it was the only place he could afford. "When I first came here I didn't have any money. I couldn't go to clubs that cost $20 or $30 bucks. So I would just go hang out." He laughed. "People would have boom boxes. We could dance, hang out, and we didn't have to pay any money. Even to go into a coffee shop you gotta pay money." In contrast, the piers, "was open public space for folks to just be."

It was like a club without an entrance fee. Donald Yearwood recalled a similar feeling arriving in the mid 1960s: "I was 16 when I first came. I had no idea where I was. But I knew when I looked around and saw all these other happy faces, this is where I can be happy and be free."

Yet, freedom was always mediated by interactions with the larger public.

Boo-boo explained: "My routine was that I would sleep half of the day. And no sooner than 6 pm I would get up." Resourcefulness was part of the life. "Now this was the wintertime. Believe me, it wasn't cold cause inside my house I had my kerosene stove." Yet, it was home. "And I was with, like, ten other residents, homeless people there. But we didn't think it was homeless, because we was inside this big old warehouse, which was made out of metal and wood that floated over the Hudson." Police interference within his routine was a norm: "The police used to come in there and wreck our homes and turn down our camps and things. And tell us we had to leave." Homeless, Boo-boo and her roommates would migrate to Tompkins Square Park, another space in the city where they could sleep outside. "We would go down there and sit for a couple of hours and come back and fix our homes again." It was all part of the cat-and-mouse routine. "And I would get up and prepare for my night, that I called my workin' hours. It was called witchin' hours. I would get up, wash up, throw on some clean panties, lay out my outfit." This included, "stockings, my heels, and my wig on the side," Boo-boo explained. "I would put my makeup on and pin on my wig and get my gear on, which is called dragging. And then I would head for the streets. We would come out and walk along the West Side Highway. It was like a "truck stop." Trucks came in from Connecticut, Baltimore, Washington, Los Angeles, Cleveland, Jersey, "all parts of the world and that was the scene." Boo-boo continued: "And there were 60 or 100 of these people that you would have thought were females, but really they was drag queens. And you would be amazed at how they would look because they would look so feminine." Yet, it was also her work. The highway was her office. "We were dressing so nicely you would have thought that we were Sixth Avenue whores, but really we were working alongside of a highway. . . . I would work Monday through Sunday. I was fascinated with what I was doing." It was the best time of Boo-boo's life. "Plus, I was young at the time."

Public Space

A central tension of narratives of public and private space involves what belongs in public. Questions about the meanings of public and private space remain at the heart of discussions about the piers and their surrounding areas. Contrary to conventional wisdom, for many queers, public space was more appealing than private or domestic space.[5] "See, for me the public made it easier," Steve Rodgers, a 39-year-old African American former pier goer, recalled of his first days on the piers from 1978 to 1981. "In the beginning, I defined that public space as an area to do things that you wouldn't do at home. That's public space to me." When asked about what he couldn't do at home, he explained. "More or less, I couldn't bring another male home and have sexual activities. I was still living with my parents." Here public space functions in contrast to the restricted heterosexual terrain of private space at home. "I couldn't do that," Rodgers elaborated. "I wasn't secure in my sexuality growing up. It was male-female, growing up in that heterosexual life. I just don't think my parents understood anything else."

For many years in New York, public space was a place for sexual contact. Author Allan Bérubé explains that queer public spaces, such as the piers, are places "sexual outcasts have created some of the most imaginative, creative, varied, unruly and long-lasting forms of gay sexual culture." For Bérubé, such spaces represent "cracks in our anti-sexual society," where he found "creative moments of intimate sexual adventure with strangers I never saw again. These erotic spaces have been little utopias of Whitmanesque camaraderie" (quoted in Wockner,1997).

Interviewees elaborate on the point. "There was a time when the subways had bathrooms at every station. That was another public space to go and do things," Steve Rodgers recalled. Those who make use of the piers and other public sex spots tend to occupy a worldview of outsider status; the places they occupy for sexual and social contact are understood as queer spaces. The notion of queer space emerges as a subaltern public sphere in contrast to the ideological and material organization of the dominant public sphere (Warner 2002). In this way, this space becomes community space involved in an interplay between dominant and subaltern publics.[6]

Those who used these community spaces describe that use in terms that cast them as members of a subaltern public. "Public space is so important, especially for this particular community. We are not recognized in mass culture," Mervyn Marcano, with FIERCE, explained. "Queers are not recognized. Sure, gay white men are on TV and assimilating into the mainstream culture. But we have a whole different culture. And we've actually been left behind by the gay movement. It's not even a liberation movement anymore."

By "left behind," Marcano refers to a mainstream gay culture barely resembling its liberationist roots (Shepard 2001; Warner 1999). Class, race, and gender lines tear at many gay communities as a split only widens between radical queers who rely on public spaces such as the piers and assimilated gays who own property and pay for leisure.

Yet, the need for public space remains. Samaj, a nineteen-year-old young Black man, spoke for a younger cohort of pier users. Wearing pink shoes, a cardigan sweater, a pink oxford cloth shirt, and a gray do-rag, he described public space as a place "where people of all cultures come together to enjoy a safe space." He drew a clear distinction between his queer counterpublic and the dominant public: "Others have other senses of public space. . . . We have ours." Like Samaj, most interviewees principally recognized public space, such as the piers, as a place for the pursuit of happiness. L. P., a thirty-four-year-old Latino man and former pier user, elaborated. For him, the piers were about, "drugs, sex, excitement, the possibility to meet someone who is sort of like myself."

David Gonzalvez suggested the piers could be considered "free space from our oppressive families, from our oppressive schools, from the negative environments where we come from." The theme of family, from which one needed to escape and rediscover, permeated the interviews.

Family

At the Reclaim our Space rally, activists called out the names of lost family members. Some famous queer martyrs and heroes—Sylvia Rivera, Matthew Shepard, Martha P. Johnson, Audre Lorde, Harvey Milk, and some less familiar names, such as Amanda Milan, a transgender woman killed in 2001—were remembered. Co-Co Richards began her testimony explaining, "Marsha P. Johnson was my gay mother from the streets." Years earlier, Johnson perished in the water off the piers. Johnson's lover, Sylvia Rivera, another Stonewall veteran who died of liver-related complications in 2002, was remembered as the patron saint of transgender activism. Kohler, who had known her since June 1969, was a "father" to Syliva. She, in turn, was a "mother" to many street "children." It was Sylvia's children from her STAR House days of the 1970s who later helped her find housing at Tranny House in the 1990s. "Sylvia was my gay mother. And I loved her to death and I promised her that I would continue the fight," mused Mariah Lopez. She was not the only speaker to refer to Rivera's legacy (see Shepard 2004).

During the early 1990s, Rivera, homeless and battling chemical dependency, formed a squat on the piers. She was also an advocate for others who used the space. Rivera spoke out on September 5, 1997, when SexPanic! held its own rally to save a distinctly "queer pier." The group's literature condemned "the fencing of the piers, curfews and other restrictions imposed on the right of assembly there; and increased arrests and harassment of gay men and lesbians by the Hudson River Park Conservancy, the park police, the Port Authority, and other police agencies" (Nichols 1997). Like many pier users, Rivera expressed mixed emotions about the space. The piers were a source of sadness for her as the place where Martha P. Johnson, her long-time partner, was killed and her body dropped into the Hudson River. On the other hand, she viewed the space as a sort of "safe haven, for the homeless. . . . They can sleep on those piers and know that the presence of non-violent gay men surrounding them at night provides them a kind of protection" (ibid.).

Yet living on the piers was never ideal. For those such as Rivera hustling and living on the streets or the piers, daily living was often consumed with the struggle to find those essentials one needs to survive, producing innovations in locating spaces and seizing opportunities. Abandoned public sites, such as the piers, are quickly reappropriated as living shelters, squats, and such (Hagan and McCarthy 1997). Like many dealing with such circumstances, Rivera built intensely close social networks. Many homeless youth do so, forming close social networks of several individuals, which they refer to in terms of family and kinship (Ibid.). These street "families" help make the day-to-day tasks of survival more manageable, even possible. Speaking at the Reclaim our Space rally, Richards recalled how such networks are born: "So, I came to New York thinking that it would be free-er, gayer. But the only thing that happened here in New York is I got busted up-side the head with a motherfucking billyjack club." She described the scene after her arrest. "It was 20 fucking drag queens in one fucking bullpen. That was not a pretty sight, wigs were coming off and makeup was all over the place." Yet, within this she also found solidarity. "If a sister didn't have anything to get her on the train, those girls in the bullpen came together and put a sister on a train." If someone didn't have money for something to eat, the others would pitch in. "You never know when you are going to be needing it . . . when you are going to need a brother or a sister." For her, this was a solidarity that was hard to shake. Many street youth establish such strong bonds that they may have little desire to leave street life (Kruks 1991). L. P. elaborated, "I basically didn't spend the night at the group home. I just stayed in the streets or with friends and so-called aunts and uncles and cousins."

References to children, cousins, and so forth speak to a form of family constellation for many queers of color. When he arrived at the piers, Adonis recalled, "You met the house children, competed against the other children." The "children" were other black and Latino men (Hawkneswood 1996). A "house," Baough explained, ". . . is like a group. There's different names. There's the House of Channel, Oman, Ebony, Patricia Fields, the house of everything. And these houses are like a clique, a group, and they're treated like a family. They're protected like they are family."

Like all families, these queer constellations face their own struggles. A number of interviewees were less enamored of the scene. Steve Rodgers found the social events "less appealing" and did not stay long. "I saw that the lifestyle included so many facets. You know, they have all these little balls and stuff and they have all these categories. That sort of thing just loses me." Others, such as Dakota, simply shrugged when asked if there was a community on the piers. "No, uh uh. Nope." Samaj elaborated: "Yea, I knew a lot of people there. But it wasn't so much of being a community. Gay people, to me it's so funny. The black gay person, it's funny, you have to pick and choose." Instead, he explained. "It took me years upon years just to know that they were my friends. Black gay men, it's all about dick. Were they friends? Would they be your friends?"

Violence

Bob Kohler was the last to romanticize the lives of queer youth such as Rivera. "They had their own benches. And god forbid if you took one of their benches. . . . One of them killed another person." Violence was a part of the very nature of the space. Boo-Boo explained:

Sometimes, it would get to the point where it would get vile down there. Guys would come down there and wait till you turned tricks and beat you. The violence was too hard for you to imagine. We had certain guys that would pretend to be your johns, and after turning tricks for them they would turn on you, just start pounding you in your face. Or sometimes a guy would pull out a pipe. And start beating you and you would just suck his cock and then he would make you take off your panties and just constantly rape you. And then take your money and your drugs and mess you up for the night. Then you have to end up going to Bellevue Hospital for a couple of days. And then after you get yourself back together, you are back to your life back down there at the piers.

One of my best girlfriends, she went out one Friday night. It was the three of us. She was a transvestite. And she was in the process of having her sex changed. She had been saving up a lot of money. She had it hidden in a hole in the ground, in a can. She went out to see three guys in Jersey. They had conned her. They said they wanted to go with her, but really they was out to brutalize and hurt her. So what happened, they ended up slitting off her nuts and her penis and stuffing it into her mouth, slit her throat and threw her into the Hudson. The cops found her just like she was, with her penis laying outside of her mouth, with her throat split. We identified who she was.

Those were just some of the horrors. One night, another girlfriend was doing a john and he threw kerosene on her and set her on fire. And she had to run and jump into the ocean, the Hudson. She was burnt and unrecognizable, but she's still alive now, if she didn't die from the virus. Then I had another girlfriend that was with a guy from Baltimore when two guys jumped out of a trunk, took and tied her to a fender of a car, and drove her almost six blocks down the street, while one guy cheered with his rectum hanging out the car, calling us queers and screaming, "We're going to kill you all." She didn't make it. She was dragged to her death. That was on a Friday night.

To cope with it, you have to turn to drugs just to survive such horror for your naked eyes to witness. (Stutters and shudders) And then some nights you be so afraid that you just saw a guy taking a knife out and he's just pulling out her guts. She tooked and swallowed the drugs and they fighting over the crack. And he cut her open to get the crack out of her body.

Paradoxically, the danger was in part produced by the same conditions that made the space accessible for alternate uses. "That particular public space there was no patrolling," Steve Rodgers recalled. "They found dead bodies in the warehouse or the water. Those things happened." For as long as any interviewees could recall, danger had been part of the story of the piers. A copy of the anonymously published *Warehouse Newsletter* from July 31, 1975 specifically warned: "STAY OFF THE PIERS AT NIGHT!!!!! MUGGERS CONTINUE TO PLAGUE PIER 48—WAREHOUSE PIER MADE TO ORDER FOR MUGGERS."

The danger of public gathering places such as the piers, the Central Park Ramble, and "the inevitable subway 'T' rooms" was a recurrent theme of the *Newsletter* throughout the summer of 1975, particularly the August 14 edition. For the author, the danger of public sex had more to do with its proximity to unregulated, outdoor spaces than the sex itself. In a homage to his times, the author of the *Warehouse Newsletter* concluded that sex in private spaces—such as backrooms in bars—offered little risk beyond "a case of the clap."[7] Still, he acknowledged that gay men were resourceful enthusiasts. "Many times I have thought the motto of promiscuous gays, including myself, should be a variation of the Post Office motto: Through rain, hail, sleet and snow, the 'gays' will get through!!!" While the anonymous author's newsletters acknowledged the dangers of public sex, he clearly offered his support for these spaces. "Am I against the piers or nite activity in this area??" he asks in the July 31, 1975 newsletter. "No, certainly not. My days of the trucks, street cruising, fucking, and all the rest have been right along with some of the rest of us who are 'charter members' of the truck cruisers club."

Death of an Autonomous Zone

The piers were a community space rather than a TAZ space, because participants created them as a way of enacting a community. The spaces were controlled by users, occupied by a specific community. Unlike a TAZ, this space proved tremendously resilient, lasting for decades. Autonomous zones are transitory by their very nature (Bey 1985). As early as 1983, pier users remember the space changing and state control being reasserted. Rodgers recalled: "Then they knocked down this warehouse in 1983. They took that off. Then they started building up the pier." Over the next twenty years, flux was constant. AIDS was a central part of the change. "I'm one of the last of my kind from that group down there, of the 100 or so drag queens that grew up with me," Boo-boo mused. Most were lost to either violence or AIDS. Throughout all of her years of work there in the late 1970s and 1980s, she failed to see the disease she called "The Killer" or "The Four Sisters"—AIDS or Debbie,

Allan, and Susan [she failed to mention a forth name]. Boo-boo did not start hearing about the disease until 1987. "We never knew that there was a horror out there till it started to kill us." She recalled early signs. "From '82 to '85, a few of my friends started getting sick. And you could see the changes of the piers." By the late 1980s: "The disease was so fierce that it wiped out all of my girlfriends." Boo-boo recalled a pall of silence at the piers with the AIDS years:

> The piers started looking like a ghost town, grungy, like bodies just started disappearing. People was dying. The beauty of the piers started looking like a dull darkness. You had a disease that was out there wiping away a lot of people, not just the drag queens but the johns. And still we were not knowing what was up.
>
> One of my girlfriends died right there in my tent. We went in one night and . . . I will tell her name 'cause she would like for me to tell her story 'cause she was a legend. Her name was Nicole. She was mixed with Indian and Spanish and white and she was a very beautiful child. It's a shame, 'cause she was only about 19 or 20 when she passed. She was being eaten up by cancer. That's what the hospital told her. She told them she didn't want to be in the hospital. She wanted to be in the street. She wanted to be with her family. She came back to the piers. We was her family. She died right there in my tent. I woke up, she was laying beside me cold as ice. And I just started rubbing her hair and I started crying.
>
> The piers was beautiful from 1981 to 1986. It started changing from '86 to, well, about '90. Then it was no more. From '89, it was no more. And the piers just absolutely rotted down in '88 and '89. All the gay people were all gone—literally all gone. It was like a big hurricane just swooshed all the people away.
>
> And then straight people started living down there. And it used to be all children. And by children, it was nothing but gay people. Then the piers [started] deteriorating. It was falling down. The wood started eating up. The warehouse started falling to the ocean floor. It was time to make a change down there.

"Now, of course, their property has increased. Its money," Kohler acknowledged. With the 1990s economic boom, property values increased at the expense of social tolerance. "They just don't want you on these streets," Kohler continued, because when youth hang out, "their money, their property, is going to go down." Propelling the controversy was the status of the Hudson River Park between highly developed Battery Park and the cleaned-up Times Square (see HRPT 2002). For years, this space was debated at the Community Board, where landowners were pitted against homeless youth and public space advocates. "During a period of economic crisis, development should meet the needs of the communities who are most vulnerable," argued Alexa Kasdan, of the Urban Justice Center, in 2009 when FIERCE published its White Paper which found the Hudson River Park Trust favoring private development, rather than community use of the space. "The Pier 40 redevelopment process presents a timely opportunity to fill critical social service gaps while improving New York's infrastructure."

Community uses favored by FIERCE ran in stark contrast to a quality-of-life campaign to clean up New York, which began in 1994 (Burr 1998;

Dangerous Bedfellows 1996). Favoring law enforcement rather than community needs, the quality-of-life crusade was implemented with an aggressive "broken windows" approach (Harcourt 2001). This meant targeting the smallest possible signs of problems, some of which were determined by aesthetics as much as policy. Cleaning up the city meant sweeping away many of the undesirables, and subsequently much of the color and pulse of New York's street life. Much of this began when the homeless encampments at the piers were torn down during the David Dinkins administration. "The police came down there and started cleaning it up," Boo-boo recalled. Her home was physically destroyed: "They came down there with the city and the city had an army. They had trucks and they told us that we would be arrested and locked up for trespassing. This was in '89." For Boo-boo, simply attempting to connect with a space that had been her home was considered trespassing:

> They tore down our tents. They just bulldozed them. They took our stuff and threw it up on dumpsters. And some people actually went to jail because they refused to leave and they sat down. They fought back by saying, "No, we're not leaving." And a lot of people laid down so the trucks couldn't come up in there. And the cops just came in and handcuffed them, lifted them, and beat them up, and police brutality. And they got away with it. Dinkins told them to clean it out, "by any way necessary" is how he said it. Really. And then they started locking people up for turning tricks for like a year. It wasn't any more two days or three days. He started giving them six months to a year. A lot of people got tired of going to jail back to back. One time I got out after six months and I was out not even two hours before I was back in the precinct facing another year. And they gave it to me. So it was like a revolving door for me, from jail to Rikers Island, and back. Not even getting to turn one trick or suck one dick. And I was back in jail doing another year. By the time that I got out, the piers were gone. When I got out there was nothing. It was a fence up there and everything was torn down. And to me, I was betrayed, I was like, "Where is everybody?" I asked people. And people was looking at me like I was crazy. There was no more of us down there.

Despite these barriers, the need for public space to connect with like-minded people remained. "The pier is a sentimental place to me," explained Kenyon Farrow, the executive director of Queers for Racial and Economic Justice, who was an organizer with FIERCE. "When I first moved to New York, it was one of the first places I was introduced to as queer space. I remember the first day that I came down three years ago when the fences went up. It was really depressing."

Fences, Barriers, and Lost Networks

"It looks just the same to me, but they got a big-assed fence all over the place. You can't get in there anymore," James Place recalled from his last trip to the pier. "I think they are giving out tickets," he concluded, alluding to the changing character of the space. FIERCE organizer Kenyon Martin elaborated,

"I've been kicked off of the Pier with other folks at 10 o'clock at night. Even that is subjective depending on whatever they feel at the moment." While recent barriers included the metal fence surrounding the area, pier users described countless others—including the use of AIDS as a justification for the crackdown, the ongoing quality-of-life crusade, and gentrification. David Gonzalvez of FIERCE explained: "The fences, the so-called redevelopment, the revitalization of the Village. It's crass. It's another way to say, 'Yeah, we want more white people in. Why don't you just leave?'" Improving "quality of life" for the people who used the piers need not have involved denying space for their community, and users of the piers would no doubt have welcomed real improvements in the quality of their lives and of the spaces in which they could exist. But the goal of the renovation was to reinstate police control and redistribute the space to a new group of users—not improve it for everyone or acknowledge multiple communities' need for safe, vibrant space.

"Every year, it [the police patrolling] gets worse," Samaj elaborated. "They are trying to fix it up, but at the same time they are kicking us off of our own space, our own home. . . . What are you trying to balance out here?" This mode of policing was a citywide problem. Within its darkest expression, this aggressive approach towards policing public space meant people of color—including Patrick Dorismond and Amadou Diallo, whose only crime was to fit a racial profile—lost their lives to police bullets. Samaj continued: "That's their only place of comfort. That's the only place they can come to . . . to meet their friends at the pier. They don't have anywhere else to enjoy their self." Samaj was not the only interviewee to ponder the implications of the dispersed networks lost in the wake of Hudson River Park's arrival on the once abandoned piers. "It breaks my heart to see that it's no longer there, to see that people will not have that opportunity to find people who will teach them that it's ok to be who you are," Dennis noted wistfully as he finished speaking at the speak-out. "Why couldn't you do it to any other spot?" Samaj wondered. "It's not like they don't know that that place was gay central. That's our space."

Without the safe haven presented by the piers, "you lose a bit of community," Steve Rodgers noted. While the space may not have been perfect, "you were seeing familiar faces, and once you saw a few familiar faces, you felt a little bit safer as opposed to going out and seeing people doing maybe the same thing you are doing, but when you are out there with unfamiliar faces, it's not as safe." Many of those who did sex work at the piers kept an eye out for each other. Kenyon Martin wondered, "What happens to people once the space is gone?" Imani Henry offered an answer: "I definitely know from folks that when you don't have any place to go, it isn't as safe. It is more dangerous. And people are in more jeopardy. And they don't have a sense of community." Without this community and community space, street hustlers were forced to work in more isolated private spaces including cars and escort services. Henry continued, "You're now disconnected. You're now working alone. And things can happen to people and we don't know it." The concepts of community space, community, and belonging and safety are highly valued by respondents. Alternatively, isolation and lack of safety are described as consequences of displacement.

Without access to the space where she had built a family, "I did something ridiculous," Boo-boo explained. She felt lost when she found the piers cleared out and fenced off after returning from jail. "I went down there and copped drugs from an undercover and went back to jail for six years. I was lonely. And at least I could be in jail where I was loved and around people who could respect me." To Boo-boo, jail was better than outside:

> You was lonely. The piers was changed. There was no more balls. All your friends was gone. You go down into the park and there were all the people down there with dogs. You couldn't really make a tent. You just had to live on the ground. You couldn't live like that 'cause there were straight people who would go down there and hassle you, put urine in your face. It was happening because the 1990s were getting ready to come in and it was changing.

"When they put the fence up, they closed everything off," James Place explained, elaborating on how the environment for hustling changed. "You can't get in there. Now you have to go to the arcades. But since 9/11, there are more DTs [detectives] in there. They got machine guns. You can get arrested just for answering, 'How much?'"

The question of safety speaks to a number of dilemmas. "My fear is that without open public spaces," HIV prevention is compromised, Kenyon Martin said as we discussed where else the pier kids could go. "Part of it is that this was where people came to do outreach to people and those people are now going underground," Martin elaborated. "If they don't have anywhere else to go, then we can't do our work to reach them. Then they are going to participate in higher risk behavior because they don't have the tools to practice safer sex with the information." Sex clubs and the piers were spaces where prevention activists and peer outreach workers could reach people where they were having sex and establish healthy patterns as well as community norms grounded in peer-based approaches to HIV prevention and mutual protection (see Crimp 2002; Dangerous Bedfellows 1996).

"Today, you have Prospect Park; you have Central Park. You have the Ramble," Rodgers noted. Many pier users have moved to the countless other "spots" for sexual contact and commerce—the train stations, the Port Authority bathrooms, the parks, the McDonalds at 34th Street, and so forth. "Well, all those old spots. They still exist and people still go there in the pitch black," Rodgers continued. "Today, there are few spaces as opposed to in the past. You had so many different options in the public spaces to go to. Today, those spaces are limited."

Different Identities

Countless permutations of queer identity have taken shape and been altered within the shifts in access from open public towards restricted or filtered spaces. Without safe spaces, many have resorted to more closed expressions of their queerness. L. P. referred to men of color who have sex with other men, without being openly "gay": "Now they call them 'mo thugs' or a 'thug mo.' Like a homo thug. And that means he's a homosexual but he's a thug. In other words, he'll take you out and rob you, beat you, but he's a homosexual on the low," L.P explained. "If you go to the warehouse up here in the Bronx, there are these boys running down the street with their baggy pants on and their Sean John jeans and coats and their bandanas and their glasses." These young boys are dancing with each other. . . . Then they go home to their high school life and nobody knows. And they are as hard as any thug you want to run into."

Interviewees commented on the "mo thug" or "down low" phenomenon. Adonis explained that even Brooklyn had a pier, but people were more "down low" there. "It was tired," he sighed. "Everybody was so in the closet. It wasn't the same as the regular pier. You see 'homeboys' walking past, but you didn't know that they were cruising because everybody was acting like a homeboy in case they ran into somebody they knew."

Others expressed concern about being seen as "being like that." Different interviewees have different readings of what "being like that" means. For many, it is any association with mainstream gay consumer culture, the rainbow flag, etc. AIDS prevention workers have long been aware of a counterpublic of "men who have sex with men," often men of color, who have no interest in relating to or being associated with the trappings of "gay" life. Rodgers noted that it was more fun for him to be in the closet and keep things secretive at home, especially in African American communities where many associate gayness with being effeminate, or "wearing hot pants and boots."

For others, the explanation involves the ongoing reality that some three decades into the epidemic, AIDS still creates fear, which generates hysteria and stigma. L. P. explained: "Although they have drugs that will keep you alive longer, its still very hard to function in society today with AIDS and not be ostracized. People are still scared to death." Panic triggers control cultures and restrictions of movement in public space—more fences (Shepard 2009; Thompson 1998). In turn, many interviewees specifically suggested AIDS was used as a justification for closing queer meeting spaces such as the piers (Crimp 2002; Dangerous Bedfellows 1996).

AIDS fear still prevents possibilities for openness. "Running around, you gotta be hard," L. P. continued. "You can't be ladylike anymore," outside of safe havens like the piers, where there was room to "waltz around." Outside of queer spaces, "you can't let it out. 'Cause then you'd be like, 'Oh shit, I let this thing out to my crib and my crew.'" L. P. was arrested and went back to jail shortly after the interview, a destination that has become the fate of many former users of this queer community space.

— —

"Now the kids are about to get the piers back," said Boo-boo. Again, the piers stretch out into the water facing New Jersey, creating a striking urban caval-cade. Yet, much of the context has changed. Today, more affluent people walk their dogs and ride their bikes there, something that would never have hap-pened before. Unlike previous years, this area is now "safe" for the affluent. Further, their very presence acts as a type of policing and normalizing force—they are backed by the police, but the policing is not exclusively done by cops. At the same time, white middle-class gay men have taken public sex indoors (via the Internet) rather than depend on outdoor venues such as the piers. Those with means have been able to re-create the spaces they desire, while the spaces available to those who are marginalized have been further reduced. Yet, with a dose of tenacity, many have remained and fought for access to this space.

"LBGTQ youth call for stronger public space provisions in Hudson River Park Development," declared a 2009 press release by FIERCE. "White paper finds Hudson River Park Trust favoring private development. Stronger lan-guage needed to protect community uses in Hudson River Park."

In the decade since it was formed, "FIERCE! has been able to change the terms of the public debate about quality of life and public safety in the West Village," (quoted in FIERCE 2007). As result, "the voices of merchants and residents, politicians and police, are not the only ones that are heard" (ibid.). Thanks to their advocacy, the City of New York, including its police depart-ment, must now justify tough policing tactics and policies rather than act in a shroud of secrecy (Amateau 2006). Much of FIERCE's success is built on advancing workable alternative solutions, communicating their aims, mobiliz-ing a wide constituency, working with allies such as ACT UP, the Audre Lorde Project, and the Radical Faeries, as well as well placed supporters such as Bob Kohler, doing research on the issues, making use of play, theater, speak outs, and creative direct action to lay out their claims. In so doing, the group and its allies articulated a different standpoint on urban life than the predominant suburban vision of public space taking hold of New York (Harstock 1998). When the community board pushed for a 10 PM curfew at the pier, FIERCE countered that this was not a solution to the issue of noise at the piers. The problem was everyone leaving at once. Thus, the group argued the park should close later. The group took the message to the media, their allies, politicos, and the community board, stacked community board meetings with group members and sought a compromise. In so doing, they reshaped debate from a focus on criminalization towards service provision.

The community board supported their proposal. "The overall idea is to have a balanced response," explained Maria Alvarado, from the office of City Council Speaker Christine Quinn. "At the same time we try to address resident and community concerns, we are using this as an effort to expand outreach and get social services to these kids" (Eleveld 2006). The city has changed as has its response to the needs of those who organize to build community in public space.

Throughout the years, social movements have remained intimately connected to ongoing changes in public space. In the days after the birth of gay liberation, many turned to the piers where liberation was first won, within shouting distance of the Stonewall itself. Inspired by the narrative of liberation, many constructed new identities and worlds around this story. Throughout the 1970s, narratives of sexual liberation created new identities and community spaces. Queers created a public sexual culture of baths, a burgeoning gay press, and emphasis on community organization. This narrative shifted in the 1980s and 1990s as spaces for liberated stories shifted and dwindled, fenced off like the piers themselves. While affluent queers made use of virtual space to arrange sexual encounters, others continued to make use of public spaces. Here different sorts of stories and movements flourished.

As the *Warehouse Newsletter* explained back in 1975, gay men are very resourceful. "The West Village is by no means the only safe haven in the five boroughs," L. P. explained. Others report crawling under or through holes in other fences blocking them from public spaces to be reclaimed. This determination ran throughout the interviews. Resistance continues, because people continue to organize to create their own autonomous zones and communities.

CHAPTER FIVE

"If We Can't Dance It's Not Our Revolution"

Reclaiming the Streets and
Creating Autonomous Space

Contemporary suburban spaces suggest a confident, elite hegemony over public space. But in order to establish suburban spaces, different kinds of public space had to be taken back from the people who used them, and behaviors that were once allowed had to be forbidden. In the 1990s, the City of New York, under the direction of Mayor Rudolph Giuliani, began that reclamation stage in the recolonization of the city, unleashing an uncompromising attack on the exercise of basic civil liberties in public space. In a reciprocating reaction characteristic of battles over public space, local activists responded to this effort to suburbanize spaces of the city not only with legal efforts to defend their rights, but direct actions in public space to reclaim some measure of the lost latitude of action in public. This chapter examines this period in the mid-to-late 1990s when the city implemented dramatic changes in policing and regulation to recast popular and community space into suburban space. From this era, two valuable insights emerge. First, while Part 1 focused on the transition to suburban space in terms of private capital's evolving objectives, this examination of the transformation of New York public space in the 1990s reveals how the state played a central role in suburbanizing public space. Second, the effort to tamp down public activities led activists to resist and identify a variety of seemingly unrelated new city policies as a collective assault on public space. We consider how one group, Reclaim the Streets, created temporary autonomous zones as part of a strategy to liberate the public space of the city at large, and in the process made the case for why cities need public space. Making use of participant observation, interviews, and the group's publications, we see how Reclaim the Streets articulated the need for popular and community space and linked the repression of such spaces to the prerogatives of global capitalism.

The administration of Mayor Rudolph Giuliani imposed dramatic new restrictions on a range of public spaces, activities, and people in the spaces. Giuliani, a former federal prosecutor, had an aggressive, vindictive style, particularly against those he saw as political opponents. But while this personal style was evident in many of the changes he imposed during his administration (from 1994 to 2001), those shifts were no less structurally necessary to the process of introducing suburban space to the city.

The Giuliani Administration's assault on the free use of public space was uncompromising. From the South Bronx to the steps of City Hall in Lower Manhattan, the City of New York attacked public space in over twenty different cases in just two years during the nineties. Defeated in court almost a half-dozen times just trying to stop parades and marches, the administration of Mayor Rudolph Giuliani prompted activists to file a record number of civil rights cases against the city. The New York Civil Liberties Union alone was involved in at least twenty First Amendment cases, winning almost all of them (New York Civil Liberties Union 1999; Sachs 1998, B1). But free speech rights do not describe all the rights that people claim in public space. Therefore, challenging the city's restriction of space on First Amendment free-speech grounds—the strategy initially used to defend government intrusions into public space—proved limited in its application, and failed to express all the ways in which public space was necessary. To defend public spaces, and the vital, basic activities that occur in them, activists needed to develop languages with which to talk about public space in the United States.

A New York branch of a mid-nineties global movement called Reclaim the Streets (RTS) warned that "The Mayor's 'Quality of Life' campaign is fast privatizing scarce public space, squeezing the pockets of diverse communities and stealing our freedom to express."[1]

RTS made their first public appearance in New York on October 4, 1998. Lured by a flyer emboldened with dancing bodies, which declared: "Reclaim the Streets: Sunday October 4th, meet at Astor Place Cube," Shepard arrived early, not knowing what to think. The Astor Place Cube was clogged with street youth. There anarchist crusty punks from Tompkins Square Park mingled with members of Fed Up Queers, Times UP!, and Lower East Side Collective, as well as members of Moving Equipment, an underground syringe exchange program, and a few Village hipsters. A fair portion of those on hand looked as though they were better suited for a rave than a street action. One man wore a bunny suit. Everyone mulled about chatting. A young woman passed out a flyer declaring that we should move when we heard the sound of a horn. It was all very secret and clandestine. Suddenly, the horn blared, and several people screamed "run!" The group of a hundred or so sprinted West from the Astor Cube over to the corner of Broadway and Astor Place, where a few men hoisted a young philosophy student named

Louis up on a tripod, where he sat thirty feet above looking at the bodies disrupting traffic. As the activists filled the street with bodies, members of the group screamed with delight, as music blared from boomboxes and a sound system broadcast to 88.7 FM. A few breathed fire and danced. Drivers looked mildly annoyed. The police who were just arriving looked befuddled.

As I (Smithsimon) walked towards Broadway, pulsing dance music began to overwhelm the midday calm. When I arrived, the block between New York University and the nightlife-rich East Village was filling with people. Most of them were young. Some stood around, appraising the scene and unsure what to do. Others were already dancing intently to the music that boomed out of the mobile sound system. At first, it was hard to feel in the mood for a party in broad daylight, in the middle of the street. But as the crowd grew, its excitement did as well. Passersby had a range of reactions: staring at the crowd, ignoring it, or joining in. Police gathered at the edge of the event. A helicopter began to circle overhead. The uncertainty of a temporary autonomous zone—the promise of a big, free party, the possibility of police response, the exhilaration of creating something new and bold, and the recognition that the event surprised or inconvenienced some bystanders, all imbued RTS's first street party in New York with the nervous energy of a TAZ.

Two college-aged women wearing orange and yellow t-shirts shirts that read "Mayor Giuliani made me do it" said they had heard about the event from flyers that had been passed out. I asked them why they had come. "Because I feel that Giuliani's been dictating this city for too long," said the first. "I mean, as a woman, and a minority, as a young person, he's just been fucking this shit up." The second said, "Well, we're here because we want to take back the streets, because it's not New York anymore, it's a big touristic Disneyland." People at the event had been straining against their firsthand observations that the city's possibilities were being restricted and narrowed. In New York, RTS was influenced by RTS groups around the world, the experiences and politics of activists and the other organizations to which they belonged, and very strongly by the antipublic space policies of the Giuliani Administration.

With the reports of the action finding their way into the *New York Times, The Villager,* and *The Village Voice* (Ferguson 1998), as well as across the world via the Internet, the action quickly became a part of Lower East Side activist lore. While countless groups—from garden activists, to strippers, to sex shop owners, to guerrilla theater actors—had participated in the debate over the privatization of public spaces, the RTS action created a do-it-yourself space for these actors to connect, check in with their bodies, and demonstrate what a democratic image of public space could really look like. For many, it was a tonic for the hyper-regulation they saw taking place throughout the city (Shepard and Hayduk 2002). Members of RTS themselves also contributed to this mythmaking, connecting the October 4th action within a larger movement narrative. "On October 4th, 1998, without asking for permission, over 500 people took the streets," read a flyer on the history of Reclaim the Streets.[2] "Costumed crowds, fire breathers, soap box dilettantes and curiosity finders celebrated a moment of freedom as a mass of police assembled." Several hours "of free form expression" later, the police halted the party with arrests. "But the event woke those present to what is possible when creative forces merge with a community political consciousness. New York is ready to reclaim the streets," the report declared. This moment of liberation catalogued the abuses of the so-called quality-of-life measures:

> Public space is rapidly privatized, pleasure is policed, street artists are locked up, diverse communities are priced into extinction, schools are stagnant; immigrants are harassed; racial hostility grows in our police forces and government; alternative forms of transportation are not cultivated. The list goes on. . . . The mission of RTS/NYC is to continue bringing the message back to the streets. Through direct action, we demand that a different philosophy govern our lives and, at least for a moment, we free ourselves to what life could be like.[3]

Over the next few years, people from all walks of New York life moved from private clubs to semipublic warehouses to help support this new movement in public space. RTS pumped new life into environmental/social justice movements by successfully organizing street dance parties/actions, mobilizing gyrating bodies into the streets (Duncombe 2002; Jordan 1998).

RTS advanced New York activists' understanding of space by developing language to describe attacks against public spaces and their need to defend and reclaim them. A group that included articulate, experienced activists, RTS was one of the first groups in New York to understand and describe a wide range of city maneuvers as components of an assault against public space. The history of Reclaim the Streets is significant to the study of public space because the language the group developed is vital to promoting and establishing the need for public space and the right to the city.

RTS's spatial strategy was also significant. Recognizing the growing control of urban public space by globalization or neoliberalism, RTS sought to liberate such spaces. Identifying spaces members felt were increasingly privately controlled to serve narrow corporate interests (including privatized, filtered, and suburbanized spaces), RTS worked to renew their public character by transforming them into TAZ spaces, from which those and other spaces might be transformed from increasingly filtered or suburban spaces into more broadly usable popular or community spaces. In New York, RTS thus initiated explicit contests *over* space, not just in space.

From Festival Marketplace to Disneyland

The Giuliani Administration's relentless assault on public space further cemented the suburban strategy in public space. It was unprecedented.

Norman Siegel, then head of the New York Civil Liberties Union said, "I've been here 13 years, and my legal director has been here even longer, and we've never filed as many cases involving one administration." Neither Koch nor Dinkins, the previous mayors, provoked nearly as many suits, and many of those filed opposed central components of the mayor's agenda. This agenda, explained Siegel, was "authoritarian, repressive and antithetical to our rich tradition of tolerance for the right to protest and dissent. It's inconsistent with what the city has been" (Sachs 1998).

A portrait of such a tyrannical privatizing mayor, promoter of property and corporate interests over people and more democratic space, emerges in a review of the assaults on public space and the disregard for constitutional protections of city residents exhibited by the Giuliani administration. The significance of these policies is that they paved the way for the more restricted concept of acceptable behavior in the suburban spaces that followed. Even treating key incidents briefly, the list is significant.

City Hall: Keep Out!

At the very heart of the Giuliani administration, control and exclusion took the place of respect for the rights of the public. City Hall Park was barricaded by metal fences, concrete barriers, and yellow police tape; pedestrian routes through the park were arbitrarily blocked (and later entirely closed as part of the "renovation" of City Hall Park); and the public was discouraged from entering City Hall by a barrage of metal detectors. Police were given the discretion to bar any potential visitor from City Hall itself, and security guards demanded identification. "They are there," explained columnist Bob Herbert, "to insure that none of you give even a moment's thought to the foolish notion that City Hall is a place that belongs to you, a place where you might be welcome. It once was, but that's over. Rudolph Giuliani is the Mayor now. City Hall belongs to him and the changed atmosphere reflects his personality—cold and remote and unforgiving" (Herbert, 1999).

The mayor expanded his control over City Hall by prohibiting groups from holding press conferences in front of the building. The steps had been a traditional spot for such announcements because of their symbolism, their proximity to the administration that speakers wanted to take heed—and not least of all, for their position just outside the offices of City Hall beat reporters. The mayor's prohibition was ultimately ruled unconstitutional in part because of selective enforcement that let certain politicians use the steps (as Giuliani had used them to announce his own campaign) and not others (Weiser 1998).

After the policy prohibiting public use of City Hall's steps was overturned, the issue demonstrated the vindictiveness one *Times* reporter suggested the mayor displayed towards public dissent (Sachs 1998):

The danger that security measures can repress dissent was seen in the administration's handling of a press conference by an AIDS service organization this week. Members of the group, Housing Works, won a court order giving them the right to hold a public event in the City Hall parking lot. The demonstrators, who numbered less than 200, were sent through outdoor metal detectors. Their spokesmen were then corralled into a small pen surrounded by barriers, separated from their hundred-odd supporters. The media were herded into another pen. Inspectors from the Department of Environmental Protection bearing noise meters monitored a reading of the names of people who had died from AIDS, to make sure the roll call of victims was not exceeding official decibel limits. A reporter who attempted to watch the activity from the City Hall porch was ordered to go inside by officers who asserted that there was a danger the demonstrators might rush the building.

The administration's actions were not honest attempts to maintain security, but frank statements to citizens that dissent would not be tolerated civilly, but repressed by any means, constitutional or unconstitutional, necessary or not, with no respect for democratic rights in public space.

The closure of City Hall Park was one of several instances where Giuliani attempted to "domesticate" the threat of terrorism. The fact that Giuliani sought to close public spaces in defense against terrorism *before* the attacks on the World Trade Center on September 11, 2001 might be taken as evidence of prescient preparation for real threats to New Yorkers. But in two respects the rhetoric was preparation for the crass application of the fear of terrorism to justify unrelated agendas that many more politicians practiced after September 11. First, "terrorism" was served up as a post hoc justification for restrictions on constitutional rights. When the City Hall press conference ban first became an issue in the press, in March 1998, a police spokesperson had initially claimed that there had been no change in policy, but instead that the rule had been "longstanding." Even after a federal judge ruled the policy unconstitutional, the City did not mention fears of terrorism. Only later was terrorism used as a justification for isolating City Hall from the public. Second, the threat of "terrorism" was used as cover to restrict or surveil the actions of groups who legitimately opposed administration proposals. In 1998, for instance, administration officials attempted to prevent taxi drivers from protesting by branding them "terrorists" (Lueck 1998). The prohibition of groups based on their opinions of the mayor's policies had nothing to do with security. Having seen how effective a justification "terrorism" already was on the national level for measures that restricted citizens' freedom and movement, the Giuliani administration was a trailblazer in inserting it into local debates, even when there was no association between terrorism and administration opponents.

The mayor's defenders might still argue that hindsight shows just how appropriate Giuliani's strict control of City Hall—which critics came to describe as a bunker—was in the years before 2001. The objective was not public safety, but the administration's war on dissent and public expression. From the barricaded, depopulated, guarded, and controlled space at the center of the city government, the mayor took aim at parade routes, parks, and every borough of the city. Many aspects of this tighter control of New York public space were undertaken for the explicit benefit of corporate interests. New York City activists mobilized to defend rights in public space in part because the mayor's own style was so hostile to popular dissent and so uncomprehending of the importance of public space and civil rights.

Parades of Protest

The blossoming of suburban space during the Giuliani Administration required that the city take a position regarding the rights that were and were not to be respected in the suburban space of the new Imperial City, and to identify what behaviors and people would no longer be tolerated now that the space had been suburbanized. The administration's actions made clear that it did not want suburbanized spaces to include the full complement of civil rights that public spaces traditionally had. In its handling of parades, the City showed contempt for the most common of public expressions in public space. In over a half-dozen cases, the City tried, in almost all cases unsuccessfully, to prohibit groups the mayor deemed unacceptable from holding marches.

The City clearly did not want political activity to be part of the new regime of suburban space. The City refused permits for antipolice brutality marches, restricted a memorial march for gay bashing victim Matthew Sheppard (which directly resulted in clashes between marchers and police), went to court repeatedly to stop the Million Youth March (and, as with Housing Works, harassed it mercilessly when the event was held), and resisted so strongly Housing Works' efforts to get a permit to march down Broadway and speak in front of City Hall that a federal judge found New York's entire parade permit law unconstitutionally vague and open to abuse (Flynn 1998).

The battles continued: a marijuana legalization group called the Million Marijuana March was lied to about parade application dates so that another group, at the prompting of a City official, could first reserve Washington Square Park on the date the marijuana group traditionally held its march there. Once the marijuana-legalization group arrived, they were filmed by police, had their signposts seized, and were hustled out of the park (Trebay 1998). Despite the fact that the marijuana group's suit against the city resulted in another parade and rally permit law being ruled unconstitutional, the City denied the group's parade permit application for the following year. Another group was denied a permit to march down Broadway in commemoration of the thirtieth anniversary of the death of Martin Luther King, Jr. The group agreed to march instead down Eighth Avenue, and even agreed to a police request to minimize statements about police brutality. But the group balked when police officials not only restricted their speech, but tried to direct the focus of the march by requesting that the ministers organizing the march lead a prayer in front of an adult video store that was targeted by the City's antipornography ordinance (Flynn 1998). When taxi drivers planned a caravan through the city to protest new taxi regulations, officials tried to limit the action to twenty cars, and hundreds of police physically prohibited cabs without passengers from entering Manhattan from Brooklyn or Queens (Lueck 1998). The challenges by the city in this period became so intimidating that some stopped trying to obtain permits. Arab-Americans protesting anti-Islamism in the movie *The Siege* outside a theater did not seek a permit because they believed they would have been pushed to a remote street, and stuck in a prolonged legal battle (Flynn 1998).

Protesters eventually prevailed in many of the suits they brought. In one four-month period in 1998, federal judges in separate cases found that police restrictions against a police brutality march were based on the march's message, that the Million Youth March could not be relocated out of Harlem, and that the mayor had to allow an AIDS service group to march down Broadway and hold an event at City Hall for World AIDS Day (Flynn 1998). But regardless of the outcome of individual suits, the City effectively won many of the skirmishes since groups were stopped in their tracks, tangled up in legal proceedings, and in some cases deterred from taking to public space. About this time, activists from across the city fought back under the banner, "Stop the Mayor" and his plans for future political office.

In their plans for the city, the administration opposed real political debate and public political activity. Dissenters and activists were pushed out not only for the political benefit of the mayor; corporations displaced citizens as the trustees and users of public space. In suburban space, real political speech and public uses of public space were replaced with advertising messages and corporate promotions, and the public was squeezed offstage to make room for private interests. The City apparently had abundant space and resources for tickertape parades honoring the Yankees, and adequate police to permit a large street presentation by Disney. As Norman Siegel of the New York Civil Liberties Union said, "If Disney or Warner Brothers with Mickey Mouse and Bugs Bunny want to do something in the street, it could be just as noisy and crowded, but it's all right, because it fits into his [the mayor's] vision of what the city should be about." While activists and civil liberties lawyers opposed restrictions by the Giuliani Administration, such efforts suffered in part from a lack of compelling arguments against not merely each infringement of civil rights, but more broadly, against the persistent and intentional assault on public space. A more expansive definition of the purpose and function of public space was needed.

Parks and the Limits of First Amendment Arguments

Some assaults on activities in public space can be successfully defended by invoking rights to free speech. So it was that a street musician successfully challenged a city ordinance that charged forty-five dollars for a one-day permit, which a judge found excessive for a constitutionally protected activity (Sachs 1998). But even in similar cases, First Amendment protections have not protected other artists, and point to the need for a broader defense of public space. In front of the Metropolitan Museum of Art, Parks Department officials carted away over sixty works of art and arrested artists repeatedly for displaying their work without permits. While a Federal Court ruled in 1996 that artists could not be required to obtain licenses to sell their work on the street, the Parks Department argued that the sidewalk in front of the Met— even though it abuts Fifth Avenue—could be more stringently regulated because it is park property. Zhang Wei, one of the artists who continued to display his work in defiance of Parks Department raids (and who first had his artwork destroyed by Chinese officers in Tiananmen Square over a decade earlier), drew a connection between his situation and the city at large. "No one listened to our fight back then—no one supported us until people died years later," he said of his protests in China. "Just like then, no one cares about what our group is doing. They don't realize if the city can take our art, our right, they can take the rights of all New Yorkers" (Christian 1998). For artists in front of the Metropolitan, the issue was about more than First Amendment rights. In reference to vending rules that would have restricted artists as well as food and merchandise ven-

dors, Robert Lederman, a painter who became notorious for his Metropolitan protests and portraits of Mayor "Adolph Jailiani," said, "This is not just about hot dogs. Mayor Giuliani's war on vendors is virtually eliminating free expression from large areas of New York City's public streets" (Allen 1998). While First Amendment arguments were sometimes used successfully to defend people's use of public space, they were not sufficient.

Because a language for defending public space is lacking in the law as much as in public discourse, many of the objections to the City's policies have been couched in the language of free speech rights. "In his pursuit of a 'civilized' New York of small-scale protests and huckster-free sidewalks, Mayor Rudolph W. Giuliani keeps bumping up against the First

One of Robert Lederman's portraits of New York's then-mayor (here dubbed Mayor Ghouliani), is hoisted above a crowd.

Amendment and getting bruised," wrote Susan Sachs in the *New York Times* (Sachs 1998). But free-speech arguments, necessary as they are in the court-room, captured only part of the crisis of public space restrictions. In many cases, free-speech protections make sense only abstractly. To reverse the broad assault on public space, rather than challenge individual cases, a description of the necessity of public space, and compelling, passionate accounts of assaults against it, needed to be developed.

Free speech was an inadequate position from which to defend public spaces like community gardens, which fell to bulldozers and were put up on the auction block in large numbers by the City during the Giuliani years. Even while many members of Reclaim the Streets pointed out that the sites first targeted were those that represented a culture opposed to Giulianization, and that they were regularly sold to developers who were supporters of the mayor's reelection campaign, demolishing gardens was much more tangibly and immediately a public-space issue than a free-speech issue. Similarly, even a supporter of the privatization of park management predicted that the privati-zation of event scheduling at places like Bryant Park would result in restric-tions of events like impromptu speeches, the distribution of materials, and street entertainers that, while never licensed, had been tolerated by public law enforcement (Kim 1987, 180). More than free speech rights were being vio-lated when private security forces disrupted uses of public space that were previously tolerated but never officially recognized. Such actions expanded a deadening control over public spaces.

Most of the City's actions against public space during this time helped reshape the city in a form more thoroughly compatible with the uses of corpo-rate capital. Community gardens were sold to real estate developers; efforts were made to restrict street vendors, to the perceived benefit of restaurants and stores (as well as their landlords); the magazines sold by newspaper vendors were restricted, further "Disneyfying" the city by reducing it to the plainest common denominator (a process often referred to as "sanitization"). Marches were opposed that might draw attention to the City's retreat from the provision of public services, while corporate promotions in, and management of, public space were embraced as consistent with what the city should be for and about. While some City policies seemed to reflect the mayor's vindictive and defensive personality, actions that seemed particular to this mayor served a larger systemic function. As with the "shock doctrine" that allows long-term systemic changes to be implemented during short-term crises, the long-term shift towards subur-ban and policed space benefited from the short-term presence of a strong mayor who threw public space into a state of crisis (Klein 2007).

In the face of this assault, the language available with which to defend public space, limited as it was to First Amendment arguments, was inadequate to defend groups across the city from the city's restriction of their right to function in public space. These antipublic politics complemented corporate efforts to exercise control over the city and see that municipal actions were more singularly determined by the priorities of investment capital. In response, Reclaim the Streets was one group that tried to articulate the vitality and necessity of urban space.

Origins of Reclaim the Streets

Before developing in New York, Reclaim the Streets was founded in London in the fall of 1991, at the beginning of a movement there to oppose road building. The group described themselves as being "FOR walking, cycling and cheap, or free, public transport, and AGAINST cars, roads and the system that pushes them" (Reclaim The Streets, London 1998a). From the start, RTS in London unified behind an "anticar" banner that was not waved as prominently in New York. But even in London, the car was seen as symbolic of a larger problem:

> We are basically about taking back public space from the enclosed private arena. At its simplest it is an attack on cars as a principal agent of enclosure. It's about reclaiming the streets as public inclusive space from the private exclusive use of the car. But we believe in this as a broader principle, taking back those things which have been enclosed within capitalist circulation and returning them to collective use as a commons (Jordan, 1998, 139–40).

From the start, RTS used its opposition to the car as a symbol of its broader opposition to the systems RTS groups around the world variously identified as capitalism, neoliberalism, privatization, and the domination of corporations. Even in its earliest, primarily ecological focus, RTS identified capitalism as the root cause of the symptoms it opposed.

Initiated by environmentalists seeking to protect wildlife from road encroachment, RTS expanded to encompass urban issues when the group opposed the building of the M11 road near London during the fall of 1993, a road which would destroy homes and communities (see Jordan 1998; Shepard 2011). A definitive element of RTS was added to the environmental/urban issues nexus in 1994, when the Criminal Justice and Public Order Act attracted a new group to RTS's work: The fight of the anti-road activists became synonymous with that of travelers, squatters and hunt saboteurs. In particular, the suddenly politicized rave scene became a communal social focus for many people (Reclaim The Streets, London 1998a).

Thus, from quite early on, RTS connected environmental opposition to expansion with both urban issues of community and public space, and England's popular rave/techno music scene in a ludic critique of the stultifying effects of capitalism. While Reclaim the Streets movements developed in other cities, the ideas articulated in the original London group's materials were the biggest international influence on New York's Reclaim the Streets.

Activists were inspired to start RTS in New York after reading an article about RTS events, which happened in over twenty cities from Bogota to Tel Aviv on May 16, 1998 (Duncombe 2002; Hines and Evarts 1998; Shepard 2011). Like an article in the *Earth First! Journal*, which ranked cities' events by police response (from "cranky to swanky"), New York activists paid close attention to police. As Alex explained after the first event, "The whole key was to fly under the radar of the police. The thing was a success because the police didn't know about it ahead of time. . . . That's the thing that everyone was losing sleep about: how do you advertise it broadly without letting everybody know about it?"[4] He explained that one of the advantages of holding

Eventually police, riot gear, and scooters were rounded up to face the dancers at a weekend Reclaim the Streets event.

the event on a Sunday was that the organizers knew that the Manhattan South Taskforce, which was assigned to protests, wasn't on duty on Sundays. As a result, RTS knew that there would be minimal police response for at least thirty minutes while police in riot gear were cobbled together. Organizers did not seek permits for events (which were unlikely to be granted anyway) since the purpose of their movement was to make public space be available for use by all without police restrictions.

Members' Influences

RTS in New York soon came to have many similar constituents, organizational influences, and attitudes as the original London organization. New York organizers were frustrated by how, as Alia explained, when protesting "you apply to the city, and you're surrounded by cops, and you walk in a circle, and you hold your signs and you preach to the converted—how your protest is completely controlled by the people you're protesting!" They readily adopted RTS-style actions, and involved music, pirate radio, and members of the techno/rave music subculture that had fueled much of the party atmosphere of London events. Members of Earth First! taught the group how to make tripods (made of three metal poles over twenty feet high, on which protesters perch to foil police efforts to clear the street) that had been used in London.

Of equal importance to understanding the direction and content of RTS were the political influences of its participants, which also resembled those of

RTS activists internationally. While the composition of the group changed from meeting
to meeting, the inaugural Broadway event was
planned with people from the following
organizations: Blackout Books, an anarchist
bookstore; anarchic cyclists' movements like
Time's Up!; the Lower East Side Collective
(LESC), a radical community group fighting
for workers rights, affordable housing, and
community gardens; Wetlands, a political and
environmental performance space; a pirate
radio station; and others.[5] Thus, not only were
planners experienced activists, but they
brought with them organizational affiliations
that reflected similar influences to those of
London's RTS. Brooke thought of the group's
composition as "an even split between LESC
people and Blackout Books people," with
others from Time's Up! and Wetlands
involved as well. This characterization repro-
duces the "red, black, and green" combination
of socialist-style community and labor
activists, anarchists, and environmentalists of
the London-based group.

During the street party on Broadway,
a participant climbs a metal-pole
"tripod" to slow removal of the
revelers by police.

This constellation of organizations also meant that RTS was predominantly white, made up of young people with activist experience and college
educations. While RTS's literature made clear its desire for the movement to
represent a broad swath of the city's disenfranchised, it isn't clear how much
outreach the group undertook, or whether it planned to actively build coalitions with groups outside its political and geographic neighborhood. But the
confrontational theatrics of street takeovers were likely to attract groups
already comfortable with this approach. While RTS was effective at beginning
to describe the broad assault on public space, and rhetorically connected the
disparate groups that had come under attack by the Giuliani Administration,
its coalition involved only a portion of the much larger universe of people
and groups impeded by a particularly restrictive city government. Over time
this coalition grew as the group connected itself with both local and global
organizational forces (Shepard 2011).

The Person Most Responsible for RTS

It is hard to overestimate the importance of the Giuliani administration in
mobilizing New York's RTS movement. In any extended interview with RTS
members, the mayor's policies were given as a crucial motivation for the

group, and were the most common thread in a half-dozen interviews. Of course, the great variety in assaults on public space made by the administration meant that each speaker and publication listed a different collection of attacks: Louis mentioned enforcement of antiloitering laws, real estate issues, ticketing for "petty crimes" like public drinking, and cops coming through his neighborhood at night and selectively telling Latino kids to go home. Alia pointed to the central importance to RTS of the City's bulldozing of neighborhood gardens, the impending sale of the Charas Community Center to a private developer, and crippling fines for artists who posted advertisements for their performances on city street lampposts. Dan described Giulianization as a strategy to take away the public space necessary for a democratic public. Each constellation of policies was unique, but many of the issues given as catalysts for the formation of RTS were associated specifically with Giuliani.

The mayor's policies were also mentioned in everything written by the group. An explanation of the first action published afterwards opened by declaring that the Broadway takeover was "In response to Mayor Giuliani's rampant privatization of public space" (Reclaim the Streets, received January 9, 1999) A flyer distributed before the event cited administration policies as the provocation for the action, and provided a laundry list of potential RTS allies:

> The time for "Reclaiming the Streets" is ripe, especially given Mayor Giuliani's "Quality of Life" campaign, which targets the working poor, community gardeners, immigrants, people of color, gays, young people, bicyclists, skaters, booksellers, artists, sex workers, students, homeless people and political activists of all stripes. The mayor's campaign has been combined with efforts to privatize public spaces, which are already in short supply. If Giuliani is successful, his vision of a whitewashed, Disneyfied New York of the future will replace the diverse, exuberant, exciting New York of the present (Reclaim the Streets distributed before October 4, 1998 event).

While RTS activists, in interviews and in their writing, identified other influences as well (including the anticar theme of older RTS groups and neoliberalism), the particular virulence of attacks against public space, progressive activists, and noncorporate viewpoints by the Giuliani administration was what galvanized so many people to take to the streets with RTS. Though Giuliani personified and magnified many of the trends RTS opposed, activists' linkage of those actions to larger forces of globalization and neoliberalism made clear that the group saw its work as opposing a historic transformation in the balance and practice of power in New York City's streets.

Comparing New York and London RTS

Looking at the differences in focus, rhetoric, and tone between RTS in New York (Duncombe 2002) and London (Jordan 1998) better defines the organization, illustrates its international connections, and points out its indigenous influences.

From the outset, the two groups defined their territory differently. In London, it was the street. "The *road* is mechanical, linear movement epitomized by the car," they intoned. In contrast, "The *street*, at best, is a living place of human movement and social intercourse, of freedom and spontaneity" (Reclaim the Streets, London 1998b). This focus led naturally to a focus on the car and celebrations in a pedestrian street. In New York, the broader goal was to "reclaim public space from the corporations that are turning our cities into a shopping mall" (Reclaim the Streets 1999). The disputed turf was much more frequently described as public space rather than as "the streets" (the group's name not withstanding), and allowed RTS in New York to address a host of real estate and development issues. Public space was also tied directly to a political ideal. As Dan explained, the importance of public space was that "I don't think a public, at least the kind that's theorized about in writings about democracy . . . can thrive without ample space and public forums for the free exchange of ideas." "Public space" encompassed housing, gardens, street vendors, artistic expression, police abuses, and the importance of democratic participation. It allowed a group like RTS to respond to a wide range of concerns, and relate them to each other under a common rubric.

Similarly, while the London group had a unifying anticar theme, New York's RTS rallied around an anti-Giuliani theme. Alia noted that the anticar theme was present in New York, where the groups wanted to "reclaim spaces that are traditionally public but have been infiltrated by cars and businesses." But she added that cars were a stronger focus in Europe. Louis concurred. "I know in Europe a lot of it is anticar. We downplayed that a little bit," he explained, adding that some participants were disappointed that they did so. But New York RTS's reasons for doing so went beyond the fact that several members owned cars themselves. Most of them described getting involved because of disagreeable changes the city and their neighborhood had undergone, and they tied these changes not to the automobile—now a decades-old fixture of city streets—but to the much more recent tactics of Mayor Giuliani. The New York group's focus was thus a response to their local conditions. (Not that the role of cars was never addressed. In 2000 the group would hold an action, which overlapped with Critical Mass, under the banner "Reclaim the Streets for a World without Cars.")

Because RTS New York had a more distinct opponent (and perhaps because of differences in the mood and political cultures of the two cities), the tone of the two groups' writing differed as well. While RTS events in New York shared the festive atmosphere of their London counterparts, their overall tone, reflecting their context, was more defiant. In contrast, the London group often struck a whimsical, playful pose, imagining "an explanation for this collective daydream."[6] "Beneath the tarmac, the forest/ sous les pavés, la plage," they wrote, in a propaganda piece that in many places resembled poetry.[7] RTS New York did make use of as highly whimsical an approach, paraphrasing Emma Goldman ("if we can't dance, it's not a revolution") while bringing fun and celebration to their events. The group explicitly contrasted their events to the seriousness of typical protests. Certainly, the "fun" approach could be a useful corrective both to Giuliani seriousness and protest-politics-as-usual; it was still not the dominant tone of the New York group. Still, the group recognized the subversive nature of pleasure in the face of a Comstock-like morality campaign. Yet, the street actions were not a collective daydream, but "a mass action of civil disobedience."[8] They "fought back," to "counteract Giuliani's 'Quality of Life' campaign," and worked towards "making ourselves visible" and "refusing to be swept under the carpet."[9] While RTS New York was not untouched by the ideology of the playful revolution that informed much of RTS elsewhere, the immediacy conveyed by the City's assault on public space cast their work in more urgent language. Still the group organized in ways that allowed fun to connect dancing bodies with social protest, in a low-threshold, highly participatory carnival of social action (Shepard 2011).

Reclaim the Streets announced their protests with the type of postcards used to promote dance clubs and parties, mixing play and politics.

Both the immediate themes of opposition to cars and to Giuliani were situated in a larger critique. The London and New York groups saw those themes as symbols of a systemic assault by the economic system, worldwide, against the people for whom RTS defended streets and public space. (Several RTS members also equated this to a "big picture/small picture" distinction, in which New York City policies were the immediate target, global ones the causes shared with other RTS groups.) Even in this domain, however, the vocabulary was different: in London, the system was called "capitalism," or described as "development"; in New York it was "neoliberalism" or "privatization." Even as the two groups described a shared analysis of the situation, there was a difference in language. On its web site, RTS London contextualized its opposition to the car in a fight against capitalism, arguing that "The struggle for car-free space must not be separated from the struggle against global capitalism—for in truth the former is encapsulated in the latter. The streets are as full of capitalism as of cars and the pollution of capitalism is much more insidious" (Reclaim the Streets, London 1998b).

Though conversations with RTS members and discussions by people at meetings suggested that members wouldn't disagree with this evaluation, members rarely referred to capitalism, but rather to neoliberalism and privatization.[10] *Capitalism* was not that common a word on the US left at the time, and fighting *privatization* had more currency and may have sounded more realistic in a political climate rife with Margaret Thatcher's refrain, "there is no alternative." For instance, Dan, who spoke the most about RTS's opposition to a larger system, described RTS this way:

> My take on it was always that it was a response to neoliberalism, really. And that it was civically a direct action that was sort of flying in the face of a trend we can trace to privatization. . . . Symbolically, cars on the street are a perfect example of all of these neoliberal reforms.

The quotes from London and New York described the same relationship—of cars as a symbol for an economic system. But while it is unlikely that Dan, nor many of the other participants in RTS, would have objected to describing RTS as opposing capitalism, that's not the word they most often chose. As a result of local conditions and history, the London and New York groups used different language even while they fundamentally shared an analysis of the "big picture."

A comparison of London and New York RTS creates a clear portrait of the New York group: energized and defiant, they opposed a host of changes in the city and attacks against public space that they tied to the Giuliani administration. But as much as he was a personification of these policies, the group recognized that New York's transformation was a local manifestation of broader forces, which they attributed to multinational corporations, and the economic system in which they operated. The assault on public space was not a local matter, for not only did the privatizing opposition come from beyond New York, but it threatened cities and citizens around the globe. Like the enclosure movement in England (a touchpoint in critiques of the privatization of public space) that took away longstanding rights people had enjoyed in public space, the shift to suburban space required a historic restriction in the activities permitted in these public spaces of the Imperial City. The City rewrote the rules governing who could occupy public space and what they could do there as part of a process in which the scope of activities allowed in these spaces of the city were narrowed and more intrusively observed. With such a regime of space imposed, the individual-level barriers of filtered spaces could be lowered, to transition to suburban spaces, because the state, through stricter policing, higher arrest rates, and more restrictive permitting, had effectively taken over responsibility for the exclusive functions that individual filtering designs had previously played.

The Street Continues

The tactics of Reclaim the Streets were striking because they were quite unlike what the city had come to expect from protest actions. But activists involved in RTS soon felt the need to alter their approaches. The element of surprise that was central to street parties was lost as the police began closely monitoring the group, and as the issues and political climate shifted, activists altered their focus as well. Members of Reclaim the Streets took with them the theatrical, ludic approach to activism that RTS had celebrated, and developed pranks, campaigns, and an evolving series of affinity group projects including, among many others: Students for Undemocratic Society—for the Bush Inauguration, Absurd Response to an Absurd War—during the buildup for the Iraq War, Patriots Against the Patriot Act—against the squeeze on dissent, and the Clandestine Insurgent Rebel Clown Army—when the Republicans came to town for the RNC (Bogad 2007a; Duncombe 2002; Shepard 2003, 2011). The group remained active from 1998 to 2004 (Shepard 2011). In the years to follow the final actions of its New York affinity group, RTS ceased to be as an organization, but street parties much like those the group organized on Broadway continued to erupt on the streets of New York year round.

In presenting the multifaceted ways in which the Giuliani administration's campaigns negatively affected city residents' quality of life, RTS initiated a public discussion about the centrality of public space; their actions embodied the often overlooked, living alternative to the mayor's vision of the city as a place for private, corporate interests to do business. Although much of the work of putting this vision into practice was not completed, RTS undertook the necessary project of identifying a constellation of policies that collectively threatened "public space," and of catalyzing a public dialog about that space. Additional groups, issues, and perspectives could be included within the public's conception of public space. To this day the need to defend public space and people's right to use it for a wide variety of purposes has not been effectively communicated to a wide enough audience so that public space is recognized as important in its own right (and not just as a site where First Amendment rights are practiced, or people's need to make a buck are recognized). RTS was not alone in establishing the importance of public space and demonstrating the creative potential of this framing of a disparate group of issues. Other groups did so as well, further defining public space and its place in democratic society and in a healthy urban environment.

Groups like RTS were not fighting for one single, undifferentiated type of space. Implicitly, the groups that came to be involved in spatial politics, like

FIERCE, RTS, and community garden defenders, recognized the need for a range of alternatives to suburbanized space, such as community and popular spaces. Additionally, the public value of privately owned spaces was not lost on activists. Spaces such as shopping malls, after all, are used as public spaces even though courts have often refused to recognize First Amendment protections there. In all these situations, and even under the best of circumstances, control of public space is contested and the public operates within it under some restriction. But understanding public space as the primary bulwark against the replacement of social interaction with privatized consumption begins the process of defining public space as vital, and defending it as a necessary component of social life that needs to be expanded, re-created, and revitalized. It is a story taking place in thousands of corners, vacant lots, forests, and streets around the globe. The account of these varied efforts continues in the next chapter. Reclaim the Streets opened the debate, but far broader involvement remains necessary to protect public space—and through it, ourselves.

CHAPTER SIX

Gardens, Streets, and Convivial Places

The Struggle for a Ludic Counterpublic

During the McCarthy years of the 1950s, C. Wright Mills suggested that the increasing homogenization of US life resulted in a shrinkage of a democratic public (Aronowitz 2003). Without a space for discussion of differences of opinions, thoughts, alternate solutions, or even daydreams, democratic culture only recedes. Without some sort of local community space where citizens can act together, there is little room for civil society to take shape. Without a space where people can share common interests and pleasures, it is difficult to imagine citizens linking their needs to political participation (Dewey 1954; Shepard 2002).

Only when citizens are mobilized and connected can communities create change; conversely, only when citizens are organized can we consider ourselves living democratically. After all, democracy, it is frequently noted, is not a spectator sport. It needs space to breathe, grow, and thrive. For many, it does so through a series of social networks—which link neighbors and friends to larger, social and cultural trends (Putnam 2001). In this way, spaces where these connections grow—gardens, community centers, parks, group bike rides, unpermitted parades, underground parties, even play spaces—serve as vital places for citizens to cultivate skills crucial to live democratically.

This chapter considers the stories of an overlapping cohort of New York direct action groups—the Reverend Billy and the Church of Stop Shopping, Reclaim the Streets New York, Lower East Side Collective, Time's Up!, the More Gardens! Coalition, and Radical Homosexual Agenda—each connected in their efforts to organize, enjoy, play, and preserve public space for authentic, direct democratic experience. A prime purpose of this social activism is to support improvisational experiences in democratic living. Such practices reject positivist models of urban planning and development by emphasizing uses, not ends—pleasure and expression rather than profit. These practices are sparked by amusement and affect, rather than logic or political calculation (Adams undated; Merrifield 2002; Shepard 2006). Here beaches really do unfold within city streets and people no longer bowl alone (Putnam 2001). More than play, these are spaces where citizens defend and revel in a right to self-determination and autonomy.

Consider the Lower East Side's old Charas El Bohio, a squatted school house, where bike activists collaborated with anarchists; garden activists shared spaces with former Young Lords busy organizing against the US Navy bombing on the Island of Vieques (Melendez 2003). Everyone enjoyed the fundraisers and dance parties at Charas, which supported their movements. Play was part of it, yet there was more to it than that. The right to play, speak out, and build community represented something larger and more authentic in terms of democratic living.

Yet—in order to create and sustain spaces of imagination, play, and autonomy—users must contend with constant duress from a range of forces from hyperdevelopment, to aggressive policing, to corporate globalization and homogenization. With each encroachment, activists have responded in telling, compelling ways. Sometimes the aim is to create autonomous space; in others it is to change laws and social mores. While the groups chronicled here mobilize in response to different issues, several themes tie them together. These groups see public space as both a resource they seek to preserve and as a space for expression that serves as a contrast to work and social control. In doing so, these seemingly disparate groups have come to share an analysis of the changes to public spaces. Each group sees their specific issue as part of a larger assault on New York's tradition of diverse and tolerant public space.

Part of this ethos includes a recognition of uses of play and creative direct action to upset the workings of power that operate against them. The possibility for ludic experience, allowing for multiple authentic expressions of the pursuit of happiness, represents a highly democratic dynamic of urban living. By supporting multiple users to express their own versions of happiness, autonomy, and democratic expression, it engages contrasting views of urban space. While developers view urban geography as an opportunity for economic growth, many of those who live in such spaces look for more. Within their neighborhoods, they hope for conversations, acquaintances, the mingling of ideas and friends, and spaces to slow down or even to play chess (Jacobs 1961; Talen 2003). Such intersections where citizens meet, build social capital, and plant the seeds of caring social relations counter the soul-crushing monoculture believed necessary to create a stable business climate (Holtzman et al. 2007; Logan and Molotch 1987). Within such spaces, tribes expand and conviviality thrives. "A modern society, bounded for convivial living, could generate a new flowering of surprises far beyond anyone's imagination and hope," writes Ivan Illych (1973, 14). Here the roots of a new embodied democratic experience take shape through shared play, autonomy, conversation, and performance.

For community gardeners, cyclists, queer activists, and others whose stories intermingle throughout this chapter, such space is more than a place on which community is enacted. In the face of a concerted threat by real estate developers, corporate gentrifiers, and pro-business city government, activists defend their community spaces by seeking to disrupt the recolonization of the city. Here, activists reclaim areas that have fallen under private control and turn them into community, TAZ, and popular spaces. In this way, the untidy range of groups and issues, and the seeming disarray sown by their actions helps community members forge monkey wrenches to sabotage the gentrifying growth machine. Sometimes this takes shape as a street party, in others as an impromptu radical street performance. While not an end in itself, such gestures inject ludic unpredictability into the normally serious business of extracting exchange profit from the land of the capitalist city. With community gardens threatened, community space became a base from which to sally forth and challenge the hubris of those intent on expanding the range of suburban, highly policed spaces throughout the city. A few words on the context of the homogenization of such spaces situates the stories which follow.

Disappearing Commons, Regulated Spaces

The final weeks of Rudy Giuliani's term as mayor of New York City revealed as much about urban life under Giuliani-ism as any month in the previous eight years. In early December 2001, the City began arresting homeless people for sleeping on the steps of the Presbyterian Church at Fifth Avenue and 55th Street. Vice-President Dick Cheney and Israeli President Ariel Sharon slept in hotels nearby as the police beat those sleeping outside and sent them to New York City's de facto shelter system: jail. The Church sued the City on behalf of the homeless, but was rebuffed, stifled by the new regulatory infrastructure taking hold of the public spaces of American cities (Goodman 1998).

The Charas El Bohio Community Services Center in the East Village lost its request for a stay of eviction the same month. In response, its supporters began a twenty-four-hour vigil. Charas had been sold, without competitive bidding, to a Giuliani campaign contributor back in 1998. By 2001, *The Village Voice*, in its "Best of New York" issue, dubbed Charas/El Bohio "the Best Place to Rally Around and/or Resuscitate." Noting that rehearsal space at Charas cost from eleven to fourteen dollars an hour, the *Voice* explained, "CHARAS serves the Lower East Side community, not the Big Apple Tour Bus, and that is why, partially, it is in jeopardy" (Sottile 2001).

Charas and Lower East Side activism had a long history. Civil disobedience training for countless community struggles, including a successful campaign to save the Lower East Side's community gardens, had been held at the former school. That made Charas a target. Protesters, squatters, garden activists, and requisite East Village vagabonds screamed, "Man of the year, get out of here!" (referring to the mayor's recent award as *Time*'s Person of the Year), as they watched the NYPD shut down access to this space where much of the do-it-yourself spirit of their neighborhood had thrived. Both Charas and the steps of Fifth Avenue Presbyterian had served as meeting spaces for marginalized groups. While for years, the mayor had battled communities of difference who fought his agenda of privatizing New York's public spaces, September 11 neutralized much of the official opposition to his plan to evict the neighborhood community center where the enemies of neoliberalism converged.

Even before 9/11, Giuliani-ism, as a mode of urban governance favoring suburban blandification of public space—replete with elaborate security functions, racial profiling, and "stop and frisk" policing—had become a model (Hammett and Hammett 2007). Pro-growth opponents noted that the underside of quality-of-life campaigns was increased police brutality and social control (Sites 2003). Recent histories of police violence in New York City dedicate considerable attention to Giuliani's aggressive policing of countless elements of urban life (Johnson 2003). The litany of complaints is not short, yet the former mayor's pro-growth and social control model of urban governance has been emulated across the country—most recently in Los Angeles, and even in Mexico City (Harcourt 2001; Lipton 2004).

If Disneyfication is the future of the American physical and psychological landscape, creative community building offers the best possibility of a detour off the one-way suburban superhighway towards the mallification of the American imagination. Here is where activists create different kinds of spaces for engagement through do-it-yourself (DIY) community-building. Within such spaces, use is valued over commercial exchange. "DIY as a form of activity creates value outside of capitalism" (Holtzman et al. 2007, 45). This chapter illustrates the distinctive ways activists reclaim areas that become suburbanized or otherwise fall under private control and turn them into community, TAZ, and popular spaces (45). DIY projects thus reject the predominant vision of urban spaces as growth machines (Logan and Molotch 1987). DIY projects cultivate a highly participatory, low-threshold approach to democratic engagement. One does what one can do to build a better world—one garden, zine, party, or bike ride at a time (Duncombe 1997). Holtzman et al (2007) maintain, "DIY reconstructs power relationships differently than those found under capital by abandoning the institutions of capital and the state, and constructing counter-institutions based upon fundamentally different principles and structures (45). Operating outside of typically alienating means and modes of production, the DIY ethos emphasizes the creation of new social relations.

Food Not Bombs and the Green Guerillas are two such DIY groups that build on these simple gestures of direct action—Food Not Bombs gives away free food and the Green Guerillas are community gardeners who transform urban rubble into green space. Both groups have encountered new mechanisms of control from the state. Members of the anarchist collective Food Not Bombs were arrested on multiple occasions for giving away food without a permit to the homeless (Vitale and McHenry 1994). Urban gardeners have been arrested again and again for trespassing on their own gardens (Kauffman 2000a). "Something is happening here in the streets of America and beyond," notes anthropologist Jeff Ferrell (2001, 3), "and while what it is may not be exactly clear, it is clear that it involves contested practices of public life and community." Ferrell's reading concurs with Michaels Hardt's (2000) contention that Western cultures have moved beyond a disciplinary era towards an era of social control. The result of these controls is the transformation and hyper-regulation of physical spaces. Throughout cities around the world, we witness methodical steps used to target "communities of difference" as urban centers have been redesigned with an aim towards marginalization on the basis of race, class, gender, and political opposition to the new suburban vision of urban life. Tools utilized include anti-vagrancy, zoning, nuisance-abatement, and "quality-of-life" statutes—all organized together to cordon off public spaces utilized by prostitutes, the homeless, gang members, green gardeners, anarchists, and countless other groups that deviate from normative notions of citizenship and political participation. The assumption is that city spaces should function like for-profit entertainment parks. In order for these entertainment zones to thrive, the state must regulate their use. Advocates of this new model of hypercontrolled public spaces—businesses, political leaders, and even some civic groups—argue closed spaces are necessary to cultivate a better, more secure business climate. Those who transgress such administrative controls are often subject to the disciplinary weight of the state (Ferrell 2001; Logan and Moloch 1987).

Much of the new hypercontrolling of public space is a response to the politics of fear, which had overwhelmed the ways New Yorkers viewed public space during the early 1990s. With his election as mayor of New York in 1993, Giuliani initiated a series of efforts to "improve the city" and enforce quality-of-life policies that facilitated middle-class renewal of mixed-income neighborhoods such as the East Village. Giuliani skillfully played on this feeling to deploy a series of panic narratives related to mugging, race, and sex to justify hitherto unacceptable encroachments into public space in the name of redevelopment (Chambliss 1995; Crimp et al. 1998; Hall et al. 1978). Giuliani's tactical manipulation of social anxieties was consistent with a dominant theme of urban political thinking. As geographer Neil Smith (1996) explained, "In the 1990s an unabated litany of crime and violence, drugs and unemployment, immigration and depravity—all laced through with terror—now scripts an unabashed revanchism of the city" (211).

At its core, the new regulation of public spaces has to do with questions about difference. The new regulatory infrastructure seems to specifically target difference, with thousands arrested and put through the system for "loitering in any public place . . . with no apparent purpose. . . ." (Ferrell 2001, 4). While charges are often dismissed, the message remains that to use public space is to take a chance. Those arrested never get back the time they spent in the system. At its core, the new "class cleansing" of public spaces aims to attack and marginalize unpopular ideas and those who harbor them (Ferrell 2001).

In response, public space groups have fought the new spatial controls and "countered new forms of spatial exclusion with the inclusive politics of liberty, diversity, disorder, who've been able to create communities of difference and inclusion" (Ferrell 2001, 19).

To the extent that the new regulatory infrastructure is aimed at squeezing certain groups out of public space, it involves core questions about pluralistic democracy. While many of the new anti-assembly, "xxx" zoning, broken windows, and "quality-of-life" ordinances are viewed as isolated city ordinances, "programs designed to police cultural spaces, to restore civility and community in such spaces, in fact reinforce patterns of special inequality, day-to-day economic and ethnic apartheid, and street-level abuse" (Ferrell 2001). In the face of such hyper-regulation, one is forced to wonder who has access to which conversations, who can or cannot walk in which areas, who can drive without being profiled by police. Without access to public spaces, any talk of democracy feels profoundly limited. And the point is clear: if you can't walk in the street, how can you be considered a citizen? (see Ribey 1998). Freedom of assembly and democratic participation are intimately connected. Such freedoms are under duress, but opposition to such politics abounds. Within the following narratives, one can trace the lines of a class war between corporate control of public space through privatization, filtering, and suburbanization, and a burgeoning do-it-yourself global justice movement aimed at using TAZs to unleash a new "liberatory urbanism" for a new century (Ferrell 2001, 231).

A Space to Play

Brian Sutton-Smith (1997 134) writes that, "play, like dreams, is not a secondary state of reality . . . but has primacy as a form of knowing." In recent years, activists within various camps, including the AIDS, global justice, and public space movements, have turned from a more conventional rational approach towards a strategy of play, creativity, and performance as a response to a burgeoning politics of panic, privatization, and control. Much of this organizing overlaps with the upsurge of a global justice movement comprised of many different social movements (Mertes 2003). These activist groups seek a more pluralistic form of democratic political engagement, and have embraced the idea of playfully engaging power, rather than confronting it (Solnit 2004).

To do this, social actors use play to communicate truth through illusion, performance, prank, and rambunctious expressions of political performance (Nardi 2006). Here, the stage becomes a site for activist engagement. For many, this play serves as an effective tool in group development; for other groups, it served as an instructive mechanism aimed at communicating move-ment messages (Shepard 2009; Shepard 2011). Here, actors, activists, and citizens (and for that matter noncitizens) cultivate theatrical imagery of regular life where art lives in a street made up of many different types of actors (Marcos 2001). They can either remain on the sidewalk or they can step into the street, onto a different kind of stage and performance in democracy where they no longer listen to their directors. Social movement action takes place when actors start improvising with their roles and their everyday lives become arenas of struggle and performance, public space serving as a place for subversive possibilities. After all, play's the thing which Hamlet used to grab the attention of the king. Such thinking finds its political manifestations in the politics of play, performance, and creative freedom and direct action (Marcos 2001). If reality is but a series of fictions, then the task of social movement actors is to create more compelling dramas, more inviting stories for citizen participation. While the Zapatistas, and the global movement they represent, assert there are different ways of thinking about political power (Marcos 2001), this book asserts different kinds of social formations and community resources are produced when people play with politics and power. The emphasis is on play elements, which not only sustain community, but also cultivate movement action.

Conceptualized as play, the cat-and-mouse game of protest takes on new meanings. "Direct action introduces the concept of play into the straight, pre-dictably grey world of politics," wrote movement sage John Jordan (1998). He writes:

> People being chased by a bunch of uncoordinated security guards through thigh-deep mud on a construction site; figures jumping onto the machinery, laughing, blowing kisses to the digger drivers and D-locking their neck to the digger arm; driving the security off a piece of the land, re-squatting it; climbing to the top of a tree and singing at the top of your voice. It's all fundamentally playful, a fantastic game: a game of cat and mouse, or, rather, David and Goliath. . . . (133)

Jordan borrows from Victor Turner's (1969) paradoxical view of play as both unserious and as a liberatory force with total disregard for social controls. "The playfulness of direct action proposes an alternate reality but it also makes play real; it takes it out of Western frameworks of childhood make believe—and throws it in the face of politicians." Such forms of direct action are difficult to reconcile with other more serious forms of political engagement. Jordan concludes, "The state never knows where this type of playing ends or begins as it seeps from construction site to construction site. . . . Its unsteadiness, slipperiness, porosity and riskiness erode the authority of those in power" (134).

Even a few social movement scholars have come to frame direct action as a form of play. "When you are locked arm in arm with your friends and you are running into a line of police and you tell them to screw off, why wouldn't that be play?" Frances Fox Piven (2006) commented recently during a panel on the new activism. For Piven, the point is that fighting authority can be a joyous endeavor. A few expressions of such gestures are instructive.

Fighting Starbucks, Supporting Charas

"God is the absence of gentrification," the Reverend Billy of the Church of Stop Shopping has frequently proclaimed (O'Neil 2004). And it is hard to argue with him on this. Through his joyous, self-deprecating street persona— a preacher guilty of the sin of shopping too much—Bill Talen has created a playful messaging device effectively used in campaigns addressing sweatshop work conditions, protecting community gardens, preserving historic sites, and defending the First Amendment. In response to the diversity-crushing gentrification steamroller, the Reverend has organized neighborhood defense actions to prevent the corporate big boxes—such as Wal-Mart and other megastores—and such as Starbucks, from planting their "sea of identical details" in once vibrant neighborhood spaces. The problem with Starbucks is that "they seek out community," the Reverend explained. Starbucks' encroachment into neighborhoods was efficient and startling. There were no Starbucks in New York City in 1994. By 2002, 124 outlets had popped up on the island of Manhattan alone (Prestin 2002). In the same period, the city bulldozed countless community gardens and locked up countless sex clubs, both unique places where community members could meet and share space. As New York City becomes more welcoming to tourists, it becomes more like the shopping malls in the hometowns from which the tourists came (Hemmett and Hemmett 2007). In response, the Reverend Billy and his Church of Stop Shopping Gospel Choir engaged in "retail interventions" in neighborhoods where Starbucks planned to open new outlets. Many of these interventions depended on a politics of play and performance in which regular life took on the complexion of a theatre of the absurd.

Shortly before the Republican National Convention protests in New York City in August 2004, the Reverend traveled to Barcelona to defend a small community there. He reflected on the trip:

God in heaven, we need a place like Barcelona on the earth. . . . We were met at the airport by sixty laughing radicals who wanted to go straight to a Starbucks. We had to shake-and-bake a sermon just to get to baggage claim. 'Our neighborhood is our body. And when our heart is cut out and a new heart is cut in, then our body accepts the new love muscle or throws a fit. CHILDREN, STARBUCKS HAS COME TO BARCELONA!! That is preemptively preposterous, we are outraged —but let us give the Green Mermaid With No Nipples the chance we would give a cut-in heart. Let's find out if our neighborhood, our body, will accept this foreign object. What does the immune system think? Let's have a test. LET US NOW EAT THE FAKE CAFÉ!! LET US TAKE IT INTO OUR BODY! LET US LICK IT!! . . .' And so we did. It was a breakthrough moment in our comic theology advancing toward us through a jet-lag fog; we knelt before the transnational corporate mermaid in the public square, as the mildly interested tourists and Bobos (Bourgeois Bohemians) watched us go native. We shouted LICK A LULIAH! LICK A LULIAH! LAM ER LULIAH (in Espanola)—and rushed the stage [the store itself]. We licked everything, really everything, including the cappuccino spouts and latte sippers' computers (Talen, undated).

While this playful spirit may seem irrelevant to social activism, it has inspired many actors to stay engaged and involved. The Reverend Billy project finds its inspiration in a number of sources, including an Emma Goldman, "if I can't dance" type of ethos. "I would believe only in a god who could dance," Talen (2005) preached, borrowing from Nietzsche. "I do not want to be pushed before moving along. Now I am light, now I fly, now I see myself beneath myself, now a god dances through me." Witnessing a cavalcade of bike riders careening through the streets of New York City, he paraphrased these lines: "Let the spirit of the ride flow through you." Yet, much of this creative spirit is threatened within a homogenization wave paving the social landscape.

"We are witnessing now the suburbanizing of New York City, in which America finally swallows it," Talen (2005) explained. The front lines of the conflict began in neighborhoods where a liberatory urbanism was threatened by a blandification steamroller.

Ascendant "developers" and transnational chain stores accomplished this, in their relentless destruction of our neighborhoods. But realize that New York City equals its neighborhoods. . . . The deluded believe New York City is actually a gathering of elites: Wall Street, the Fashion District, Madison Avenue. We have co-existed with those elites for some time, but now they want forty-story condos in Williamsburg, gated communities along the East River, bulldozed community gardens in the Bronx, a nineteen-story corporate dorm where Charas Community Center once stood—if the elites assimilate our neighborhoods into an endless monoculture, then New York City will no longer be a voice of peace, a voice of tolerance, a voice of imagination. New York City cannot converse with the culture of the world if we allow its neighborhoods to die. . . . New Yorkers yell at each other in the doorways of diners along 10th Avenue, the gossip makes them laugh in barbershops in Fort Greene. We live in the gardens and stoops and bars (with unlicensed dancing, even) and eccentric little shops and farmers' markets and basketball courts and the F Train on Saturday night—that scathing music is the real city. . . . In that music, I see the flight Nietzsche wrote of. Public space hijackers oppose our flight. (Talen 2005)

Within this passion for authentic experience, opposition abounds. Recent suc-
cesses cited by the Reverend Billy and his Church of Stop Shopping include
the victory by the citizens of Inglewood, 113,000 of whom recently voted to
ban Wal-Mart from their neighborhood. Yet, for every step forward, a step
backward seems to follow.

In recent years, the Reverend Billy has preached about the fate of the old
PS 64, longtime home of Charas/El Bohio Community Services Center,
which was sold off to a developer in 1998. Charas/El Bohio was a former
public school building, which functioned as a community center on 9th Street
between Avenues B and C (Moynihan, 1999). Between its founding in 1979
and its takeover by the City of New York in January 2002, Charas offered
affordable classes, studio space, tutoring services, after-school activities, a
recycle-a-bike program, and meeting space for community groups.

Charas' origins can be found in the squatter movement of the 1970s and
1980s. Charas/El Bohio began when directors Armando Perez and Chino
Garcia moved their group, Charas, into the then-abandoned school building
in 1979. At the time, the building was in disrepair and functioning as a
"shooting gallery" for heroin users. Charas rechristened the building "El
Bohio" (the hut) and renovated the building with sweat equity. By 1982, their
efforts were so successful that Community Board 3 recommended Charas be
given a lease on the property. The New York Department of City Planning,
the City Planning Commission, and the City Council all upheld this request.
But in 1998, the building was sold to real estate developer Greg Singer for
$1.71 million (Moynihan 1999). Resistance to the sale among community
members continued over the ensuing years. The building was taken over by
the City in January 2002.

In the years between the building's sale and its final occupation by the
developer, the space became a symbol of the hazards of neighborhood gentrification. In the days right before the City evicted community members from
the space, Reclaim the Streets passed out flyers asking: "Do You Ever Walk
Around The Neighborhood And Not Recognize A Fxxxxxxx Thing?"
(Reclaim the Streets, New York 2001). The RTS broadsides continued:

> It's funny. There has been so much progress in the last decade that there is almost
> nowhere to go to organize a meeting, put on a play, or sit down without paying an
> entrance fee. In the days since September 11th, people all over the world have com-
> mented on the sense of common purpose, their appreciation for community of New
> Yorkers. So why is the city fighting to take away one of the bedrocks of the East Village
> community?

In response to the eviction threat, RTS threw a street party to defend the space
and called for activists to contact the mayor to push for help. Yet, more than
anything, the street party was a final moment to enjoy what Charas had meant
to the community. The broadside described the coalition supporting Charas:

This rag-tag group of vagabonds, dot-comers, anarchists, newcomers, and old-school
neighborhood hang-abouts is here to call for something simple: that we SAVE CHARAS.
We're here to dance, make noise, and create a bit of the carnival of community Charas
has always inspired. RECLAIM THE STREETS AND SAVE OUR COMMUNITY
CENTER! (Ibid.).

While Charas is gone, many of the squats and community gardens that were
also born of its spirit of community engagement remain. They still exist,
despite threats to the neighborhood, because organizers fought for them.
When activists fight, they don't always win. But if they do not fight, they do
not stand a chance of winning. Quite often they do win if they put up a fight.

Charas was a central part of the East Village, which stretches north from
East Houston Street and eastward from Broadway towards 14th Street. Since
the late 1970s, this area has also been referred to as "Alphabet City," due to its
lettered avenues (Mele 2000). One description of the neighborhood always
seems to remain constant: the East Village has become a model case of urban
gentrification. The literature on the area's history and gentrification is extensive (Smith 1996; Mele 2000; Sites 2003). While many of these studies con-
centrate on the loss of community sovereignty to market forces, corporate
globalization, and gentrification, a few consider how competing groups of
urban actors have successfully brokered compromises that allowed them to
survive despite immense pressure from corporate globalization. Consider the
Lower East Side Collective (LESC)—a community coalition comprised of
neighborhood gardeners, trade unionists, public space advocates, and a "Min-
istry of Love" to handle process issues and help people get involved—which
successfully worked to thwart these trends.

The Lower East Side Collective

A primary example of activist engagement that found its inspiration in the
regressive policies of the Giuliani years was the Lower East Side Collective
(LESC). LESC was born in 1997. An advertisement for one of the group's
"Radical Love" benefit dance parties in 1999 described the group:

> LESC is an activist group based on the Lower East Side. We have been fighting for com-
> munity gardens, defending community arts centers, disrupting City auctions, organizing
> immigrant workers, unfurling guerrilla billboards, jamming phones and faxes, demanding
> affordable housing, sponsoring poetry readings, holding fabulous parties, working for
> real "quality of life" in the Lower East Side, and generally making life miserable for land-
> lords, bureaucrats and developers since 1997.

The flyer ends with an invitation to a new sort of political ethos: "Come celebrate the neighborhood's vibrant political culture with some of its most
unruly elements." For years since the legendary Tompkins Square Park police
riot in 1989, people had suggested that the battle against gentrification in the

Lower East Side was lost. Yet, for others, the long history and culture of activism in the Lower East Side presented an opportunity. Many contributed to LESC's new ethos of activism. In so doing, they borrowed from the history of the battle against gentrification in the Lower East Side, carefully picking and choosing elements to embrace and others to reject (for more on LESC see Shepard 2011).

One of LESC's greatest campaigns involved the struggle to save the community gardens in the East Village and throughout the city. In many ways, the East Village thrived as a somewhat anachronistic—perhaps even utopian—experience in community building in the midst of hostile market forces. The neighborhood continued to produce social relations and representational spaces of opposition, despite market pressures from corporate globalization, gentrification, and the increase of hip cultural capital. While use values found themselves at odds with the exchange values that could be realized in real estate throughout the East Village, the rules of community and collective consumption occasionally sustained themselves despite the pressures of the rules of individual consumption, which turn urban spaces into commodities (Logan and Moloch 1987). Such a politics of community can thwart the politics of fear and panic propelling the logic of primitive globalization (Sites 2003; Smith 1996). No better example of such a politics exists than the campaigns to save the community gardens.

Community Gardens and a Space to Play

"This is a free market economy: welcome to the era after communism," Mayor Rudy Giuliani taunted activists and garden supporters after announcing plans to sell off dozens of Lower East Side community gardens in 1999 (Kifner 1999). In response, community members cried foul, using every tool at their disposal to launch a multiprong sustained campaign to preserve the community gardens. The struggle to save these gardens took many forms over many years. Those involved included the Lower East Side Collective, the Bronx Urban Gardeners (BUG), the Guerilla Gardeners, the More Gardens! Coalition, as well as many other squatters, homesteaders, and community residents. Tools involved within the campaigns included clear demands, research, mobilization, direct action, fundraising, and legal and theatrical resources (Ferguson 1999; Ferguson 2000; Will 2003). Community garden activists provide an excellent example of the use of play in community organizing. Much of their organizing took place during meetings at Charas. "Gardening helps people with dynamite in their pants to change the world: it sustains us as we prod the world along," garden supporter Donna Schaper explained (2007, xiv). For Schaper, growing gardens worked in tandem with growing social change.

Community gardens were established in large numbers in New York beginning in the 1970s. As a result of urban disinvestment, redlining, and "planned shrinkage," the city's population fell; landlords allowed buildings to deteriorate, or they incinerated them; and the city left vacant lots to rot and accumulate trash. Local residents, including both small groups of ethnic working-class residents and counterculture newer arrivals, began moving into these abandoned spaces and making community gardens out of them. Eventually, the city responded to this unexpected response to planned shrinkage by institutionalizing the gardeners' right to the spaces they had reclaimed (Zukin 2010).

The gardens served important roles in their neighborhoods. In many cases, they reinforced the identity of the groups that ran them, whether Puerto Rican families and neighbors, radicalized groups in the neighborhood, or other constellations of local residents. As community spaces, they carried the risk of exclusion, and Miranda J. Martinez expertly detailed the conflicts, particularly between long-time Puerto Rican users of the gardens and newer "artist gardeners" (Martinez 2002). The fact that gardens were public spaces but also sites of exclusion has been a confounding paradox—or even a damning shortcoming of the gardens for many who have observed, written, and even defended the gardens. Differences of class, ethnicity, age, gender, and tenure frequently needed to be negotiated in the gardens, and these differences complicated both the use of the gardens and locals' efforts to protect them. In addition, gardeners were forced to contend with the struggle with garden hours. "It was difficult because they were incredibly suspicious of anyone from the outside, and since none of us had a garden we were definitely not gardeners," explained LESC member David Crane, who helped organize to save the gardens. "So that was partly how Francoise [Cachelin] was very useful because we were able to really prove ourselves with the Creative Little Garden on 530 E. 6th Street. We decided to open up the gardens, and we did something called 'Spring into the Garden.'"

Recognizing the gardens as community space helps us identify their exclusive aspect as an inherent conflict to be expected (because users control access), not a paradox to be explained. This account does not focus on those important dynamics within the gardens, but instead examines the ways in which garden defender groups used space to defend their spaces. Yet, in sharing organizing tasks as well as playing together, activists and gardeners found common cause in the direct action of building and defending green spaces (Will 2003).

As gentrification expanded across new parts of the city, Mayor Giuliani obliged real estate speculators by trying to sell off any city-owned lots that developers might want, including community gardens. Gardeners and the groups that supported them responded in force (Ferguson 1999; Martinez 2002; Shepard 2002; Shepard 2011; Zukin 2010).

Garden activists found a range of inspirations for their work. New York City garden activist Tim Becker worked with a number of garden groups, including the Lower East Side Collective Public Space group as well as the More Gardens! coalition. Aresh Javadi, one of the founders of More Gardens!, had helped create a profoundly theatrical quality within the defense of the gardens. Becker recalled the day the gardeners rode a giant homemade bike to City Hall dressed as a giant tomato to defend the community gardens under threat:

> I helped them build the tomato on the bicycle. That was put together as well at Charas before the caterpillar. More Gardens! got more and more ambitious with their creations-on-wheels campaign. First they had the tomato. It was two bicycles welded together, and it was a huge monster tomato. I remember riding that from Aresh's house to City Hall one day, and it was the most fun I've had in my life. You know, we were going down Allen Street. The thing was held together by wires. It could move but it was a little shaky. You had to look out [of it to] see. It was hard to drive. But people's jaws were dropping. They couldn't believe a tomato was going down Allen Street. It was big. Two bikes, as big as your couch and eight feet high. People saw it, loved it, and they couldn't believe it.

Caterpillar bike. (Courtesy www.timesup.org.)

Throughout this period, garden activists such as Becker brought many different forms of puppet theater to the public conversation. In another example, gardeners brought a dragonfly whose wings went up and down when the bikers inside pedaled.

There are some six hundred gardens in New York City and fifty in the East Village. In 2002, after years of direct action and civil disobedience, Mayor Bloomberg helped cut a deal with then Attorney General Elliot Spitzer (2002). A portion of these spaces were designated as park space. Yet, the deal would only last until 2010, when community spaces were again put in jeopardy. The confusion about the garden agreement was that many believed that *all* the gardens had been made permanent. Yet, in the ensuing years, support for the agreement began to erode as individual gardens continued to face a threat.

Over the years of the garden struggle, garden supporters sought to theatrically represent the spirit of the gardens—through a series of rituals, parades, and pageants. Through play and performance, these yearly events sought to highlight the social drama of the garden struggle. From 1991 through 2005, Felicia Young helped organize a collective one-day pageant called Earth Celebrations, which zigged and zagged through the various fifty-plus community gardens in the Lower East Side. The point was to highlight the beauty of the gardens and the dire straits they faced—from bulldozers, developers, and waves of redevelopment. Yet, the gardeners struggled onward and so did their spirit. Earth Celebrations was a pageant comprised of giant flower puppets, samba and marching bands, as well as a panorama of supporters dressed as garden spirits, nymphs, and fairies with flowers in their hair. The eight-hour panorama typically began at Forsyth Garden. The parade included blessings at each garden plot (as well as memorials for a few casualties). The celebration included a theatrical birth, kidnapping, and saving of Gaia, who was forced to battle robots and developers before her libation. The drama of the attack was so vivid my (Shepard's) older daughter Dodi asked to leave the parade. As the years continued, the numbers of gardens casualties—Chico Mendez, Eperanza, Little Puerto-Rico—mounted (Ferguson 1999; Ferguson 2004a). And fatigue set in with the drawn-out struggle.

By 2006, word on the street was that no Earth Celebrations would take place. So members of Time's Up! collaborated with the More Gardens! Coalition as well as a few veterans of the Lower East Side Collective Public Space Group to coordinate The Roving Garden Parade (RGP), a garden celebration to be held in the spring. The event would include the theatricality of Earth Celebrations, yet cut the length of the route. The RGP would conjure old and new battlegrounds to bring attention to the sixty-five endangered community gardens across the city that need to be saved. Implicit was the recognition that community gardens play a vital role in New York City's diverse neighborhoods as places to set and maintain roots. The Roving Garden Party would urge people to start, support, and save all open spaces for growth and nurturing in their communities.

The action was to call attention to New York's endangered community gardens: "Coalition of Activists, Gardeners And Performers will Loudly Celebrate NYC Gardens in a Traveling Party which Concludes at a Rally for the Endangered Children's Magical Garden," press materials declared before the action.

"*The Roving Garden Party* encourages everyone to loudly support and celebrate their community gardens by gathering together to dress up, play music, dance and march," declared the press release. "We call on everyone to make some noise for the gardens and to remember that our fight to preserve them is not over!" It concluded: "Let's do what we have always done when faced with a threat: dress up, play music, dance, and make some noise as we call for support from the garden creatures!" A scaled-down alternative in lieu of the annual Earth Celebration, the afternoon of the Roving Garden Parade was full of ritualistic gestures.

Stop, Go, Grow and exercise the bulldozer. Photo by Gaylen Hamilton

Roving Garden Party Celebration at Children's Magical Garden in the Lower East Side. 2006. With members of the More Gardens Coalition! Lower East Side Collective, Reverend Billy and the Church of Stop Shopping, Times Up!. the Rude Mechanical Orchestra, and the Radical Homosexual Agenda present, this photo captures much of the spirit of freedom and possibility of the movement for public space in New York City. (Photo by www.timesup.org.)

"The event began in Tompkins Square Park.," Ellen, a Time's Up! garden supporter, wrote in a report back. "The Rude Mechanical Orchestra and the Roving Garden Party was announced from the stage of a salsa music concert which took a break to allow us to loudly march out of the park." Those attending included nearly a hundred garden supporters, and Ellen recalled, "kids dressed like fairies, flower-people, a few bugs (including a fantastic ladybug), pedicabs, cargo bikes, a bulldozer, garden bikes, decorated bikes and dogs, etc." Others wore green banners with the words, 'Go Grow!!!" spray-painted in pink on the back. After a playful ritual in which members of the crowd exhorted the bulldozer to "Stop!?" "Plant!" and "Grow" as if they were plants themselves, the Rude Mechanical Orchestra led the dancing crowd out of the park. "As we exited the park, we were greeted only with happy faces from the community," Ellen recalled. The NYPD notably skipped the Saturday afternoon action. "Our numbers swelled to over one hundred as the parade went on and the vibe went from fantastic to ecstatic."

Gardeners danced and remembered gardens and gardeners who had passed. They passed out flower seeds and threw seed balls—comprised of dirt, wildflower seeds, and cat litter—into vacant lots. And a cardboard bulldozer chased down the garden creatures, threatening to bulldoze them. The Reverend Billy and the Church of Stop Shopping blessed the gardens. In El

Jardin del Paraiso on East 5th Street, members of More Gardens! led participants through a spiral dance.

After visiting several Lower East Side gardens and remembering community gardens and activists recently lost, the Roving Garden Party included a rally to support the endangered Children's Magical Garden de Carmen Rubio on the corner of Norfolk and Stanton Streets. The afterparty included a picnic, songs by the Rude Mechanical Orchestra, and fire spinning and a little rain. Bread and wine flowed during the afterparty, which ended with a crescendo of rain. In a notable absence, few police were anywhere to be seen for the unpermitted parade.

The central concern of many of the garden supporters during the garden parade was the fate of Children's Magical Garden. In 1980, longtime Lower East Side resident Carmen Rubio and art student Alfredo Feliciano had transformed the space from a vacant lot full of junk and debris into a garden for the neighborhood's youth. Since 1982, the land comprising the space had been owned both by the City of New York and by developer Serge Hoyda. Over the years, Lower East Side garden support groups including the

Roving Garden Party flyer by Caroline Shepard 2007. www.timesup.org

More Gardens! Coalition and Time's Up! worked to stack community board meetings to call for support for the garden. Even local politicians called for the garden to be preserved.

Speakers declared their support for the garden still facing the threat of bulldozers.

"The Children's Magical Garden de Carmen Rubio is in Danger," speaker after speaker lamented.

"So far this year, five New York City gardens have been damaged by developers; many others are endangered—this could happen to any garden in light of unchecked development city-wide," said Time's Up! volunteer and Children's Magical Garden member Christine Halvorson. "This garden is one of over fifty gardens that are now in danger of destruction."

"I am here because community gardens are important to the environment, the quality of life, and the future of New York City," another supporter declared. "They should be included within Bloomberg's plan to make New York a sustainable city."

"Most people in New York are not aware that the gardens have not been saved," another speaker explained. "The Attorney General agreement of 2002 was only temporary. Already developers have been attacking even protected gardens. We have to save our green spaces in light of unchecked development and rising asthma rates," he continued. "When we lose our gardens, we lose all that makes the city unique, colorful—its vibrant city's character. Our communities, the public commons—this is what makes New York City unique."

Most of the support for the garden stemmed from its long history as a community space for children to hang out, chat, share an afterschool snack, learn to garden, and play. Located between two schools, the space long functioned as a convergence space for a wide cross section of neighborhood youth, who benefited from Rubio and Feliciano's work to make the garden a safe space for the neighborhood. Two generations of kids and adults loved the mulberries, apples, peaches, tomatoes, pumpkins, and sunflowers, and the low-key communal spirit that grew in the space. Ground rules for the space were minimal: no cursing, fighting, or disrespecting anyone. "I have met kids of kids who grew up in the garden," Feliciano told me (Shepard) during one of the garden working days in October 2007. "From the very beginning, it was children—so they could learn how to garden, how to plant," Feliciano recalled in a 2006 interview (Siegel 2006). "I really love the fact that it's for kids," Kate Temple-West, the garden's director, recalled in the same interview. "I can't imagine being a kid and not being able to run and play." Temple-West helped coordinate and organize events and teach-ins at the garden. Themes included topics such as planting and composting. Temple-West suggested young people thrive when exposed to the natural environment. "Makes for sane, happy adults if they have a chance to play in green spaces as children" (Siegel 2006).

Time's Up! began providing volunteers and support during the garden's fall work days. On October 6, 2007, Children's Magical held a work day and pizza-making party. I (Shepard) brought my one-year-old daughter Scarlett to play with the younger kids. She and a group of children, from a wide range of backgrounds and ethnicities, danced to Santana rock-and-roll tapes on the stage, played with dolls, swung on swings, and helped spread a pile of compost and mulch throughout the garden with the help of Feliciano and other volunteers. I wheeled Scarlett, who sat perched on a pile of compost, to and from the compost pile to the bushes. In between stops, she dug in the compost and romped around with the other kids. "Scarlett, come play with me," some of the children screamed as we zigged and zagged back and forth throughout the garden. "*Que pasa*," one of the other volunteers greeted Scarlett as she ran through the space, her face and clothes covered in dirt. It is hard to not feel welcome in such an environment. The experience of playing in the dirt in the garden is a stark contrast to the rough-and-tumble concrete jungle's rough edges and its asphalt playing fields where children regularly experience scraped knees and occasionally, bruised egos.

Later in the afternoon, the children and volunteers made a dinner with the vegetables grown from the garden. One volunteer brought a juicer and made carrot juice for everyone. Many other children's spaces throughout the city involve a dynamic of endless competition or anonymity. An entirely different ethos existed at the garden. Few of us had ever made pizzas outside in a garden. The children worked collaboratively to pound pizza dough, chop tomatoes, pick other ingredients, and grill their own pizzas. "My job is to teach Kate what I don't yet know," gardener Donna Schaper (2007)

Scarlett and Benjamin Shepard at garden clean up day at Children's Magical Garden. Fall 2007. Photo by Jefferson Seigel.

wrote about a similar experience of working with her daughter in their garden. "It is yet another repentance isn't it, to raise our children better than we were raised ourselves?" (16). For many garden supporters, time in the gardens opens the possibly to contemplate a few mysteries. Gardens help open up minds and points of view.

"If they want to try to destroy this garden, it's not going to be so easy. This garden has a long, strong history in this community as a place that kids can go and have a break and learn about community," Bill DiPaulo, the founder and director of environmental advocacy group Time's Up! declared during the October 15, 2006 work day in the garden (Siegel 2006). Time's Up! had a long history of garden advocacy. DiPaula helped organize the long defense of the Chico Mendez Community Garden, one of the first significant garden defense occupations in the Lower East Side in the late 1990s. The defense would serve as a model for the El Jardin Esperanza Defense in 2000, which profoundly radicalized a generation of garden activists and laid the groundwork for the 2002 garden settlement (Ferguson 2000; Shepard 2011).

From the 1990s onward, the garden movement served as innovation space for activists to experiment with different tactics, strategies, and practices. L. A. Kauffman helped organize the Lower East Side Collective's Public Space Group. Her coconspirator David Crane described the group's ethos:

We were providing propaganda for the defense of the public space movement. We called ourselves the Public Space Project. It wasn't just gardens, it was community centers. And what other kinds of public spaces are under attack at this point? How can we defend them? How can we help groups that are trying to defend them get together and see that they've got common interests.

Kauffman described some of the passion propelling those to defend the city's public spaces. "In New York City, for example, where I live, there has been a longstanding battle against private luxury development on publicly owned community gardens," Kauffman (2000a) wrote. "The other night, several hundred people calling themselves the Subway Liberation Front staged a raucous outlaw party, taking over first an L and then an A train." The "outlaw party" Kauffman referred to was a moving subway party, which had begun downtown earlier that night. It is one of the many playful innovations in street protest party culture to tap into the simultaneous ambitions for people to meet, create a public commons, and seek something better with their world. "A large part of the crowd, juiced by its own defiance, proceeded to the recently bulldozed Esperanza Garden on Manhattan's Lower East Side, where they tore down the developer's fence and began replanting the land," Kauffman (2000a) recalled. "This impromptu action came at a high price: With no news cameras or legal observers to provide cover for the radical gardeners, the NYPD swooped in, badly beating a number of the participants."

William Etundi described the feeling of inherent freedom that often accompanied these carnival-like parties:

> Another element to New York City, which is kind of specific perhaps to this town, but the feeling of even a semi-legal party in an alternative space is liberating. If it's an explicitly illegal party on a subway or on the street, that is liberating. Just dancing in the street is a liberating moment. And we should never underestimate the power of these liberating moments. It's really self-sustaining. I mean, even if you get arrested after it, you feel like, wow, you stood up and took something. And sometimes being arrested is the most politicizing thing that can happen to a person. And hearing people's stories and having other people realize, "Oh shit, I never thought I could get arrested for dancing in the street." Suddenly a person's life has changed from that, which is interesting and exciting.

Within Etundi's narrative, the street party becomes a transformative public ritual, creating the kind of liminal spaces capable of shifting the way people approach their everyday lives (Turner 1969). San Francisco activist David Solnit concurred: "I think as I get older that there is no difference between a ritual, a performance, and an action. You are trying to shift consciousness and change reality, and change how people view reality. And communicate ideas." As an example, Etundi referred to the work of the urban garden activists who worked so effectively to bridge the local/global praxis divide:

> I think More Gardens! is an awesome example of that. Around Esperanza, that was a campaign that was quite clearly lost; the garden was destroyed. But that really gelled a whole lot of people around a specific thing, a lot of specific connections between people. It was an emotional everything. It was challenging. It was growth. It was building connections, networks. It really catalyzed different sectors of people around one thing.

The garden struggle is consistently mentioned as a model of creating community and community space, while linking local and global issues. Garden activists remember the Esperanza campaign, in which activists made a giant bullfrog—a Coqui—to watch over the garden, as one of the more memorable displays of community resolve in recent memory. Play was a centerpiece of the long campaign. Squatters shared the space with street performers; community members and activists cooked dinner and commiserated by the winter campfire; and closer friends created their own heat during countless sleep-overs within the larger-than-life Coqui overlooking the garden (Will 2003). One part art piece/love-den, the Coqui also served as bulldozer watch. To add a tragicomic dimension to the story, the garden itself was bulldozed on Valentine's Day 2000. Thirty-one activists, including Shepard, were arrested during the day-long siege (Ferguson 2000). As the garden was being bull-dozed, the Attorney General called for a temporary restraining order to prevent further destruction of the gardens.

From the struggle for gardens to spaces for nonpolluting transportation, the fight for a place to play, specifically to ride, became another flashpoint in the ongoing battle over public space. "We don't need a permit," said Bill DiPaula of Time's Up! during the first Roving Garden Party. "The gardens and the streets represent public space for the people. People have a right to use them without a permit," (quoted in Villager 2006) DiPaulo would know. For the twenty years since the founding of Time's Up!, DiPaulo has helped organize group bike rides throughout the city. Here the struggle for community took a mobile dimension as conflict between public space activists and police intensified.

Critical Mass Bike Rides and Roving Communities

In August 1999, the New York City Parks Department altered the City's Parks Rules. The regulation stated that groups of twenty or more would be required to obtain permits to assemble or face arrest (City Record 1999). Representatives from public space groups from around the city, including Time's Up! and LESC, testified at the hearings over the new park rules. They pointed out that the rule would stifle freedom of assembly and could be selectively enforced against activists. The rule presented a great challenge to gatherings for community bike rides. "This is an illegal gathering," a policeman told me as I stood with a group before a Fall 2000 ride. A friend noted that there were far under twenty people and the policeman left, for that moment (Shepard and Moore 2002). The cat-and-mouse game over the new rule would last well into the next decade.

The struggle over the right to unfettered access to public space for group events was perhaps most intense for Critical Mass, the monthly bike ride that since 1992 was part of the urban experience in cities around the world. With public space movements overlapping between campaigns involving gardens, neighborhoods, cities, and transnational spaces, these monthly rides became incubators for movement cross-pollination and innovation. Some days New

York riders borrowed from London's RTS; others they borrowed from San Francisco's bike messengers organizing Critical Mass rides (Ibid.). One of the most popular themes of the monthly Critical Mass bike rides called for activists to create a garden in the streets of New York City. For Tim Becker (2005) and other garden activists, this call offered a compelling challenge:

> They did different things. They just got more and more elaborate. And people would kick in. All the artists and people who had good ideas would come over and bring ideas and tools. They would say to Aresh, I know what we'll do. We'll make the wing move. It reached its peak with the caterpillar. That was made of six bikes welded together. And papier-mâché. It had two big plastic eyes you could look out of. One night it went on a TIME'S UP! Critical Mass ride. And the whole ride was waving. This was back in the fun days of Critical Mass before it became like a layer of Dante's Hell. We were waiting at Union Square before the caterpillar came down 14th Street. And everyone was waving and clapping. And then we headed down Broadway. And the caterpillar goes through a movie shoot. And the people are like yelling and screaming because they want the authentic look of New York. They want the cars and the taxicabs. But they don't want the twenty-five-foot caterpillar. They are not shooting a horror flick. We went right through the movie set. It was hilarious. The caterpillar didn't make it too far before the police arrested it.

As Becker noted, a certain hostility also accompanied the convergences, where social actors helped cultivate these forms of creative play.

From the mid-1990s until August 2004, the Critical Mass rides took place in New York without much fanfare. For many, this convergence was an opportunity to meet friends, ride, and revel. Official hostility appeared to be attracted to this spirit of playful connection. Matthew Roth, a regular participant in the rides, explained:

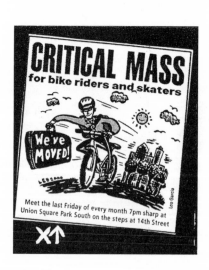

Last Friday of Every Month! 7PM sharp, meet at
Union Square South, on the steps at 14th St.
Tell a friend, spread the word!

Critical Mass New York by Fly
www.timeup.org

All I think about bikes is that bikes are about adolescence. They're about childhood. They are about that first. You can play and you can run pretty fast. But when you get on a bike, when you are four or five or six, you get on a bike and it's just a totally different sense of freedom. It's a totally different sense of play. You are going four times faster than you did before—depending on how steep that hill is you are going down. This is play. This is that sense of freedom. And every single car commercial tries to mimic this . . . but children get it inherently. You get on a bike, that's liberation. You're on your bike, you're exploring, suddenly your neighborhood grew geometrically. Maybe you saw a couple of yards, now you see maybe four, five, ten blocks or more. So there are these very intensely, deeply rooted childhood memories associated to bicycles. And that is something that people still get. Even when you get on a bike in this ferocious city where there are no acceptable lanes, you are completely crammed in and cars are whizzing by you at forty or fifty miles an hour, there's still this sense of "Ahhhh, (sigh), I'm on a bike. This is fun." It harkens back to something more innocent. Anyone who rides, despite all the sense of terror, you still sense that deep play. And when you get a hundred people riding together, a thousand people riding together, there's screaming, there's hooting, there's hollering. It is a playground on wheels.

Roth is hardly the only bike supporter who feels this way. "I guess it connects with the playfulness and the child in everyone that you have to let go of to get a paycheck every Friday," Tim Becker (2005) concurs. "That becomes more important to you. And people are torn."

Much of this changed during the Critical Mass ride before the Republican National Convention (RNC) in New York in 2004. After being labeled "bike hooligans" by the local press, Critical Mass participants endured a crackdown that which had evolved into a decade long battle. Time's Up! felt the brunt of the crackdown. Barbara Ross, a forty-one-year-old human resources manager and urban bike commuter, who volunteered with Time's Up!, explained.[1] "The NYPD has arrested me twice and confiscated my bicycle three times for the so-called-crime of bicycling without a permit." Throughout the Republican convention, the city amplified public hysteria to justify preemptive arrest and control of public space. "The rule that long week was preemptive arrest," explained Eugene Karmazin (2005). "Simply put, anyone seemingly dissident was forcibly removed from the streets, effectively removing them from public discourse as well. More than 1,800 arrests where made during the RNC, more than at any prior Republican or Democratic Convention in US history." This preemptive approach has become *de riguer* for policing public space. "The last Friday of every month, the NYPD turns Union Square Park into a prison yard," Madeline Nelson, a bike supporter, explained before the May 2005 Critical Mass ride. "They line the park and surrounding streets with scores of police vehicles and hundreds of uniformed and undercover cops waiting to scoop up anyone who happens to be there. Who is authorizing the use of taxpayer resources to suppress a public gathering?" Before a ride in March of 2005 the Reverend Billy asked a group of policemen, "Why are you doing this?" as they prepared to arrest a group of bikers. "Well," one officer is said to have declared, "everything changed after 9/11." In fact, it was not until August 2004 that the police behavior at the rides really changed. As with Critical Mass in San Francisco (as described in Chapter 1), in New York the event grew in response to heightened efforts to repress the ride. But, in New York City, the police response was more protracted.

August 27, 2004: The Attack on Critical Mass

The Friday before the Republican Convention, a helicopter pulsed overhead as nervous activists meandered around St. Mark's Church in the minutes after several hundred bikers were arrested for participating in a community bike ride. Earlier in the evening, some five thousand bikers had formed a cavalcade through the summer night. The ride was the culmination of nearly a decade of bike and public space activism (Shepard and Moore 2002). After years of theme-based Critical Mass bike rides supporting community gardens, nonpolluting transportation, even a commemoration of lost firemen after 9/11, the summers of 2003 and 2004 brought thousands of new members into New York's public space/environmental activism. Throughout the Spring and Summer of 2004, activists across the country recognized that the last Friday of August dovetailed with the RNC protests. Critical Mass rides took place around the world on the last Friday of every month. Anticipating the RNC, riders careened across the FDR freeway during the July 30 ride—the last ride of "the fun old days" of Critical Mass. By the next month, everything would be different.

By August, organizing efforts were met with government surveillance and attempts at total control of the monthly Critical Mass rides. During the last week of the month, police began making routine visits to the headquarters of Time's Up! (which was involved in local bike activism), where they asked about the whereabouts of a number of organizers who were on their radar. Surveillance, such as visits to the homes and workplace of activists known to be effective organizers, was common during the days before the RNC.

Two days before the August ride, organizers were informed that they could not hold their planned afterparty at the Frying Pan, a regular venue for political parties and fundraisers, including many previous dance parties after Critical Mass rides. Apparently, the police, the Coast Guard, and others had flooded the Frying Pan owners with phone calls. Under heat from the federal government, the owners canceled the party. The Critical Mass rides and afterparties were events at which the roving activist social world converged on a monthly basis. Without opportunities to get together, such communities are threatened with oblivion. Once again, a community event was being attacked under the auspices of "zero tolerance" policing. That night, organizers distributed a flyer with the following message:

> Important Message to Our Community.
> Our beloved Critical Mass Ride is under attack!
> All threats, intimidation tactics and harassment, however, will not keep us from going forward with this amazing community ritual! We have worked hard to build this dynamic community and to advocate for the rights of those that use alternative modes of transportation! We have worked hard to reclaim our rights to public space in our city of New York!

The message implored ride supporters to come out in force. It emphasized community interrelatedness, play, and pleasure as responses to the impending panic, and specifically called on riders not to cave in to a culture of fear and intimidation:

> Tell all your friends. Bring family, neighbors, lovers and strangers. Bring noisemakers, musical instruments, face-paint, flowers, and your energy and joy. Bring things to juggle and to share and also your conviction that we have a right to converge and ride throughout this glorious city. Bring video cameras.
>   We will not be intimidated!
>   We will not be threatened and harassed!
>   This is our city! This is our community!
>   Let's make this the biggest, loudest, most joyful Critical Mass ever!

That Friday night, five thousand riders—both locals and itinerant activists in town for the Republic National Convention (RNC)—responded to the call. It was the largest Critical Mass ride in New York City's history. Those who participated encountered the brand of demonization of protest and community building that had become a typical feature of the Patriot Act Era. Over 250 riders were arrested that night; another 150 bicyclists were arrested by the time the RNC had ended, totaling over 400 bike arrests during the RNC alone.

"Police hate to be upstaged," one observer involved in radical gardening and bicycling activism noted. Both groups had become targets of government crackdowns because they seemed to advocate a vision of urban life in which care and connection with neighbors was prioritized over policing, the security culture, and entrance fees. Community gardening and bicycling both challenged notions of the city as profit-making machine.

In the case of Critical Mass, the police appeared to be responding to the prefigurative "Yes"—the community-building process and the spontaneous ritual of community that unfolded the last Friday of every month. Activists had created an image of urban life built on affective play: bike riding amongst friends and neighbors in a healthy, sustainable city. These rides functioned as open-ended, leaderless and democratic free-for-alls—fostering spaces open for more and more bikers to participate. The police seemed upset that a group of citizens was not interested in asking for permission, or asking them to play a role in helping organize their leaderless community. For many, the ride had become a sort of living example of noncommodified possibility. Critical Mass represented a powerful "Yes" to life, community, and authentic fun in a world of "Nos." While the police formed a security detail for the malling of Manhattan and the suburbanization of New York, Critical Mass rides represented a form of community building that had nothing to do with citizenship as shopping endeavor.

Tim Becker, who participated in many of the Critical Mass rides, including the August 27 event, commented on the sentiment shared among riders that the police seem like they were out for blood. "I think they know they have this window in history when they can try to crush it." Much of the momentum for the attack on Critical Mass dated back to that ride. "I guess it's the payback for 3,000 people going to ride during the Republican National Convention," Becker noted. "It was a sea of people. I couldn't even find anyone I knew. I went on the ride. It was like one of those Charlton Heston movies where he plays God and just wades out into the people."

September and October 2004: A Legal Fight Intensifies

"We are not blocking traffic. We are traffic," was the motto of Critical Mass. Cars make up traffic, and so do bikes. Few people expect car drivers to ask for permission to clog the streets. Bicyclists were claiming the same space for themselves. The arrests preceding the RNC were only the beginning of a long legal fight between bikers and the police over the definition of a "procession." Police added a new element to the fight during the September 24 ride: cutting chains and confiscating forty parked bicycles. In response, those whose bikes had been taken retained civil liberties attorney Norman Siegel, who had successfully fought Giuliani over similar First Amendment cases in the 1990s, and filed an injunction against the city. For many bikers, the debate about Critical Mass spoke to core constitutional rights, including the First Amendment right of the people "peaceably to assemble" and the Fifth Amendment right not to be "deprived of life, liberty, or property, without due process of law." Cases involving the Fifth Amendment are routed to federal court. Thus, the riders filing for the loss of their bikes learned that US District Judge William H. Pauley III would preside over their case.

Caught in the Act: NYC police stealing bicycles. This day they cut over 30 locks and confiscated bicycles.

CYCLISTS BEWARE!!

Although cycling in NYC is a beautiful form of non-polluting transportation, which is steadily on the rise, some corrupt city officials are not appreciative of the positive effects that increased cycling will have on the cities infrastructure.

In the last couple of months the police and city employees have been harassing bicyclists all over the cities 5 boroughs: more tickets, more arrests, more organized harassment and cuttings people's bike locks without any prior or subsequent notice, which is stealing.   Cyclists beware.

If You See Something Say Something.

Take pictures, interview people, it's important that we document these events. The press and lawyers are taking notice. Stand tall and fight back. *Still we ride.*

If you have any information of harassments or city employees stealing bikes contacts Phil at rnclostbikes@hotmail.com

Friendly cycling organizations:
TIME'S UP! at timesup@panix.com or 212 802 8222
Transportation Alternatives at info@transalt.org or 212 629 8080

In response to the bikers' lawsuit, the NYPD filed a counterinjunction against Critical Mass, demanding that the leaderless ritual obtain a permit for the next communal bike ride. The police asserted that Critical Mass was a parade without a permit. Arriving just days before the next scheduled ride, the city's argument presented a number of questions and conundrums about the nature and definition of a procession. Was it possible for a community event without a leader or a sponsor to apply for a permit? If so, who would do the applying? Most important, how and in what way did the First, Fifth, and Fourteenth Amendments to the US Constitution apply to specific New York City traffic ordinances? (Karmazin 2005).

On October 28, 2004, Judge Pauley ruled that the city had violated the bikers' right to due process by confiscating their bikes without charging the riders with a crime and called for the ride to go on. "[T]he city and its police officers and agents are preliminarily enjoined from seizing bicycles used by participants in the October 29, 2004, Critical Mass bike ride unless said participants are provided with notice of the reasons for seizure or they are charged with a crime or violation of law" (quoted in Karmazin 2005).

With this victory in hand (see Moynihan 2004), the Critical Mass ride went forward without a permit on the last Friday of October, on Halloween 2004, and just days before the November 2 elections. On this evening, police arrested thirty-three bikers. Battered but determined, bikers and their friends danced the night away at an afterparty held at the Time's Up! space on Houston Street. Outside, police circled the party, confiscated more bikes, and raided the party.

November 2004: Buy Nothing Day in a Police State

The next month, the Critical Mass ride was scheduled to take place the day after Thanksgiving. Many activists know the day as International Buy Nothing Day. The Reverend Billy sponsored a series of pranks and zaps throughout the day. Throughout the summer, the Reverend had used the First Amendment like garlic to protect himself as he led thousands in reciting the amendment at the World Trade Center site. The police seemed to have a hard time arresting a group of people reciting words from the US Constitution, "the right of the people peaceably to assemble, and to petition the Government for a redress of grievances," so the same talisman was employed on Buy Nothing Day.

But the charm did not work as well that day. The Reverend spent a night in the Tombs after being arrested for his performance inside a Starbucks coffee shop. Later in the evening he was joined by a group of seventeen bicyclists. After coming home from Reverend Billy's show, I picked up my (Shepard's) daughter Dodi, and we went to wish the Critical Mass riders well. Union Square—where the bicyclists usually converge before the ride—was surrounded by police. "White shirts," the commanding officers, talked with detectives. There must have been twenty-five patrol wagons surrounding the park. Gloom filled the dark night air, particularly as the nervous crowd read a flyer passed out by the police:

NOTICE TO BICYCLISTS

- THE NEW YORK CITY POLICE DEPARTMENT REQUIRES YOUR COOPER-
ATION IN COMPLYING WITH THE LAW AND PROTECTING THE PUBLIC
FROM HARM
- IT IS DANGEROUS AND ILLEGAL TO RIDE A BICYCLE IN A PROCESSION
ON THE PUBLIC STREETS WITHIN NEW YORK CITY, IF A PERMIT FOR THE
PROCESSION HAS NOT BEEN ISSUED BY THE NEW YORK CITY POLICE
DEPARTMENT.
- NO PERMIT HAS BEEN ISSUED FOR THE A BICYCLE PROCESSION
TONIGHT, NOVEMBER 26, 2004.
- IF YOU CHOOSE TO RIDE IN A PROCESSION THIS EVENING, YOU WILL
BE ARRESTED AND YOUR BICYCLE WILL BE SEIZED.
- THANK YOU FOR YOUR COOPERATION.

Dodi and I wished everyone well, hoping they would not face a night at Central Booking. While the police had not identified which laws the bikers were ostensibly breaking, this did not stop them from presenting an ominous show. As Dodi and I left, we hoped to avoid police ire as we walked along the sidewalk to the subway entrance. Discussion on the Indy Media website that night invoked images of a city that felt like a police state.

December 2004: Finally, a Win

As fall turned to winter, the police and the bikers continued to spar over the definition of a public procession. The struggle marked yet another in an ongoing series of skirmishes in what amounted to a class war over liberatory urbanism versus control of public space (Ferrell 2001).

The year ended on an up note. Judge Pauley threw out the city's counterinjunction over Critical Mass, suggesting that the conflict would be best handled in state court. Pauley, who was careful not to appear to support the bikers, specifically noted that the City had tolerated and even supported the rides in years past. "After allowing Critical Mass rides in Manhattan for ten years without permits," he explained, "the police department has acquiesced to the very conduct it now seeks to prohibit" (Bray vs. The City of New York: 20). Further, the judge highlighted the testimony by assistant Police Chief Bruce H. Smolka, Jr., who confessed that the NYPD "can enforce the laws without an injunction, but an injunction would be helpful."

Pauley rejected the city's push to require Critical Mass to apply for permits and wait for approval from the Parks Department before the rides. He noted that since there was no organizer for the event, the application for permits would not be possible for such an amoeba-like entity (Associated Press 2004). Thus, the city's claim could not be sustained. "The City does not aver that it seized Plaintiff's bicycles on September 24, 2004 to redress violations of the special event permit requirement," Pauley wrote. "There is no logical connection between the claims, other than the fact that they both relate to the Plaintiff's status as Critical Mass riders. This is not sufficient" (Bray v. The City of New York 2004, 12).

Pauley specifically addressed the definition of permitted actions at the heart of the controversy. "The applicability of the parade permit requirement has not been adequately delineated by any federal or state court decision," he wrote. Therefore, the judge concluded, "the city's counterclaim presents novel questions of state or local law, which militate strongly against exercising supplemental jurisdiction" (Bray v. The City of New York 2004, 16). Pauley noted that the bicyclists were right to claim that they had the same rights to use the streets as cars did. Two bikes in a row is not a procession, it is traffic—exactly the argument Critical Mass riders had made for years. "We believe that the judge was legally correct, and hopefully the strength of his legal argument will deter the city from seeking to appeal," said Siegel (Associated Press 2004). But the City said that it would appeal the decision. For the bikers, the final ride of the year, on New Year's Eve, was a thrilling victory lap with no arrests.

March and April 2005: The City Responds by Muzzling Dissent

As the winter turned to spring, however, there were more arrests. In March 2005, the City responded with another effort to control the Critical Mass ride, filing a new lawsuit in state court. This time, they sought to prohibit primary organizers within Time's Up! from speaking out about the ride, thus muzzling those speaking out against the City. The City's actions could also have set a precedent that would allow the police to set the terms for the number of people who assemble in a city park. If the City won, the police would have been allowed to disperse any gathering it wished if twenty or more people were in attendance (Karmazin 2005).

Once again, the plaintiff's attorney, Siegel, responded to the charges presented by the City. "No court has said that it's unlawful to stand in Union Square Park without a permit," he explained. "If the City of New York succeeds here, it would have huge implications for social protest movements, not only in New York, but throughout America," Siegel continued. "For example, the idea that SCLC [the Southern Christian Leadership Conference,] and Dr. King could not publicize and tell people to gather, to sit in at lunch counters, would have been unlawful at the time. People were challenging the idea of segregation. So the idea that you could not publicize the gathering to challenge unlawful laws is alien to what American history is all about and we will vigorously oppose that in the state court" (Siegel 2005a).

Eugene Karmazin, a Critical Mass supporter, wondered how long the NYPD could continue to battle with the citizens of the city they were charged to support. "To suggest that the maintenance of a political prerogative justifies the NYPD's recent behavior would be insufficient," he wrote. "A more plausible logic might say that once defied, police forces will move to reestablish their authority, often with crushing force" (Karmazin 2005).

Bruce Smolka, an assistant police chief, confirmed Karmazin's thesis at the Still We Speak rally, an event organized by Time's Up! as a kickoff for the April 29 ride. After a parade of testimonials—from Reverend Billy, Norm Siegel, and others on the importance of the First Amendment, Smolka's response was to personally and violently arrest a bystander. "You're riding your bicycle on the sidewalk," Smolka is said to have declared. "You're under arrest." *The New York Times* captured the searing image of the officer who had once presided over the Street Crimes Unit, the same unit responsible for putting forty-one bullets in Amadou Diallo, and later made the order to start unprovoked, unannounced arrests at the Carlyle Group in April 7, 2003 during an antiwar protest (Naparstek, 2005). From Diallo to the Carlyle Group to Critical Mass, the new "zero tolerance" policing is a threat to human life, peaceable assembly—and by extension, democracy itself. In the case of Critical Mass, after ten years of relatively peaceful rides, the city's case against the rides speaks to core questions about the use of public space, the fate of activism, and creative direct action in the era of the Patriot Act.

Fighting for the Right—Movement as Party and Protest

"This event is about building the world we want to see," declared William Etundi at one of his parties before the Republican National Convention in 2004 (Ferguson 2004a). Much of the ambition of the movement between party and protest is to create an image of a better world—even for a moment. Such an ambition is part of every street action or subway party.

Etundi, who worked with public-space advocates from RTS and Time's Up, as well as his own group, Complacent and the Danger, said his "first action that mattered" was a Reclaim the Streets party. Over the years, Etundi helped organize street pranks and parties—some on the streets, some in warehouses. Some took place without a hitch. Many more drew the attention of police and were shut down for one reason or another. They were all part of an ongoing battle on nightlife in New York, part and parcel of the Giuliani quality-of-life politics, which came to define political culture in New York.

"What's the difference between airport security and New York City nightclubs?? — Nothing!!" New York party person and nightlife aficionado Sarah

Sparkles (2007) wrote. She described the current state of nightlife in New York City:

> It is now nearly impossible to have a warehouse party without it being shut down by the police. On the special occasion that an event goes until dawn, there is a sweet taste of freedom that has become something rare. We have become children of the police state, with highly regulated options as to how we can engage. No unsupervised gatherings are permitted, we must be under surveillance at all times and we are told it's for our own good. We have many options on how to be consumers, yet very few options for creating new culture.

Still, activists kept on trying to create options.

In the months after the updated parade laws were announced, a number of public space groups responded. Assemble for Rights, a group formed in response to the arrests of cyclists, immediately spoke out against the rule. Time's Up! announced its opposition. And Etundi helped organize a renegade street party with a group of friends, which specifically challenged the city's new rule. Over the previous two years Etundi had helped organize renegade RTS style street parties, designed to both elude multiple arrests and provide a memorable panorama of dancing bodies and beats. The Spring 2005 "First Warm Night" was viewed as a new direction for public space activism. Joe Tuba, who had led his Hungry March Band through both RTS actions and countless street parties, was openly giddy before the spring 2005 party.

"It's gonna be brilliant," Tuba explained. "Its the next step. I kinda feel like there were all these train parties and RTS and now this." RTS organizers with the Ransom Corp used to organize street parties, which culminated with late night swims in Coney Island in 1999. "There is a long history there," Tuba recalled, reflecting on stories about street parties dating back to New York club and rave culture of the 1980s. "I was dating this girl who was kind of a raver and she was talking about how her raver friends had outlaw parties on the trains, years and years and years ago, a whole different group of people." The train party, by its mobile nature capable of moving large bodies of dancing revelers from one borough to another in a matter of minutes, was ideally suited to the cat-and-mouse game, which characterized much of New York public space activism. The First Warm Night would be held the first warm Saturday night of the spring of 2005. A series of text messages would help the crowd find a convergence location, meet, and move with flexibility and fun. The party had no clear political message beyond the simple subversive possibility of public assembly of friends. Similarly, the next year's "Night of Fire" began at sundown in the middle of the Brooklyn Bridge before the party moved back to a subway in Brooklyn for a train party to Coney Island like the Ransom Corp parties of the late 1990s. The 2007 Night of Fire, which also converged in the middle of the Brooklyn Bridge, made an explicit nod to the new parade rules. As the sun began to fade into the night, the unpermitted crowd of several hundred meandered towards City Hall just off of the bridge. There, the burlesque of stilt rope walkers, mobile musicians, and revelers dressed as angels lunged into the park in front of City Hall. Some found their way into the fountain where the dancing only intensified before the crowd made a quick exit towards a final twilight of dancing and swimming in Coney Island, which was slated for redevelopment (Ferguson 2007).

Shortly after the new rules were announced, the newly formed queer anarchist group ironically named the Radical Homosexual Agenda (RHA) announced plans for a downtown Parade without a Permit during work hours. In a playful, yet historically telling gesture, the RHA called for activists to come wearing pink helmets, a not so subtle reference to the helmets members of the Weather Underground wore to protect themselves from police batons during the 1969 Days of Rage in Chicago when police brutally beat antiwar protestors. With the support of Time's Up! ACT UP, and Assembly for Rights, the April 19, 2007 RHA action would include legions in their pink helmets, fights between activists and police who hoped to contain the action, and a series of violent arrests. The RHA was comprised of both veterans of street parties past as well as members who were newer to direct action. Activists around the world witnessed both photos and a video of the NYPD forcing activists to the ground and digging their knees into the backs of those on the ground before dragging them away. Undaunted, the RHA continued its work, disrupting, in activist parlance zapping, the council speaker with reminders about the undemocratic nature of the parade permit laws throughout the summer and fall. In late September 2007, New York City Council speaker Christine Quinn took a question about the ongoing attack on party culture in the city during a talk sponsored by the Stonewall Democrats. "When will the city and police allow nightlife to come back?" one gentleman asked the speaker, referring to the once "vibrant" quality of New York nightlife, which had become as restrictive as many could remember in their lifetimes. The man received a large round of applause. Quinn noted that New York nightlife was a billion dollar industry. Thus, there must be a "connection between nightlife and enforcement" (quoted in Fitzharris 2007).

Giuliani and Bloomberg's quality-of-life initiatives have specifically targeted queers, party people, and social outsiders. This pattern dated back well into the mid-1990s. In the fall of 1996, some fourteen hundred inspections had taken place in fifty queer businesses (Shindler 1997). Before the summer of 1997, some seventeen gay businesses, nine theaters, and eight clubs, including five in close proximity on 14th Street, were closed for violations of the state health code banning oral, anal, and vaginal sex in businesses. Cruising spots where low-income gays of color met were fenced off. A ban on dancing and obsolete fire codes were selectively enforced as part of a constant flow of legal assaults narrowing the types of clubs and bars seen as legal. A prohibition-era cabaret law about clubs and strict zoning ordinances on adult businesses were enforced to erase queer New York's face from the landscape. Countless clubs couldn't endure the legal barrage and eventually were forced to close their doors (Adkins 1997). Those that remained open proceeded with business in a highly regulated fashion.

When Speaker Quinn spoke during a session sponsored by the Stonewall Democrats in September 2007, members of RHA, including Shepard, unfolded banners declaring, "Cops Should Not Write Laws" and "Quinn Betrays Queers." The banners addressed the speaker's support for a new set of parade rules—that was brokered between the police department and the speaker's office in January of 2007—requiring permits for groups of fifty or more. As the parade rules were being debated, garden and bike activists, queers and civil libertarians, and countless other advocates stated their opposition to the new regulations on First Amendment grounds. The Association of the Bar of the City of New York (2006) published a sixteen-page statement opposing the rules. The group presented their analysis during a public hearing on the rules. "If adopted, these revisions would impose dramatic new restrictions on peaceful protests and other public gatherings in New York City— means of expression that are a cornerstone of our democratic system." The bar association argued that, given the gravity of the issue, the City Council must take the lead "to define a parade and to establish the criteria for issuing parade permits. Such a critical determination should not be relegated to a rulemaking or ad hoc decision-making body by the New York City Police Department."

The "Quinn Betrays Queers" banner referred to Quinn's ascent in the speaker's office. As an out lesbian, Quinn benefited from the work of social movements, many of which depended on acts of direct action, which would have been rendered illegal by her own parade rules. During the event at the Stonewall Democrats, Quinn failed to call on any of the questions by the members of RHA until one of her supporters chastised her for ducking the hard questions. Why did Quinn, at the head of the legislative branch of City's government, not seek to check the powers of the executive branch of government? Why, in an age with so much clear documentation of police abuse, was the city failing to reign in police powers? "As the mood grew more tense— reminiscent, perhaps, of Quinn's earlier activist days with ACT UP—the speaker thanked everyone for attending and exited for another commitment" (quoted in Fitzharris, 2007).

While Quinn was ducking questions from RHA, the NYPD was busy arresting supporters of the Sylvia Rivera Law Project who were gathering for the five-year anniversary celebration of their organization. "When will the savagery stop? How long will we have to put up with this stupidity and this thuggery?" asked ACT UP veteran and RHA supporter James Wagner (2007), who managed to get a question in during the session with Quinn, and would later reflect on the overlapping events in his blog. "Especially in a city as dynamic and sophisticated as this one is, no one should have to fear assault and arrest by the police simply because of who she or he may be." Wagner concluded, "in spite of what some people may think and say, including officials who should know better, the police are not supposed to 'control' us or our 'situations.' The police are public servants, entrusted and paid to keep us safe, not to tell us what we may or may not do."

RHA scheduled another Parade without a Permit for late September 2007. The group framed that action around the linkage between freedom of access to public space and democratic possibility. "Quinn also argued that the anti-assembly rules are fair," RHA organizer Tim Doody (2007) noted in a letter to a local gay paper shortly after the second Parade without a Permit. "Two weeks ago, in Myanmar, the military junta passed a rule that makes it illegal for five or more people to gather. Does Quinn really believe that the difference between a junta and a democracy is 45 people?" For members of the RHA, such as Doody, the new police rules represented a clear failure of the balance of powers, of the legislative branch of city government to check the power of the executive branch of government. "The anti-assembly rules are just the latest NYPD attack on civil liberties," Doody explained. The police cannot simultaneously govern themselves, write rules, and "enforce the rules governing when and how people can gather in New York City. . . . We didn't vote for Police Commissioner Ray Kelly, and he shouldn't be drafting rules behind closed doors, especially about something so essential to democracy as freedom of assembly."

The Fall 2007 Parade without a Permit 2 turned out to be a total success. The event began with a festive night time convergence of friends and veterans from ACT UP to Queer Nation, RTS to Time's Up!, among others, in Washington Square Park. The mood changed once drummers led activists out of Washington Square with a somber beat and a police escort. The police pushed for activists to stay on the sidewalk rather than the street. Activists continued west. By the time the crowd crossed Seventh Street, the crowd took the street. "We danced through the Meatpacking District," an RHA report back noted, "then we proceeded south to Christopher Street, where we picked up more people and steered towards the piers that still serve as a meeting place for queers, especially queer youth of color—though the area is now under heavy surveillance." The marched ended by 9:30; fireworks lit up the sky; everyone lay out in the grass and turned the space once more into a community space, as the legendary piers had been for queers for decades. "This is what democracy looks like," the account concluded. "We hope to see it more often in the City" (WEWANTyou 2007).

Convivial Community

After the Parade without a Permit in fall 2007, members of the squat Casa das Pombas were evicted from their home and cultural center in Brasilia, Brazil.

Earlier in the year, activists were evicted from Ungdomshuset or "Youth House," a four-story community center, which had been a home for squatters for over a quarter century in Copenhagen, Denmark. "Eviction of Danish Social Centre Fuels Anger Across Europe," declared headlines in Indy Media (2007). Like Charas, the space had served as a social, cultural, and political center for anarchists and punks, supporting concerts, debates, and cultural events for some three decades. With over six hundred arrests during its final hours, activists around the world fought the "Final Battle" for Ungdomshuset as more than just a community center, but as a symbol of a larger struggle against capitalist encroachment into public space. Writing in English, Danish activists argued that "the struggle for more free spaces, where we can show our resistance against a tendency of normalization that only wishes to make people more effective, docile and obedient, must be fought in the schools, at work and in the social security office. The energy we exhibited in the weekend, is the core in a society. It's about much more than a house. Its about our lives and the future, about how society as a whole should develop" (Indy Media 2007).

Not unlike the campaign to preserve Ungdomshuset, the cases presented here—for a community center, public gardens, a space for alternative transportation, and even to play—were all skirmishes in a larger struggle for public space. "As a gardener, I have a front-row seat on global warming and the many other idiocies of capitalism untamed," wrote garden sage Donna Schaper (2007, xx), sounding strikingly familiar to Danish activists. Garden activism allowed activists and citizens alike to stay engaged with a lighter, even ludic spirit. "You can recreate hope off the grid or on the grid. I work on the grid. Fun hope is the soil in which serious hope can grow. A lot of people are stuck in (legitimate) despair. Gardening and farming-agricultures can grow them out of it" (xxi).

When threatened, community spaces can become havens from which to challenge planned displacements of communities. Activists use community space to defend the communities that have deep, social-use value against developers seeking to maximize exchange value. To do so, in the 1990s, a host of groups, many centered in the Lower East Side yet extending out to Brooklyn and the world, used community space strategically. Reverend Billy, defenders of Charas, the Lower East Side Collective, community garden defenders, Critical Mass cyclists, and the Radical Homosexual Agenda, among others, identified community spaces as both places to defend and resources to employ in their efforts to disrupt plans to bulldoze those spaces. Disruption, then, was synonymous with struggles against community destruction. At the same time, activists not only playfully disrupted "business-as-usual," but built alternative institutions and imagined ways of interacting with others in the city different from the commodified model of suburban space. Defiant community spaces were a foundation of that strategy.

The ludic turn in activist practices highlights a difference between the narrative that can be told of privately owned public spaces—their evolution in the past four decades from privatized, to filtered, to suburban spaces—and the story gleaned from activists' use of public spaces. Unlike privately controlled spaces, activists' uses do not fit into a simple, linear historical narrative of transformation from one space to another. Because activists are sometimes fighting defensive actions, sometimes expanding the domain of popular and community space, and sometimes seeking an autonomous zone for more democratic uses of space—their stories leap frog from one type of space to another, from the defense of gardens as community space to the critique of the suburban strategy with a TAZ space down Broadway, from using popular spaces that authorities are trying to police to swimming in fountains on privatized space plazas. The different types of space are no less valuable in understanding activists' need and use of different kinds of public space, but their application of these types has been more flexible and responsive to the needs of their communities and to the threats they have faced.

The seeds of conviviality, of acknowledgement of difference, grow roots in such spaces. Thus, at their core, campaigns for gardens—and for spaces to ride, meet, and protest—involve a struggle for democratic possibility. Without such spaces—where citizens can meet, and share a moment and act together—democratic publics dwindle. Such spaces are feeling the squeeze. Wanderlust for such space endures. So does the hope for a more authentic form of democracy. While many are getting there through life-affirming forms of play, protest, and community building, their foundation remains unsecured.

CHAPTER SEVEN

From Contested to Popular Space

New York's Bike Lane Liberation Clowns

It is easy to forget that our streets are alterable. . . . Streets must be more than just a place for the movement and storage of private motor vehicles. The urban street of the 21st century will be a "complete street," accommodating pedestrians, cyclists, and transit riders alike.
—Carly Clark and Aaron Naparstek (2009)

[Bike] lanes get people out of their metal bubbles, into the streets, where people can mingle, talk, run into each other, maybe buy a slice of pizza. . . . Bikes help us get out and actually interface and communicate with each other, be healthy and enjoy our lives.
—Time's Up! volunteer Monica Hunken

Throughout the 2000s, people around the world started to conceive of "streets as great public spaces" (Clark and Naparstek 2009). To do so, they were forced to establish a more engaged, interactive relationship to these streets. As RTS declared in one of its early broadsides, when one steps off the sidewalk, one faces a fundamental choice about his or her view of the street. Is it a place for pleasure and possibility or a space in which to cower or just go to work? In recent years, a new cohort of social actors has chosen the former. And the streets of cities around the world show the difference. Much of this shift began with an impulse to play in public space.

"Whatever its shortcomings as a means to social change, protest movements keep reinventing carnival," Ehrenreich (2007, 259) notes. "Almost every demonstration I have been to over the years—antiwar, feminist, or for economic justice—has featured some element of the carnivalesque: costumes, music, impromptu dancing, the sharing of food and drink." Through such forms of play and direct action, regular people reimagine their relationship to the city. Through such direct action, activists define, organize, and defend spaces where community building activities take place. Along the way, contested spaces become popular spaces and community spaces. For the Time's Up! Bike Liberation Clowns, the subject of this chapter, play was a way to move beyond staking out community spaces towards expanding the way we understand, use, define, and defend popular spaces.

Play helped activists envision a transportation network through the city that held a different relationship to the physical and natural environment, and allowed bike activists to reestablish a public space—bike lanes—for popular use. Contrary to our image of the historical "street" as the prototypical public space, most roads are not very public at all. A typical street, four-lane road, or divided highway doesn't allow people to walk on to it and use the space. In private cars, the space doesn't allow people to have the substantial communications with strangers that defines a public space. A roadway, then, is a utility space, one owned by the government but dominated by cars. A bike path, by comparison, is a popular space. Cyclists do have interactions with each other, talking at stop lights and even while moving, and recognizing friends traveling in the opposite direction. Cyclists' social behavior is more akin to pedestrians than automobile drivers. Bike paths are not as accommodating a popular space as a park since they accommodate fewer uses. Still, cyclists share paths with joggers, rollerbladers, baby strollers, and other vehicles. On a waterfront park, a pedestrian path and a bike path would both be popular spaces. One role of play, then, was to encourage the transformation of utilitarian roadways into more popular bike paths.

But even with bike lanes freshly painted throughout the five boroughs of New York City, these routes often remained segregated and difficult for cyclists to use because cars and delivery trucks frequently disregarded the bike paths, as drivers would park in the lanes while making deliveries or pick-ups. According to a Hunter College study, there is a 60 percent chance of a cyclist being obstructed by a car in a bike lane (Nelson 2009). It was in order to more firmly transform these utility spaces into more popular spaces that a small group of bike activists adopted a strategy of play. More than an example of how to make inaccessible space more public, this case highlights play's unique ability to transform space. To the extent that ludic activity has been known to invert power relations, cross boundaries, and challenge unspoken norms, play was seen as an appropriate tactic with which to challenge the conventional understandings of the organization of a public space. Such a strategy would be more than necessary in taking on the City's newest "culture war"— between cars, bikes and a right to the road (Crowley 2009).

Case Narrative: Cars vs Bikes

Anthropologist Jeff Ferrell (2001) has suggested that while the term *hegemony* is often overused, when one talks about the influence of the automobile on the US political economy, energy, and urban policy, such a description is not unreasonable. Cars dominate urban space in countless ways. In spite of this, the environmental movement has aimed to challenge the very notion of a presumed right of cars to dominate public streets. Faced with the seemingly insurmountable task of creating spaces for bike and nonpolluting transportation in the mean streets of New York City, environmental activists made use of a politics of play and theatrics to engage others in the struggle for nonpolluting transportation. This final case narrative highlights the point that ludic activity offers a generally—but not always—nonviolent way of engaging, of playing with power, rather than replicating sources of oppression or violence.

In August 2005, I (Shepard) received a phone call from one of the activists who had been involved with the Critical Mass bike rides asking if I would be interested in participating in a new kind of ride organized around clowning. I was immediately excited and somewhat scared about the specter of another clowning project. The previous summer, New York's ever-morphing chapter of Reclaim the Streets had organized a chapter of the Clandestine Insurgent Rebel Clown Army (Bogad 2007b; Shepard 2005). "It would take a lot of work and training to start another clown troop," I observed. After a pause my friend replied, "The ride is scheduled for this Tuesday. Grab your best wig."

On August 20, 2005, environmental group Time's Up! declared August 23 "Bike Lane Liberation Day" in New York City. That Tuesday, a group of bikers wearing clown costumes started a bike ride at St. Marks Church in the East Village and rode up Second Avenue. By St. Marks Place and 7th Street, the clowns found their first culprit, a UPS delivery truck. The driver accepted his ticket in good cheer. The orange ticket placed on cars resembled an actual parking ticket. It notified owners of illegally parked vehicles that "this could have been a real ticket," and listed driving rules for New York City which supported this claim. "Section 4-08(e): Stopping, standing, parking or otherwise obstructing bike lanes is prohibited. Subject to a $115 fine." From there, the clowns continued their ride through the city, giving cars parked in bike lanes fake tickets (Siegel 2005b). On the ride, activists also ticketed a police car parked in a bike lane. Like the UPS driver, most drivers laughed and drove away; others engaged in a dialogue about cars in the city and the need for nonpolluting transportation. When a few drivers screamed, the clowns generally honked their horns and rode away.

Police Car parked in 2nd Avenue Bike Lane.
Photo by Fred Askew.

The following day, an activist photographer posted his photographs from the action on the Indymedia website (Askew 2005). The photos inspired a wide range of responses discussing the role of play in relation to social movement activity. On August 24, 2005, a person identified as "biker" posted the following observation about the Bike Lane Liberation Clowns:

I'm an NYC biker too but the NYC Indymedia coverage of all things biking when there is a lot of shit going on in the world makes it come off as a ridiculous youth clique and totally irrelevant. Please report on, oh, I don't know THE WARS, not a group of tattooed twenty-somethings irritating traffic. As soon as real "bike liberation" tactics are used, I'll be interested. Ridiculous.

What "biker" was missing was that many of the bike clowns found it a compliment to be called "ridiculous." Others responded that Indymedia is open for anyone to post news. Still others said that they loved the ride. "Branford and Chesterfield" wrote that they felt that the ride was "Lovely! Oh lovely and so much lovelier!" They suggested, "Send in the clowns—never stop clowning around." Another poster, called "g" began with an Emma Goldman-like sentiment:

> If fun is not part of the movement, it will die.
> If laughter is not part of the movement, it will die.
> If clowns are not part of the movement, than I want no part of it.

From there, "g" reminded "biker" that those involved with New York bike activism had been arrested in the hundreds and sued by the NYPD since the Republican National Convention the previous year. Thus, there was nothing wrong with blowing off a little steam. The writer explained: "Your comments are valid, but I feel you need to chill out a little. We have been chased by cops armed with deadly Vespas, helicopters, and a whole lot of intelligence and surveillance. It's been a year and we need to be able to have fun. Yes, the clown brigade had its tattooed youth, but over half of the ride was past the age of 30, and with no tattoos. Morale is a little bit higher because of the clown brigade. Thank you for your conversation. Please join us, you can help steer this movement too. Get involved and ride."

Such invitations are a core part of the politics of play. The point is of course to break down the divide between spectators and social actors. The politics of play aims to allow those facing difficult moments such as the crackdown on Critical Mass to stay involved.

The next morning, August 25, the debate about the "biker" post continued. In a message that began, "Great logic, biker," another poster, "asdfasdf," said: "I guess we should stop working against racism since the war is killing more people than lynchings, eh? Perhaps school lunches for the poor aren't important because global warming affects more people?" "Asdfasdf" followed with a call for "biker" to follow the DIY ethos and "*do* something instead of sitting at your computer being more-radical-than-thou." "Asdfasdf" then suggested that "biker" could always just join the Time's Up! contingent for the court hearing for bike activists who'd been arrested for riding in public in the last year. Later that day, a final clown supporter responded to "biker's" suggestions that riders get involved with something serious like antiwar activism. "Bent_rider" noted, "Maybe you have lost the connection between the wars and car usage, which the [Critical Mass] movement is countering. It's all connected." And "bent_rider" reminded "biker" of the bike activist slogans: "No War for Oil! Ride a Bike" and "Bicycling: A Quiet Statement Against Oil Wars." As this stream of posts suggests, bike clowning is a useful embodiment of the politics of play. And while the emphasis during this action was on its ludic quality, if asked, clowns identified real connections between that play and a range of political commitments. The point of ludic activism is to initiate a dialogue, which this action did.

At the time, bike lanes were on no one's agenda. Over the next five years, members of the Time's Up! Bike Lane Liberation Clown Block would put them there through dozens of rides. As the city shifted and convulsed, the Bike Lane Clowns commented on the scene, ever the wise fools. "Send in the Clowns: The Clown Bicycle Brigade prepares for possible transit strike by clearing cars from bike lanes," Barbara (2005), aka Babbs the Clown, posted on the NYC Indymedia website before the December 2005 ride slated to take place the same week as a city transit strike: "Nothing can shame a driver into moving out of the bike lane more than a pack of cheerful clowns. . . . All drivers refusing to move will be ticketed for violating Section 4-08(e), which explicitly prohibits stopping in the bike lanes." That December night, the clowns encountered a Fed Ex truck parked in the bike

The politics of play often leads to discussions. Photo by Joann Santangelo. (www.joannsantangelo.com)

lane on Broadway. After careening into the truck so rudely parked in our bike lane, we mocked the truck: "Silly Truck, Bike Lanes are for Bikes." Some of us moved inside the double-parked vehicle and mockingly played with the gears, etc. On his return, the driver actually found it all funny. The clowns helped him unpack the boxes from the truck so he was able to move on. Much of the politics of play involves shifting debate about who plays, "on what terms, by whose rules, and on whose playing field" (Schechner 2002).

For many involved in the long standoff between police and bike activists, the Bike Lane Liberation clowns helped bridge the space between the joy of riding free and possibilities for public-space environmental activism. Accompanied by a "sound bike" blaring Freddie Mercury singing, "I want to ride my bicycle," the dancing Bike Lane Liberation rides brought a renewed spirit of fun to bike activism. With every new ride, the clowns better developed their moving theater, inviting more and more spectators into their performance. For the most part, the clowns operated within a "you get more with sugar than salt" disposition. The majority of the cars were more than happy to move on. The clowns were there to remind everyone of the need for more bike lanes, with less cars parked in them. The Bike Lane Clowns declared they would make riding healthier and safer. The police rarely interrupted the ride, but this is not to say there were not a few bumps along the road.

In January 2006, the clowns scheduled yet another ride. Rather than the usual lighter fare, a darker Punch and Judy form of play manifested itself throughout the ride. A writer from the *Village Voice* accompanied us. "Some drivers didn't find the antics funny at all," the journalist wrote (Ferguson 2006). It was true. While the clowns had talked about making use of the Monty Python, "run away fast" approach, when confronted with violence or grumpy cars, it was not always done. Instead, road rage took over both riders and clowns. Riding up Eighth Avenue, the clowns attempted to move a car that wouldn't budge. When the agitated driver emerged, the clowns confronted him and offered him a ticket. "Are you serious?" he asked. Yes, we explained. "Well, I am an undercover cop. Get the fuck out of here!" he screamed. Shocked, few of us fell into our Monty Python run away routine. But the rest of us stumbled away in fear.

On that first ride in January 2006, most of the ride went as planned, and yet the *Village Voice* writer who had joined us remained skeptical. The writer had a long history as a tough confrontational reporter. The clowns worked in earnest to represent an authentic and compelling image of Bike Lane Liberation Clowning. We ticketed a few cars, cajoled a few others to leave. Cheers were heard all around. As the ride careened down Fifth Ave, with Washington Square—our destination—in sight, trouble hit. A shopper double-parked outside an apartment building and refused to move, honking belligerently as the clowns finally rode off. "I'm just giving you a taste of your own medicine!" the *Village Voice* quoted him screaming. Further South on Fifth, the clowns careened into yet another car parked outside a rather pricey address with a view of the Washington Square arch. Unmoved by the clowns, the driver argued he had the right to impede the bike lane because he was waiting to pick up a friend. Finally his friend arrived, and the clowns begged him to leave. His friend had brought the driver a cup of coffee and a cookie. The driver sat to take his time and enjoy his cookie and coffee, taunting, "Talk to the horn, baby!" One of the clowns retorted by honking his plastic baby horn in the driver's window. The driver grabbed the horn and broke it in half. With a red nose and a cap resembling Mac the Knife from the *Three Penny Opera*, violence simmered as Mac the Clown retaliated with a fist. Richard Schechner (2002, 107) suggests "dark play" is a heavier kind of expression. Within this form of play, gestures that begin as forms of simple bravado, such as radical clowning, can descend into a violent form of theater as it breaks its own rules. And this was exactly what took place on lower Fifth Avenue. The writer from the *Voice* was on hand to watch the whole scene. She wrote, "The driver snatched the horn and broke it, and the angry clown struck him in the face. The other clowns were horrified." "We're supposed to be peaceful gnome clowns and keep our sense of humor," groaned Monica Hunken, who had worked with New York's Absurd Response to an Absurd War as well as the Clandestine Rebel Clown Army and the Church of Stop Shopping, with her face fully pained and a traffic cone perched atop her head. "That's totally antithetical to what this ride is all about. Next time we're definitely going to have rules for bike clowns and maybe broadcast them from our sound truck before we leave" (Ferguson 2006).

Hunken's reference to "peaceful gnomes" was inspired from her reading of L.M. Bogad's (2005) *Electoral Guerrilla Theatre*, which had been published the previous fall. Many of the clowns attended Bogad's book release party and reading at Bluestockings Bookstore the previous fall. The work featured a case study from the 1960s Dutch anarchist group Provo, and the Kabouters, an offshoot of the group that formed in 1970, and borrowed from the friendly iconography of the gnomes in their run for vacant seats in Amsterdam's city council. The Provos' pranks have long inspired street activists. Recall their 1966 prank involving a group of young radicals giving out pamphlets to passersby on the streets of Amsterdam without a permit, despite a Dutch law that requires police permission for the distribution of political leaflets. "When the police moved in to confiscate the material, which turned out to be blank pieces of paper, the smiling Provos shouted: 'Write your own manifestos!'" (Bogad 2007a).

Bike activists specifically look to the theatrics of the Provo and their masterful anticapitalist, antiestablishment antics; the result often combined riots and laughter. While the immediate effect of the pranks were viewed as minimal, the group's "white bike program," aimed at decreasing car traffic on the streets of Amsterdam in the long term, offered bikes, painted white, free of charge as a transportation alternative. These playful pranks presented students and activists a vision of an alternate way of organizing urban life, while serving as an uncomfortable reminder of idealist dreams for the liberal government. For many, the aim of movement organizing is to create not only an external solution to problems, but to create a different kind of community of support and resistance. Here, play supports a prefigurative community-building dimension, in which activists seek to embody the image of the better world they hope to create. Inspired by the Provos' willingness to act on their views of political hypocrisy, a new wave of wildly imaginative political actors entered politics with an appetite for direct action and a distinctly rambunctious view of political hypocrisy. The prank political campaigns of the Provo, who ran for political office on a whim, produced a wide number of movement outcomes, the most strange of which was that a number were actually elected into office. Once there, some continued the antics. Others influenced the political discourse and public policy. The City of Amsterdam's extensive network of 249 miles of bike lanes, which make bike commuting a safe alternative to driving, is the both the legacy of this activism and the envy of bike riders the world over. The Dutch approach to drug use and security net provisions is one of the most extensive in the world (Bogad 2005). One needs to have utopian dreams to create forward thinking solutions (Duncombe 2007).

New York's Bike Lane Liberation Clowns borrowed a similar disposition to imagine an urban life in which cars made way for nonpolluting sources of transportation, such as bikes. And like the Provo, the group was willing to use direct action to act on this vision, and the city started to take notice. Coverage of the clowns started at the media periphery—at first only with independent media, a blog or two during the spring. "Clowns Take Back the Bike Lanes," a writer noted in the *Gothamist* (Chung 2006). "Clowns Liberate Bike Lanes," Will (2006) wrote on his website *NYTurf*. Later that August, a writer for *NYC-stories* noticed a group of clowns attempting to push a truck out of a bike lane on Seventh Avenue on her way to work. "Despite a lot of pushing, the truck was just too big for them to move without help," she later recounted on her

blog. As always with these rides, the clown spectacle was most effective when it provoked a discussion of unsafe riding conditions on New York Streets—which it usually did.

Yet, by the fall of 2006, attention to the clowns and bike lanes moved from the blogosphere into the mainstream media, and by extension, political debate. That fall, two articles on bike lanes would be featured in the *New York Times* (Neuman 2006; Schwartz 2006). A former New York Department of Transportation assistant commissioner bemoaned not working harder to keep bike lanes in place during the 1970s in New York (Schwartz 2006). And the *New Yorker* would highlight Time's Up! for its advocacy for bike lanes and nonpolluting transportation in a long feature on the rise of the bike movement in New York City. "The movement hopes to save the planet by creating bike lanes and overthrowing car tyranny" (McGrath 2006). Throughout the fall, debate about bike lanes was also featured in many neighborhood papers (Vega 2006).

In April 2006, the City announced plans to fortify and extend the Eighth Avenue bike lane. Most of the Bike Lane Liberation rides had taken place along Eighth Avenue, so the clowns were clearly optimistic. News only got better when the NYC Department of Health issued a press release on September 12, 2006 declaring, "City Announces Unprecedented Citywide Bicycle Improvements." The announcement specifically linked bike fatalities with lack of safety, including space on the roads, for bikes. The city also issued a report, *Bicycle Fatalities and Serious Injuries in New York City 1996–2005*. In it, the city presented plans to add two hundred miles of bike lanes within the city. The next day, the *New York Times* reported, "City Hall Promises Major Increase in Bike Lanes on Streets" (Neuman 2006). Over the months, the rides brought a lighter tone to Time's Up!, the group from which the clowns emerged. In difficult times, many activists have borrowed from and sustained themselves by incorporating ludic elements within their performances and campaigns. The clown rides helped support group morale in the middle of a long legal fight. This was profoundly important in the months before the city dropped its lawsuit against individual members of Time's Up!—grudgingly acknowledging that traffic law allowed the same street access to groups of two-wheeled as to four-wheeled vehicles only after New York State Supreme Court judge Michael D. Stallman ruled against the city's injunction against Critical Mass in February 2006 (Dwyer 2006; Stallman 2006). Stallman rejected all the city's arguments that Critical Mass or group bike rides should be regulated by the city. Most importantly, he declared that there was absolutely no legal ground for the city to consider a group of bike riders a protest in need of a permit, thereby affirming the argument made by bicycle activists that rather than interfering with traffic, "We Are Traffic." To force the riders to obtain a permit would be like asking car drivers to get a permit to drive across the Brooklyn Bridge every day. Stallman concluded that New York City had "not met the three-part test for a preliminary injunction with respect to the pre-ride gatherings for the Critical Mass rides, advertising of the rides, or the rides themselves."

Bill DiPaola, one of the named defendants in the case, expressed his appreciation for the decision. "We are extremely happy with the judge's decision. It's not only a big victory for free expression and the right to assemble, but also supports bicyclists' rights to continue riding in groups for safety," DiPaola said in a Times Up! press release. In Spring 2007, even the *Village Voice* would change their tune about the clown rides. "Despite being led by clowns, Thursday evening's Bike Liberation Ride was a rousing success," a *Voice* writer reported in May 2007. "The group of a dozen or so riders nudged, cajoled, and teased drivers of trucks, taxis, limos, and private cars out of dedicated bike lanes downtown," (Conaway 2007).

On September 20, 2007 the NYC Department of Transportation announced plans for "New York City's first-ever physically separated bike lane, or "cycle track," on Ninth Avenue between Sixteenth and Twenty-Third

Streets. The next day, the Bike Lane Liberation Clowns participated in a ride during Friday morning rush-hour traffic. The Bike Lane Liberation Clowns celebrated the new Ninth Avenue bike lane in their final ride of 2007, calling for the City to fully realize their plans for more bike lanes.

Throughout 2008 and 2009, the rides became more and more creative. Each ride built around different themes: "The Pies of March" held on the Ides of March, "The Where's Waldo Ride" in homage to the bike lanes listed by the city that few can find, and the "Love Lane" campaign celebrating the lanes in the face of a community backlash. The group also included more and more painting and stenciling on the lanes in an effort to highlight the importance of following the bike lane. These rides included a sound bike for dancing, clowns, painters wearing white overalls, and spray paint. Sometimes a clown hat would be painted on the head of the biker painted in the bike lane by the city. All the while, dancing clowns deflected attention from those painting on the lanes.

Clowns crashing into cars parked in bike lanes. Times Up environmental organization. http://times-up.org (Photos by Tim)

In Spring 2008, the *New York Times* brought reporters and film crews along for one of the rides. The paper highlighted the lack of enforcement of violations by cars parked in the bike lanes. Not only did the article highlight concerns among riders, but it also highlighted the near forty-year history of struggle for the bike lanes, which dated back to a 1970 Critical Mass-like bike ride in which then Mayor Lindsay joined a group of some one thousand cyclists for a ride down Fifth Ave, calling for the city to create bike lanes (Moynihan 2008).

Love Lane. Times Up environmental organization. http://times-up.org

The clown story highlights ways that play effectively supported parallel campaigns, those of Transportation Alternatives and Time's Up! who were making use of an inside/outside strategy to force the city to acknowledge the need for nonpolluting transportation. As underscored by periodically skyrocketing gasoline prices, nonpolluting transportation was clearly an idea whose time has come. Bike riding was part of a solution to a warming, congested planet. This is a reality that the city is increasingly recognizing. By July 2009, the City announced it had finished adding 200 bike lanes in the Bronx, adding up to 420 total miles of bike lanes in the five boroughs (Block 2006). Yet, for each step forward the spectre of a setback followed. Most bike lanes still suffered cars parked in them that were not ticketed. Even those bike lanes in place often failed to enjoy full support from the City (Crowley 2009).

While bike lanes were becoming a part of the city's transporation infrastructure, they also inspired a backlash. Nowhere was this backlash more prominent than in the borough of Brooklyn and its distinct neighborhoods. Controversy surrounded the Kent Avenue bike lane in Williamsburg/Greenpoint, Brooklyn in 2008 and 2009. The lane ran through a Hasidic neighborhood near a gentrifying neighborhood. "Hasids vs. Hipsters" became a story line told over and over again. Community residents threatened to block the bike lanes. In response, the clowns held a contentious, well-covered defense of the space. In December of 2009, the City got rid of the adjacent bike lane on Bedford Avenue altogether. The bike activist community, like much of New York, was up in arms. Immediately, a few bike supporters repainted the bike lanes; another group planned to stage a naked ride to protest those who wanted to take away the lanes in the belief immodestly dressed women rode their bikes in the lane through the religiously conservative neighborhood. The following week, the clowns planned to hold a mock New Orleans style funeral procession, followed by a vigil, for the fourteen blocks removed from the Bedford bike lane.

The action was to take place the same week as the 2009 United Nations Climate Change Conference in Copenhagen "The Mayor is back peddling on his promise to green the city and ripping out our beloved bike lanes from under us. Bike lanes need to be improved, not removed," explained Time's Up! volunteer Barbara Ross. Word of the protest and the anger went viral, as activists and media alike connected the dots between the Mayor's rhetoric at the environmental conference and the reality of his actions (Olshan 2009). "We're talking about a public street. It's for everybody," Geoff Zink, a Times UP! Volunteer, argued the day of the action (Feeney and Fursee 2009).

The action took place on a rain-soaked day. I (Shepard) rode with a soggy group of riders chanting, "Resurrect the lane! Resurrect the lane!" Given that the ride was billed a New Orleans-style march, the message was to transcend the loss of the lanes. Participants sang new lyrics to "When the Saints Go Marching In":

> Oh when the bikes, go riding in.
> Oh when bikes go riding in.
> We will all create more bike lanes,
> when the bikes go riding in.

Most everyone clapped and sang along as the ride/makeshift funeral session meandered. "Only the Good Die Young" and "And I Will Always Love You" blared from the sound bike. We played taps for the lane with plastic bugles. Little did any of us know that that same day, a younger women, Solange Raulston, was killed while riding her bike in the same neighborhood. A reporter with the *Brooklyn Paper* called me later that night to ask for a comment. "This really speaks to the reason we fight for all these bike lanes. . . . It's not about hipsters or the Hasidim like everyone keeps talking about—it's public safety. This girl should have been able to ride along and not take her life in her hands" (Campbell 2009). Throughout most of the radical clowning we have done, we've performed on a tragicomic stage.

The Sustaining Power of Play

The activist stage is in constant flux. As the Bike Lane Liberation Clowns demonstrate, savvy activists have utilized elements of play and political performance to comment on and influence modern life. These urban actors have borrowed from a range of influences to cultivate a model of political engagement that has profoundly shifted both public discourse and policy. In order to do so, bike activists continue to reinforce the notion that political protest and street theatrics remain vital ingredients of effective organizing campaigns. As activists increasingly orient their campaigns around contests over space, part of the power of play is its ability to redefine the social meaning of spaces, to transform them from one type to another.

The Bike Lane Clowns highlight the ways play embodies an alternative way of being in the world, while liberating space, generating energy, and helping activists to stay engaged in sometimes complicated policy battles. Over and over again, the ludic, clowning trickster confused hardened positions to foster new insights and challenge recalcitrant ways of thinking. For many, the aim of movement organizing is to create not only an external solution to problems, but to create a different kind of community of support and resistance. The Bike Lane Clown narrative also highlights the ways play serves as an effective compliment to a more conventional campaign. As the Clowns showed, play invites people to participate. And biking is perhaps the purest form of play. Through its low threshold for entry, it allows new participants into the game of social action.

Through participant observation, we have attempted to explore the relationship between the ludic and the political. Through play, bike activists helped transform a misunderstood, highly contested space. Through their play, the Bike Lane Clowns created a sense of community; their actions actually challenged the city to live up to its responsibility to defend a popular space—the bike lanes—for public use against obstruction by parked, private automobiles.

But there is more to it than that. In the spirit of Situationists, most of the rides take shape as guerilla activist interventions, as forms of "détournement" and "dérive." On a recent ride through Chinatown, we noted that the city had painted the lane in a swervy swoop across the street, seemingly leading nowhere but into traffic. So, the group used chalk to rearrange and highlight directions for the bike lanes, both disrupting expectations of the spaces and creating new meanings. Like most, this ride functioned to resist control-oriented patterns of urban life, remapping a city as a space for creative play as well as people's needs (Lefebvre 1974; Merrifield 2002; Thompson 2004). The point was to trigger up new thoughts, daydreams, and associations which might inspire viewers to second guess or rethink a few of the givens of modern living (Aufheben undated). As the clowns chalked and doodled along the lane, we named the new lane the Andre Breton Bike Path in homage to the surrealist hero. Through the years of rides, the ludic activity helped turn once unusable bike lanes into spaces for enactment of a collective imagination. "Its not all just about cars, bike lanes are about returning the streets to the people," Barbara Ross suggested during one ride. "Its about our right to an environmentally friendly, green infrastructure for a city of our imagination."

CHAPTER EIGHT

Conclusion

This Land Is Your Land?

> As I went walking I saw a sign there
> And on the sign it said "No Trespassing."
> But on the other side it didn't say nothing,
> That side was made for you and me.
>
> Chorus
>
> In the squares of the city—In the shadow of the steeple
> Near the relief office—I see my people
> And some are grumblin' and some are wonderin'
> If this land's still made for you and me.
> —Woody Guthrie[1]

Guthrie is said to have written "This Land Is Your Land" as he hitchhiked from Texas to New York City in 1940. During a performance at Lincoln Center in the summer of 2008, Guthrie's friend and former band mate Pete Seeger noted that while most kids learn this song at summer camp, teachers usually omit these final two verses. This, of course, is no surprise. The lyrics evoke a contested quality to public space and by extension capitalism itself. While the "no tress passin'" sign Guthrie describes indicates enclosure and privatization, he harkens to a liberatory possibility of public space, "on the other side it didn't say nothing." The lyrics evoke a "popular patriotism": land given back to the people, to be shared by everyone, land that is yours and mine (Eyerman and Jamison 1998, 69). Conversely, Guthrie hints at the sense of enclosure, of exclusion experienced by the poor fenced out of this promise, left to wonder and grumble, "If this land's still made for you and me." Public space is certainly anything but simple. This book has sought to grapple with the yin-yang–like complexity of this topic. In these notes towards a conclusion, we consider a few of the historic currents influencing this conversation.

"I think you are going to save your garden. I don't quite know how. But, I know you will," promised Pete Seeger, while performing at a Harlem community garden under threat of being bulldozed a few years ago. For decades, Seeger has been a constant fixture in the activist scene. He talked about this at the show. "There are more small groups of people in this country doing good things than any time in history . . . hundreds of thousands of groups. These are people who figure they have to do something, if only for their own peace of mind" (quoted in Tarleton 2002). And certainly Seeger has been one of them. He was there to serenade activists during a rally at Forty-Second Street and Sixth Avenue when the city threatened the gardens, bringing an ethereal quality to the event. "Beethoven's Seventh Symphony floated out over the traffic," Seeger mused. He was also there to play a show in a community garden in the East Village when the city threatened to auction off hundreds of gardens in the late 1990s. In between songs, Seeger, who once resided in the Village, mused about the garden struggle in relation to a changing urban landscape. LESC veteran Ron Hayduk, who was at the show, recalled Seeger declaring: "Here in the Lower East Side development is a mixed bag. Obviously, the buildings need to be fixed. We don't need 'em falling down." But Seeger reasoned we also don't want to lose the gardens. We don't want to suffocate the planet with concrete. So we have to fight for the gardens, clean water and so on.

"I used to go to his concerts and he would play kid songs or do folk songs, and then there would be a little message that I would find myself humming on the way home and thinking about later," explained Hayduk. He ruminated about Seeger's comments in relation to his life in the Lower East Side. "I lived on East 2nd Street and Ave B where half the buildings were abandoned. A lot of the lots were empty. And there was heroin coming out of my building. It was not a cool scene on some levels," Hayduk explained. "We needed some development. But development on whose terms? A lot of people got pushed out. . . ." Rents went up; residents "got some of the things that they needed, but . . . also got some other things that they didn't really need. And so LESC thought, OK, how can we

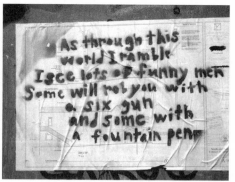

Superimposed on blueprints for a luxury loft, lyrics by Woody Guthrie were appropriated to oppose gentrification.

slow this down or stop it?" And they started organizing. In doing so, LESC, RTS, and the other groups considered in this project incorporated as much music, play, and pranks as possible into a protracted conflict over use, exchange, and sustainability of public space. The play was the food which nourished the organizing. Seeger and Hayduk's observations of these waves of activism and their ongoing engagement with the forces influencing urban development hint at a dialectic of urban space.

Throughout this study, we have considered a tension between sustainability and development, inclusion and exclusion, aesthetic and social needs, as well as social and political understandings of urban space. Cities are always going to be sites of contestation. While developers see urban space in terms of profitability, activists see alienation and displacement. This is the tale of two cities which Bertell Ollman (2003) describes in his work *Dance of the Dialectic*. For Ollman, the first city is "capitalism"; the second "communism." Yet, "[t]he rulers are the capitalistic class, or those who own and control the means of production, distribution, and exchange, and the principle rule by which they operate is profit maximalization," argues Ollmam (p.1). The tale of these two cities plays out as an ongoing conflict, a clash between interconnected social forces, pregnant within their opposites (Merrifield 2002, Ollman 2003).

"It is an eternal cycle in which matter moves," elaborated Marx's partner Frederick Engels (1883). "A cycle in which every finite mode of existence of matter . . . is equally transient, and wherein nothing is eternal but eternally changing, eternally moving matter and the laws according to which it moves and changes." Here, "[c]hange of form of motion is always a process that takes place between at least two bodies, one loses a definite quantity of motion of one quality (e.g. heat), while the other gains a corresponding quantity." And all that is solid melts into air. Marshall Berman (1982) looked to Marx to help him understand the topsy-turvy tragicomic, sometimes playful, often painful nature of modern urban living. "To be modern is to find ourselves in an environment that promises us adventure, power, joy, growth, transformation of ourselves and the world—and, at the same time, that threatens to destroy everything we have, everything we know, everything we are" (15). Yet, there is a dance to navigating such a way of living and being. "It is a paradoxical unity, a unity of disunity: it pours us all into a maelstrom of perpetual disintegration and renewal, of struggle and contradiction, of ambiguity and anguish" (15). Buildings crumble. And resistance movements are born in the dark corners of even the most colonized, commodified spaces.

Such forces churn through the waves crashing on the beach beneath the streets. This book begins with a glimpse at New York's fiscal crisis and neoliberal transformation. A predominant thesis becomes that global capital supersedes the sovereignty of local actors (Harvey 2005; Sites 2003). The first half of *The Beach Beneath the Streets* traces this argument through New York's social, political, and physical geography—its plazas, as the private absorbs the public. These chapters consider notions of space from a vantage point of exclusion, real estate, and elite controls thought to be necessary to cultivate a better business climate. Yet, almost simultaneously, resistance movements take hold, challenging the privatization and commodification of public space and the erosion of the public sector (Berman 2007; Harvey 2008; Moody 2007; Shepard and Hayduk 2002). City University students improvise with hip-hop and graffiti; public space groups reclaim streets and vacant lots with gardens and street parties. Bikers ride through streets in an example of what urban space can look like. Through such activities, different groups open up spaces to wide ranges of uses. And the city reflects their influence. These are the stories of the second half of this book. Yet, it is hard to see any of these movements slowing down or resolving themselves. Our synthesis takes shape within this participation in urban democracy: the ongoing influence of regular people in the very formation and composition, the play and feel of public space. The best urban spaces take shape when they are well used and loved. "The most used plazas are the most sociable," explained William H. Whyte, noting that regular people have a vast impact on the everyday use and feel of public space. He muses, "Lovers, incidentally, are quite regular. Contrary to plaza lore, they do not tryst mostly in secluded places. They're right out front. . . ." "Schmoozing patterns are similarly consistent" (quoted in Kaufman 1999). Play follows a similar pattern. Yet, as the city becomes focused on work and profit maximization, users only gain access by navigating through a set of gates, lines, markets, crowds, fences, filters, and barriers.

Hence the back-and-forth between inclusion and exclusion, enclosure vs openness, public vs private uses which runs throughout this book. To ground this tension, the cases included were presented within a framework demarcating degrees of public and private space—from exclusive and highly gated suburban spaces to filtered to community spaces, temporary autonomous zones and popular spaces open to all. In elaborating on this typology, we've described a recent trajectory of space in New York. Throughout the work, we considered interlocking variables of social movement activity: play and public space and their interplay between expression and control in a geography which has come to be recognized as a case example of neoliberal urban development. Along the way, we've traced the historical development of both a neoliberal spatial and social order as well as resistance movements aimed at countering the erosion of a public sector and commons. The use of these spaces hinged on competing notions of community need. As activists turned garbage dumps into gardens, busy streets into locations for a carnival, these spaces were transformed into sites for autonomy, imagination, identity formation, creativity, problem solving, even democracy renewal. Uses found expression within spaces, such as abandoned piers. As these cases indicate, the longing, not just for public space, but community space controlled by users remains. The poetry of the temporary autonomous zones created by Reclaim the Streets and FIERCE derives its energy as a direct lived expression of this longing to rescue space and transform it into space that everyone and anyone can access. These spaces remain in constant flux. The problem with temporary autonomous zones is just what their name implies: they are temporary. The party tends to recede to the alarm clocks of reality and the powers that be come to reassert control of spatial order.

Throughout the years, this boogy-woogy of aspiration and heart break, inclusion and exclusion, play and repression churned out a tense energy which manifests itself in a wide range of expressions. "[T]he weight of the city was murderous—one of those who had been crushed on the day, which was every day, these towers fell," James Baldwin (1960 4) wrote, describing a stroll through Manhattan a half century ago. "Entirely alone and dying of it, he was part of an unprecedented multitude." Given such creative and combustible ingredients, it is not surprising that the city is described as "the epicenter of postmodern cultural and intellectual experimentation" (Harvey, 2005, 47). This is not to suggest the manic-depressive peaks and valleys, work hard/play hard ethos is comfortable. Over and over again, we are left with a searing conflict between interests. Having begun with a discussion of how the city's 1975 fiscal crisis set in motion the movement towards exclusive control of public space, it is useful to reconsider the impacts of the current crises in terms of questions of urban space.

Those who care about cities have long fought patterns of displacement taking place in cities from New Orleans to Rio de Janeiro and around the world (Arreorla et al. 2010; Davis 2007; Sites 2003; Van Kleunen 1994). Faced with this pattern, David Harvey (2008) calls for urban actors to fight for their own right to the city. In doing so, he articulates a set of approaches to grapple with the real life impacts of neoliberalism (Purcell 2003). As Henri Lefebvre (2003) describes and those in FIERCE, Reclaim the Streets, and Time's Up! demonstrate, this right to the city has long embodied a raw ambition to reclaim public space for uses that favor alternative social relations to those of capitalism; for these movements, the rules of community trump those of consumption (Holtzman et al. 2007; Merrifield 2002; Muertes 2004; Will 2003; Shepard and Hayduk 2002). Unfortunately, this right is met with an equally potent countervailing force: the authority of urban police departments to control and cordon off access to public space— and, by extension, political expression (Fernandez, 2008), especially in the face of political crises.

And in New York, crises are part of the life pulse of the city. Each crisis—from the fiscal and financial breakdowns to crime and terrorism—profoundly affects the way the city understands itself. When crime was thought to be a crisis, it was used by elites to justify larger numbers of police to address the problem of disorder in public space. When social order was thought to be tenuous, many welcomed the police to move in and take control (Vitale 2008). Police are thought to be necessary to ensure the right to the city for the rich, for developers, for bankers, and for those with little interest in intermingling with many of New York's colorful actors or interests. Here the right to the city finds expression in policies which make access to the city "favorable to devel-

opers, Wall Street and transnational capitalist-class elements." (Harvey 2008). In New York, mayor after mayor has sold the city as a popular destination for tourists and business, all with the support of a police force as large as many armies. "He [Bloomberg] is, in effect, turning Manhattan into one vast gated community for the rich" (Harvey 2008). Given that Mayor Bloomberg will have an extended impact on the city, a brief consideration of this process offers a few indications about where the city is heading.

Police guarding the plate-glass window of a Starbucks underscored the store's symbolism of corporate capitalism. (Rally against the World Economic Forum. New York, February, 2002.)

When, for example, Williamsburg, Brooklyn residents put together a plan to redevelop their waterfront, which was both consistent with the neighborhood's height and bulk and maintained access to water and open public space, both their community board and city council supported their work (Williamsburg Waterfront 197–A-Plan 2002). Yet, the mayor had other plans—to rezone the neighborhood and place forty-story towers, shockingly dissimilar to any other structure in the space, along the Williamsburg Waterfront. When supporters of the community plan held a press conference condemning the mayor's rezoning plan in 2005, the mayor passed by on his way to City Hall. Activists, including one of us (Shepard), chanted "Community Plan!!! Community Plan!!!" Hearing their chant, the mayor leaned over in a guffaw, laughing. While the community plan was opposed by the mayor, it garnered support from some of the most thoughtful observers of cities. "What the intelligently worked out plan devised by the community itself does *not* do is worth noticing," wrote the eighty-eight-year-old Jane Jacobs (2005) to Mayor Bloomberg and the City Council, in favor of the community plan, rather than rezoning the waterfront just a year before her death. "The community's plan does not violate the existing scale of the community, nor does it insult the visual and economic advantages of neighborhoods that are precisely of the kind that demonstrably attract artists and other craftsmen, initiating spontaneous and self-organizing renewal," she explained. "I will make two predictions with utter confidence," wrote Jacobs:

Williamsberg residents fighting for the community plan. Photo by Fred Askew. In this skit, the towers theatrically lost to the flowers. Yet, at City Hall the developer backed towers prevailed.

1. If you follow the community's plan you will harvest a success. 2. If you follow the proposal before you today, you will maybe enrich a few heedless and ignorant developers, but at the cost of an ugly and intractable mistake. Even the presumed beneficiaries of this misuse of governmental powers, the developers and financiers of luxury towers, may not benefit; misused environments are not good long-term economic bets. (Jacobs 2005)

Of course, the mayor did the latter. *The New York Times* would sit on Jacobs' letter until after the council vote in favor of rezoning. Six years later, Jacobs' statement remains prophetic and prescient. Today, semi-completed forty-story condos stand empty along the waterfront, "half-built shells of a vanished boom"—an image of hubris and short sighted planning (Amsden 2009).

The Williamsburg rezoning was one of over one hundred rezoning measures seen over the last decade in New York. Most all of them were developer-supported and backed by the mayor, under whom construction spending doubled (Buettner and Rivera 2009), aided by financing from the festering real estate bubble. Over time, the push to support developers' agendas included payoffs to crane inspectors, subsequent crane collapses, deaths at construction sites, widespread corruption, clogged streets, and a feeling that developers enjoyed exclusive, special rights to the city (Rashbaum 2009). "He didn't steer the boom," argued Ron Shiffman, a former planning commissioner. Rather the mayor failed to publicly spread the benefits enjoyed by the real estate industry. "He did not direct it in such a way that it benefited a more diverse set of populations in the city of New York, and more diverse income groups. It was basically developer driven" (Buettner and Rivera 2009).

The Williamsburg/Greenpoint rezoning would not be the last time the mayor turned his back on democratic precedents to advance his own agenda. Three years later, the mayor, backed by Wall Street moguls, wrapped this agenda around the economic crisis, suggesting term limits would have to be overturned for the city to survive the financial crisis. During the council

http://www.jameswagner.com/

hearings on the subject of overturning term limits, activists zapped one of the mayor's supporters lifting a banner declaring: "Mayor to Democracy: Drop Dead" in reference to Ford's famous message to the city (Lucadamo 2008; Wagner 2008). Term limits had twice been approved by voters aware that power corrupts, and that it was useful to limit access to governance and the purse strings of the City of New York (Barrett 2009). Again, the mayor guffawed.

Parks, Popular Spaces, and Play Spaces

More than anything, understandings of public space involve vacillations between freedom and exclusion. At their core, many city parks are quintessential popular public spaces, open for all. Central Park, Prospect Park, and Tompkins Square Park brim with activity day in, day out. At the same time, public spaces can sometimes become exclusive community enclaves in which users bond with each other, but narrowly defined interests trump democratic calls for openness and exchange. One group dominates a space, rendering it exclusive, while pushing others away. Discussions of public space are limited without acknowledging this risk. Yet, within this risk some wonderful things happen; such is the inherent peril and promise of community space. From the annual unpermitted Drag March, which takes place the last weekend in June, to the yearly Mermaid Parades where Woody Guthrie once lived in Coney Island, New York's public spaces often function as a stage for imagination-stirring convergences of bodies and spectacle (Cohen-Cruz 1998).

To the extent that space in New York is viewed as a commodity, spaces for vernacular uses, those that challenge capitalist logic, are increasingly squeezed (Harvey 2005; Logan and Molotch 1987). In the months after the 2008 opening of a new residential complex called the Breakers in Sheepshead Bay, long-term residents were shocked to find themselves denied access to a waterfront open to the public for as long as anyone could remember. "Everybody had expected this would be open," one resident grumbled. "It's a private property, developed by a private developer" explained Albert Wilk, a broker for the Breakers. "It's going to be gated, and accessed only by members. If the neighbors wanted access, then why didn't they participate in the costs of putting in the boardwalk and the dock?" (Mindlin 2008). Community members yearning for access to public space and developers justifying exclusion—it is a back and forth which takes place every day in New York and in communities around the world.

Despite these barriers, the craving for spaces to play endures. The informal uses of these spaces by residents continues to influence policy debate and development of New York's public spaces (Campo 2002). In the years since the deindustrialization of Brooklyn's waterfront, users invented countless community uses for spaces there (Levinson, 2008). At Brooklyn's Eastern District Terminal in Williamsburg/Greenpoint, for example, users—from marching bands to skateboarders—have built a community on this waterfront space off Kent Avenue (Campo 2002). The uses were so varied that even in the middle of a vast rezoning of the space for residential uses the city built on the lessons of their experiences and turned the space into a public park. Those uses have been codified, based on community input (Campo 2002). And Williamsburg is no isolated example.

From Hunts Point in the Bronx to the West Side of Manhattan to Red Hook in Brooklyn, users are influencing and shaping debates about access to public space (Gonzalez 2007). When long-time New Yorker Ron Hayduk moved to Jackson Heights in 2007, he was immediately aware the area lacked open spaces for his kids to play. The local park, Travers Park, felt crowded beyond capacity. Doing what many do in public parks Hayduk, a political scientist with City University, started talking with his neighbors. In between changing diapers and chasing kids, Hayduk and his neighbors started working out plans to rectify the situation. Hayduk was aware of a pilot plan under the city's Play Streets program. So he proposed to residents that they request permission to shut 78th Street from 34th Avenue to Northern Boulevard to traffic on Sundays. By the next summer, the community's plan for street closures on Sundays became a reality (McCormack 2008). As a result, traffic would be diverted away from 78th Street so the neighborhood's children could have an additional space for play and games, without having to worry about cars. "A small band of residents in a dense and diverse corner of western Queens have championed their own effort to use a roadway to make more room for their children to play," the *New York Times* declared after the plan was approved (quoted in Santos 2008). Throughout the summer of 2008 the city experimented with opening streets for alternate uses, and users took full advantage. As a trial program to open streets to bikes and close them to cars showed, the push for a place to ride and play safely is on the upswing. And in recent years, the city has transformed streets into open pedestrian plazas where people can actually sit and watch the city move in front of their eyes.

But with each victory and increase in access to public space, a new form of restriction seems to follow. Later the same summer of 2008 when Queens residents opened their street, the pavilion at Union Square, a historic space for convergences of movement activity, was fenced off and slated for development as a restaurant. In a stark departure from its historic function as a place for free-speech and public gatherings, the space was being developed for diners with resources to pay fifteen dollars for a glass of wine. Activists cried foul, noting the space functioned much like Hyde Park, as a public commons, and should not be be privatized as an exclusive restaurant (Shepard 2008a; Shepard 2008b; Zukin 2010). A stay was placed on development of the space, but it did not last. In November 2009, former Assemblywomen Deborah Glick wrote a letter to the Parks Department about the proposed restaurant in Union Square: "A private restaurant is simply not a needed amenity nor is it a proper use of Union Square Park. This area is replete with restaurants but has limited park space," she argued. "We urged the Parks Department to withdraw its current intention to issue an RFP for a restaurant and instead work with the community to come up with a plan that would allow for community use of the pavilion" (quoted in Swan 2009). By its very nature, understandings of public space are contested—with parks and public space advocates favoring alternative uses, and developers favoring use of space for maximum profitability.

Because of proximity among bodies, space consistently sets up conflicts between exclusion and inclusion, expression and repression. Bodies, after all, exist in space, where they are subject to differing interpretations. The image of a queer body, of perhaps an African American body covered in a sweat suit rollerblading and dancing in Washington Square Park, conjures up a different set of understandings than that of a young white mother with a baby stroller in Carroll Park in Brooklyn. Such bodies can be viewed with any number of interpretations. While one can see such bodies as contrasting expressions of a democratic promise for the interconnection among bodies in space, others see such bodies as signs of trouble (Hunter 2005). What takes place in public space can be viewed as a sign of a healthy public commons or as a menacing indication of urban decline. Cities are organized to privilege select aspects of these interpretations; conflict results when alternative expressions or interpretations are physically excluded.

One outcome of studying different types of public space is to see that public space is shaped through conflict. If, in the Marxist formulation, conflict between a thesis and antithesis leads to synthesis—as the inherent conflict between workers and capitalists is to lead inevitably to a communist revolution reshaping the means of production—then public space is not synthesis, the outcome of conflict. Instead, public space is the conflict itself. It is the site where social groups meet, play, and quite often come into conflict. A privately owned plaza is public space to the extent that the public also seeks to establish a claim on the space. A park is public to the extent that a wide enough array of users seek to use the space and thus must resolve their overlapping plans and activities (either on the spot or in a bureaucratized setting where rules are written down). Likewise, the one-step-forward-one-step-back nature of changes to the city's public spaces—opening up play streets but closing Union Square landmarks—are not contradictory messages about the trend in public space, but evidence that public space continues to be created and contested or, to put it more precisely, created because it is contested.

Thus, the conflicts that we chronicle in these pages are not the precursor to some kind of ideal public space that will resolve these contests. It is not the outcome that will create public space, it is the conflicts themselves that *are* public space, and public space exists to the extent that people demand (either in organized groups or as individual actors in the politics of everyday life) tolerance, access, visibility, equality, civil rights, or just plain autonomy. To say public space is conflict is not to celebrate conflict without concern for the outcome of these struggles. We seek a more public, accessible and egalitarian city. The extent to which our society adjudicates the conflicts that constitute public space in ways that are inclusive rather then exclusive, civil rather than martial, egalitarian rather than unequal, and accommodating rather than censorious is the degree to which public spaces are successful, well-used, and reflect a society that can organize itself democratically to right inequality, create ludic spaces for us to imagine, create, and express our aspirations, and incorporate everyone in the social forum of public space. Public spaces are sites and instances of social conflict, but they remain successful to the extent that they also embody inclusive forms of social organization that address those conflicts.

The ongoing history of these conflicts constitutes a narrative. From Chicago to Los Angeles to New York, cities are often best understood as storied spaces. The interplay between exclusion and inclusion, barriers to difference and democracy has been become a central part of the story of public space in New York. Rather than throw one's hands in the air, we are suggesting that within this interplay, there is room for agency, for people to move, tell stories, participate, and reclaim a right to the city long imagined possible in urban space (Lefebvre 2003). To reach this vantage point, we have considered the shifting contours of urban theory within the context of changes in the way cities contend with notions of public space in a global era. Corporate globalization often represents a force for homogenizing sameness. US global cities face a rising sea of corporate demands. Yet, if their stories indicate anything, they suggest there is still room for difference and play in urban space (Abu-Lughod 1999; Abu-Lughod 2007). They help us see that people can look at the city and reshape it (Merrifield 2002). In doing so, one can see the city as a work of art: a beach beneath the pavement. The imperative to reclaim streets is born from just such dreaming. Here, play is reclaimed from work, for both adults and children, and we all enjoy the collective daydream RTS London long dreamed was possible.

Cities are places where people imagine and reflect, as well as create new identities. Walter Benjamin reveled in much of what the city of Paris offered.

Yet, he also recognized the exploitation; he loved the eros, yet he also worried about the darkness. It was a place for him to explore his life and relationship to the world (Merrifield, 2002) Within the public spaces of the city, one finds an ongoing set of reciprocal relations from temptation to exploitation, inclusion to exclusion; the elite develop buildings, and users find a way to carve out a space for difference. Within the text of the city, one finds space to think about democracy. From the community gardens to the West Side piers, from Brooklyn's vernacular waterfront to play streets in Jackson Heights, we are suggesting there is another story to twenty-first century urban life. It still takes place within a city feeling the squeeze. Social services remain inadequate to demand. Decent paying jobs were in short supply even in boom times. The housing market in New York can somehow collapse and remain unaffordable simultaneously. Destructive development continued, as Yankee Stadium and Shea welcomed their last visitors in 2008, and these storied places were replaced with stadiums that included fewer seats, higher costs, and increased debt for the city subsidizing their development (Buettner and Rivera 2009). Astroland at Coney Island welcomed the masses for one last time at the end of September 2008 (Parker, 2008). Its replacement is slated to follow a familiar, more exclusive pattern. Paul's Daughter, a forty-year-old mom and pop business on the Coney Island boardwalk, is now being evicted, replaced by corporate chain Sodexo, yet not without a fight. The contestation and the stories of the city continue.

The Joys and Promise of the Post-Imperial City

Since at least the 1990s, perhaps since the financial restructuring of 1975, capital has been ascendant in New York and communities have been on the defensive. With the concomitant crash of the financial markets in 2008 (upon which New York's local economy depends so heavily) and the New York real estate market, capital must attend to its own problems. Recessions bring difficult times. This temporary retreat is not unprecedented, and history offers indications of how to make popular improvements to public space in this period. William H. Whyte famously succeeded in pushing the city to adopt a zoning revision in 1975, which required seating, trees, water features, and other amenities in bonus plazas that previously could have been utterly barren. (Kayden et al. 2000). He did so in no small part because, as planners we interviewed recalled, the real estate industry was busy licking its wounds during a bear market, and wasn't paying much attention to what new public space regulations got passed.

Thus, the current pause in the decade-long onslaught by speculators, gentrifiers, and law-and-order politicians seeking to clear the path for corporate recolonization of the city holds a moment of opportunity. It will certainly hold abundant difficulties, with rising unemployment, hard times for already-poor people, and anxious uncertainty. But just as structural speculators look ahead to see opportunities, we benefit from anticipating structural opportunities at any moment in the urban narrative.

The age of the Imperial City was supremely self-confident. But capitalism is cyclical, not perpetual. There is no guarantee that communities can make advances in the opening that economic disorganization presents. But it provides a pause during which activists can promote popular priorities in urban space.

Communities are trying to make the best of a bear market. "Real estate's imperial rule, though still in force, is losing ground to the rising community-based, city-wide, regional and global efforts to take back the land," wrote the Center for Urban Planning and Development's Tom Angotti (2009). "People are discovering new concepts of community land—land that is outside the speculative marketplace and subject to democratic control that respects principles of economic, social and environmental justice."

There are several reasons why activists are well-positioned to reclaim public space. First, as we've seen, activists have for many years been framing their campaigns, demands, and strategies in terms of public space. Second, the spaces in which they may mobilize, even those that have been thoroughly gentrified, are often in more promising physical condition than the privatized and fortified spaces of earlier eras. Suburban spaces beg to be made truly public—to be used for play, to be liberated as lush temporary autonomous zones, to be expanded beyond the narrow uses envisioned by their developer-creators into truly public spaces that can serve broader, more diverse needs of people in the city. Until now, activists' appropriation, strategic and creative use of community spaces and TAZ spaces have rarely crossed the boundary onto privately controlled spaces. But in a moment of flux such as the one faced in the recession that began in 2008, public space activists might successfully claim suburban, filtered, and privatized spaces. If this is the moment for such a spatial revolution, it is not to tear down the old order, but to productively, creatively reappropriate it, reshape it, and imagine alternate ways of using space.

This kind of creative reimaging can often be felt riding a bike through the streets of New York. The night after a bike parking bill was passed by the City Council in August of 2009, Time's Up! held an "80s Dance Party" themed bike ride, including a roving DJ riding a "sound bike" with a makeshift sound system. The ride was an amazing celebration of the City Council moving ahead with plans to make the city more bike friendly, including a city wide bike access bill creating new parking spaces in buildings. But more than this, it was an image of the kind of joyous interaction, which takes shape when people share space in the city and actually value the kinds of lovely and surprising spontaneous interactions, which take place as this happens. A fitting conclusion, this ride passed through many of the spaces discussed in this book, and in a single evening reprised the themes we've discussed here. The ride was to kick off at Tompkins Square Park. There a group of Time's Up! volunteers, and people from the neighborhood, some parents and toddlers, others like the homeless in the park, joined us to dance. Following the sound bike, we rode to Astor Place where the party grew just it had for an early Reclaim the Streets action held eleven years prior and recalled in Chapter 5. More passers-by stopped to dance; a young woman spun the Astor Place Cube. Up at Union Square, we found hundreds hanging out enjoying the summer night. Despite the more subdued crowd, a roar of approval broke out when we played "Celebration." As we left, I (Shepard) overheard a young man say, "follow them, they have the music," and a group of young men of color with baggy pants joined us. Riding undersized motocross bikes, they ended up leading the cavalcade—all while popping wheelies, flipping their bikes in the air, and screaming in moments of revelry. As we played the dance anthem "Don't You Want Me" by the Human League, one of them announced he was conceived to this song. Laughter filled the air. Everyone roared approvingly when British punk poured out of the sound bike. Riding through New York City, one will discover any number of subcultures—some on foot, roller skates, blades and most certainly on bikes. Some bikes are fashioned like low-riders, remade as models of Southern California hot rods with sound systems and car stereos. Some are stripped down for speed, some bulked up with baskets, trailers, and extra seats to carry cargo, kids, or companions. Others ride small bikes specialized for tricks, like the young men who joined our ride. Every day, every ride is different. As we made our way west to the piers that had once been the squats described in Chapter 4, more and more people roared and cheered. As we meandered past Christopher Street, through the fountain facing the Hudson River where both Bob Kohler and Sylvia Rivera's ashes were strewn, the moon shone on the blue water of the summer night. At the westernmost end of the pier, the crowd undulated to Grace Jones' iconic 1981 hit, "Pull up to the Bumper Baby." In between gyrations, a few of the twenty or so posed for a group photo. By the time we played the disco-era liberationist anthem, "It's Raining Men," more and more of the evening crowd of queer pier users had joined us in creating our own body electric in the New York City night. The scene could have been from *Paris is Burning,* a film and subculture born of this space and the urban daydreams it inspires. We started to ride back out of the park as the beats of New Order's "Blue Monday" undulated from the sound bike. Everyone just wanted to dance, enjoying sharing space. By the time we put on Salt-n-Pepa's "Push It" the crowd was willing to show everyone what the summer night could be. The familiar words, "Oooh, baby, baby, Baby, baby. . . . Oooh, baby, baby" received an enthusiastic reception. "This dance ain't for everybody, Only the sexy people, So all you fly mothers, get on out there and dance" And dance we did, while a few of the riders and dancers helped demonstrate what the song might have meant by "push it." As we left, we experienced only mild interference from police about the sound system before we left to ride off to the Washington Square Park fountain for a dip. It is hard not to feel the energy of the streets and the people occupying them. At every street corner, people joined us to dance and take part, even when we jumped in the fountain to swim. Throughout the summer, we'd gone for rides in which we ended up reveling in, dipping, and diving in many of the public plazas throughout the city (that is until security arrived in a minute or two). This after all is our beach—sometimes beneath the streets—often right on top.

Our recognition of the vitality of ludic activist gestures should not be seen as neglect or a deflection of the exploitive forces, which con-

80s Dance Ride—Fame Shot. Photo by Benjamin Cerf.

tinue to plague urban life and cities. It is not. Instead, we acknowledge the recent crash opened the door for speculation and more predatory investment in foreclosed buildings among those displaced. These patterns contributed to social inequalities. They also opened the door for regressive social policies and practices such as bank bail outs, corporate welfare, and redlining (see Wilder 2001). During the recent blizzard, a man froze to death while sleeping on a subway platform. "Neighborhoods with people of modest incomes are paying the heaviest price relative to their assets, as we saw in the wholesale abandonment of the 1960s and 70s," noted Tom Angotti (2009). We emphasize play because we all have the right to reimagine our relationship with urban space and by extension with the city itself. Cities can still be our works of art. Yet, to create them we must rethink core assumptions about land use and urban experience. "All of this may spur more protest and activism and increase the attractiveness of community land and planning as alternatives to real estate as usual," Angotti wrote. Such thinking begins with a rejection of a model of urban space as growth machine in favor of alternate models of urban sustainability and creativity. Here, the needs of people, democracy, and land use must reconnect. Reimagining urban space and living begins with a little forward thinking about the construction of cities. People must feel like this land is really their land (Angotti 2009). Land-use policies must be reconnected with the needs of people, rather than developers (Bagli 2009).

The political activism of public space has been remarkable for its creativity—that is, for its focus on creating better, livelier, more engaging spaces and possibilities for living. There has to be more to urban living than privately controlled spaces, whose owners guard the gates less strictly while tending to their own financial concerns. The limitations of such a situation give activists any number of opportunities to rethink and influence the perpetual debate over the disposition of urban public space.

In the mid-nineties, a rumor circulated that some group would challenge Giuliani's closure of City Hall Park by smashing a van through the fence. Privatized spaces could only be liberated by knocking down walls. Even filtered space was defined by barriers that left it inhospitable to popular use. But suburban spaces can be liberated by lowering the policy barriers to broad civic interaction. Such spaces can live up to the promise that their luxurious designs suggest—becoming autonomous spaces, popular spaces, community spaces, family spaces, working-class spaces, immigrant spaces, queer spaces—never more so than when corporations are in a slump during which they can find no profitable use for such spaces. Rejuvenated, these spaces could redefine the city through the priorities of the millions of people who live here, not the developers who extract profit from it.

Such an outcome is never guaranteed; public space inherently entails risk as well as promise. But for now, people will continue occupying and using their public spaces across the city, and will likely expand into newfound spaces. As they do so, they will assign new social meanings to those spaces. If individuals, groups, and communities are able to securely plant those meanings and uses in public spaces, they can access the fantastic potential of that beach beneath the streets.

Notes

Introduction

1. Harvey used the term *bread and circuses* in this context. See Harvey 1990, and Harvey, 1994.
2. For a compelling account of planned shrinkage as a conflagration comparable to a policy-produced public health epidemic, see Wallace 1998.

Chapter 1

1. To the contrary, formal control can disrupt just such a scene: Sheepshead Bay residents recently lost access to their waterfront when a new developer gated and locked a route that had traditionally been open to the public. See Mindlin 2008.
2. "Accessible to all" comes from Hannah Arendt on the public realm, as cited in Dijkstra. Also, see Lofland, Carr. [This is not clear. Please give the author(s)' name(s) with publication date. Dijkstra recognizes that the requirement actually prompts a consideration of *how* accessible a space must be to be public.
3. While graphically similar to Harvey's "grid of spatial practices," this model seeks to identify different spaces in which action occurs, whereas Harvey seeks to identify the different practices that occur in space. See Harvey 1994, 361–86.
4. Figures regarding use from Dunlap 1999b.
5. "Quality-of-life" programs affected many areas. Those that reduced the visibility in public space of marginalized people included the closing of sex shops and heavier policing of street prostitutes that moved prostitutes indoors. Similarly, homeless people were removed from within the boundaries of the imperial city in drives that pushed them out of places like Penn Station (see Duneier 1999) or the Port Authority Bus Terminal. The Grand Central Partnership, a Business Improvement District, was sued for paying people to harass and even assault homeless men sleeping near ATM machines and other indoor spaces around Grand Central Station.

Chapter 2

1. Of the five firms that designed the most buildings with bonus plazas, we were able to interview architects at three. Architect Richard Roth was the grandson of the founder of Emery Roth and Sons. Peter Claman is a partner at Schuman, Lichtenstein, Claman and Efron. Saky Yakas is also a partner at SLCE. David West is a partner at Costas Kondylis, inheritor to Philip Birnbaum's firm. We interviewed a larger number of planners from the New York City Department of City Planning, both past and present.
2. The plaza has since been dramatically renovated, as a suburban space.
3. Thus, the spaces are supposed to be publicly accessible, but critically, most building owners have never treated them that way. As William Whyte said, "What does 'accessible' mean? A commonsense interpretation would be that the public could use the space in the same manner it uses any public space, with the same freedoms and the same constraints. Many buildings managements have been operating with a much narrower concept of access. They shoo away entertainers and people who distribute leaflets or give speeches. Apartment buildings managements often shoo away everybody except residents. This is a flagrant violation of the zoning intent, but to date no one has gone to court on it. The public's right in urban plazas would seem clear. Not only are plazas used as public spaces; in most cases the owner has been specifically, and richly, rewarded for providing them. He has not been given license to allow only those public activities he happens to approve of. He may assume that he has license, and some owners have been operating on this basis with impunity. But that is because nobody has challenged them. A stiff, clarifying test is in order" (Whyte 1988).
4. Tax and business law give family empires certain advantages over shareholder corporations like investment companies or like banks or insurance companies, or other firms large enough to finance such expensive projects. Family control provided another—the willingness to weather downturns—since the families had repeatedly seen much larger corporations threateningly enter New York real estate, only to exit when the market cooled and shareholders expected the companies to find greener short-term pastures for their investments.

The families—including Cohen, Durst, Fisher, Uris, Rose, Rudin, Resnick, and Tischman—are distinct (and consider themselves distinct) from more well-known real estate names like Trump and Helmsley in equal parts because of their greater influence and, historically, lower public profile. Another advantage was knowledge and experience. Interviewees agreed that real estate was "not a genteel business." Financial success depends on knowing something that other players do not—

whether it is a guess that the market is heating up, a way to build a larger, more profitable building on a lot for sale than others are considering, control of adjacent lots that can be combined with a property, or other things. Samuels writes that "With a few additions and subtractions, these are the same families that dominated the city's real-estate market 40 years ago. They have survived the assaults of the big insurance companies of the 60's, the near-bankruptcy of the city in the 70's, the entry into the market in the 80's of well-capitalized foreign giants like Sumitomo and Ladbroke and Olympia & York. They have expanded their fortunes as arriviste competitors have come and gone" (Samuels 1997, 37).

5. Theoretically, the architect of record is the design firm responsible for making sure building plans comply with local codes; an internationally know "brand name" architect from outside the region may not have the expertise to make sure the building complies with local regulations.

6. Our study is of the 291 spaces at 219 buildings in Midtown and Downtown. Some buildings had multiple bonus spaces, such as a plaza and an arcade, which were counted and graded separately.

7. From bonus plaza zoning archives of the City Planning Commission, in possession of Philip Schneider. April 16, 1975.

8. Interview Philip Schneider, 2003.

9. Emery Roth and Son's long list of achievements includes being the *architect of record* for all seven buildings of the World Trade Center. Minoru Yamasaki was the architect.

10. On Roth's ongoing relationship with developers: Roth is retired, and I interviewed him during one of his twice-yearly visits to New York from the Bahamas. During the interview, he suggested I talk to developer Melvyn Kaufman, saying he would put in a word for me since "I have to call Mel anyway." In a second interview, he mentioned writing a letter of condolence to a developer after the passing of his brother.

11. Sulzberger is evidently not related to the Sulzberger family that runs the *Times* (McQuiston 1988, B8).

12. Interview Peter Claman, January 16, 2004. In fact, zoning regulations for this area did not require the developer to gain City Planning's approval for this plaza.

Chapter 3

1. In addition to jungle imagery, there is the persistent and relentless inclusion of rape in these arguments, a crime that has symbolized the ultimate threat by which White America describes Black America. Whalen also conflated the civil rights movement and crime, as when he nodded approvingly to the comments of a New Yorker who writes after a civil

rights march in Alabama, "We also need a great civil rights march in our city to insure to us the civil rights to live in our homes, to ride in our subways, to walk in our streets and parks at any hour without fear of being murdered, robbed and raped" (Whalen 1965, 23–24).

2. Roth was more specific than others, and it is significant that he is retired, and no longer working for developers, even though he apparently remained friendly with several afterwards. (Philip Schneider, recently retired from the Department of City Planning, was similarly more willing to discuss developers by name. Jonathan Barnett, no longer at City Planning, was also more forthcoming than other interview subjects.)

3. *Undesirables* is a term, widely used and apparently popularized by William H. Whyte, to describe anyone whom others have decided they don't want in a space. That is, it should be taken strictly as an observed, not normative, category. Interview with Richard Roth, June 1, 2003.

4. Interview with Richard Roth, June 12, 2003.

5. Community Boards are often described as New York's most local level of government. Members are appointed by elected officials. The fifty-nine boards that cover the city have advisory power only. They consider every zoning and development change in the neighborhoods of their community district.

6. Interview with Richard Roth, June 1, 2003.

7. Interview with Saky Yakas, May 9, 2003. Italics mine.

8. "Police Stop More Than 1 Million People on Street," *New York Times*, October 8, 2009. According to police data, 83 percent of people stopped were Black or Latino.

9. For instance, the loss of tens of thousands of units of affordable housing through mass conversion of Mitchell Lama middle-income projects to luxury apartments, the massive Stuyvesant Town project—and, as of this writing, the uncertain future of the equally large Starrett City.

10. Throughout 2010, members of the New York City AIDS Housing Network (NYCAHN), a member of the Right to the City Alliance, collected data about harassment of those who participate in needle exchange programs. They helped publish a report and presented the data to the governor and called for remedy (Urban Justice Center 2010). On August 3, 2010, the NYCAHN syringe access bill was signed into law, permitting possession of syringes (see New York City Bar 2010; Urban Justice Center 2010). Still, the larger problem of ongoing harassment of low-income communities continues.

11. It is true that bonus plaza regulations were tightened in 1975, and many new plazas were required to install amenities seating and trees. But unusable spaces were still possible after 1975, and many of the post-1975 spaces go beyond what was required in the revised regulations. The regulations, pushed through by William H. Whyte, were a valuable improvement. But developers' strategies changed as well.

12. Lauded for his hard-nosed realism, Newman's "defensible" recommendations rest on an often-overlooked racist assumption about what criminals and decent people look like.
13. Anthony King has used the term *post-imperialism* to refer to global cities. But in his use, post-imperial is London after the age of the classic British Empire, whereas in the context of New York, the imperial age is the present (King 1990).

Part Two

1. "Demand a Queer Pier" SexPanic! flyer. October 4, 1998. In collection of the authors.
2. Warner is describing spaces that are "accessible for a fee," like bath houses, as public spaces because of their otherwise nondiscriminatory access. Access fees can create a filtered space; users of the piers described the piers as more accessible than indoor clubs because clubs charged a fee.

Chapter 4

1. As a city park, Hudson River Park would normally be classified as popular space. However, the intensive policing used to keep out and restrict the activities of the people who used the space before is better understood by conceiving of the space in terms of the dialectical relationship between suburban space and policed space.
2. People become "aware of the sacred because it manifests itself, shows itself, as something wholly different from the profane," notes philosopher Mercea Eliade (1957). A poem about the space reflects just this sentiment:

> Flying high above the Hudson River
> the tranquility tingly, crystal-like sensations
> . . . Heaven's Gates appear through big, fluffy clouds . . . (Xavier 1997).

3. Countless authors have written about the piers. David Wojnarowicz (1991) has come perhaps the closest of any writer to conjuring up the haunted loneliness of both the connection and separation experienced at the piers. In a later treatment of this work, Patrick Moore (2004) notes that Wojnarowicz "insisted there was a beauty to be found among the ruins of the West Village" (106). Charles Shively (1974/2001) specifically notes the "trucks" were a place where "a faggot will make it with someone he will not have to live with the next day." Within such spaces, "occasionally the vision of luxury, even ecstasy of a mutual faggot sexuality can be found." The only "decadence" involved in these spaces is if

queers leave only to emulate the inequalities of the dominant culture.

4. For activists, attacks on queer meeting spaces have historically been viewed as attacks on gay identity, spurring calls for liberation. During the twentieth century, sexual outcasts repeatedly fought turf wars over the waterfront, beginning with the seamen's strikes of the Depression, as the space became a convergence point for sexual commerce and leather communities through the 1970s (See Bérubé 1997).

5. Nothing divides the private from the public more than the notion that the personal sphere is where intimacy appropriately takes place. For many, sex is the most intimate, and therefore, the most private act of all. Recent years have witnessed a new hyper vigilance around public order, policing the divide between the public and the personal. For many, privacy is seen as an ideology of capital, heteronormativity, reproduction, family values, and privilege (Berlant and Warner 1999). The public is a place for conversations, for cross-class contact, and for community building (Delany 1999). Personal lives are categorized according to proximity to public and private space. (Rubin 1984, 110; Rubin 1999, 25–26) Those who can pay for private space and related freedoms usually do; those unable to pay remain exposed to the elements and subject to the state's whims within public space. Deviance tends to be conditioned and increasingly policed among those with fewer resources to pay for private space and cover (Wagner 1997, 5–6; Warner 1999).

6. "The bourgeois public sphere consists of private persons whose identity is formed in the privacy of the conjugal domestic family and who enter into rational-critical debate around matters common to all by bracketing their embodiment and status. Counterpublics of sexuality and gender, on the other hand, are scenes of association and identity that transform the private lives they mediate," (Warner 2002, 57). Such spaces involve an interplay between capital and community building, market pressure and pluralistic democracy, private interest (isolation/alienation) and public consciousness (interconnection/solidarity).

7. "There is plenty of cock and ass around without having to go there at nite. There are a few bars around that have fuck rooms in them. If you much participate in this type of games, go there—at least the most that could happen is you get the clap" (Warehouse Newsletter 1975, 2). This statement was written years before the onset of HIV/AIDS.

Chapter 5

1. Quote is from a handbill advertising Reclaim the Streets' inaugural October 4, 1998 action.

2. Reclaim the Streets New York City. Flyer. 1999. In the collection of the authors.

3. Ibid.
4. At the time this ethnography was conducted Mayor Giuliani was displaying a clear pattern of vindictiveness toward public space activists, such as Housing Works. In the interest of protecting the respondents, last names were never collected.
5. While I (Smithsimon) was told that members from these groups were involved in RTS, there is no evidence that the organizations themselves endorsed or participated in RTS actions. This distinction is important because of the potential for state reactions against planners of some RTS events.
6. Reclaim the Streets!, London 1998c.
7. Reclaim the Streets!, London 1998d.
8. "Reclaim the Streets" (2nd flyer with that title) n.d., received January 9, 1999.
9. "Reclaim the Streets" n.d., distributed before October 4, 1998 event.
10. The political context that discouraged the rhetoric of "anticapitalism" shifted over the years. As the group evolved and became increasingly linked with a global movement, more and more group members articulated their critique in terms of explicit anticapitalist discourses. (Shepard 2011).

Chapter 6

1. By October 2010, the city would agree to pay Barbara Ross and some eighty-two other cyclists $965,000 to settle a lawsuit by those who were wrongfully arrested by the NYPD during Critical Mass rides from 2004–2006. This win was by means an isolated instance. In the years since the beginning the crackdown, the city had been forced to pay out countless activists. For example in March of 2010, the city agreed to pay $98,000 to Critical Mass participants wrongfully arrested on the March 2007 ride. Yet, the costs for activists were many, as the Times Up! Declared after the October 2010 legal victory. The arrested cyclists spent hours behind bars, made numerous court appearances to fight the charges, and had their bikes taken from them as evidence. The NYPD used huge amounts of resources at taxpayers' expense during the 2004–2006 Critical Mass rides. Detail reports verify that large amounts of NYPD resources were used during the 2004–2006 Critical Mass rides, including the over seven hundred police officers assigned to follow the ride and thirty-five rolls of orange netting to trap cyclists as they rode down the streets. Despite numerous losses in court, the NYPD continues to show up at the monthly bicycle ride with a disproportionate number of police officers specifically assigned to follow the Critical Mass. "Dozens of officers on motorized scooters follow the ride for

hours, says plaintiff and Critical Mass participant Barbara Ross, who made eleven court appearances until all charges from her February 2005 arrest were dismissed fourteen months later. "High-ranking officers and NYPD's video team intimidate cyclists by driving closely behind in marked and unmarked cars. The number of police following the ride will often equal or exceed the number of cyclists on the ride each month." In addition to this recent nearly million-dollar lawsuit payout, the NYPD continues to spend huge amount of expenditures without any credible justification or oversight by the city council. Rosie Mendez and eleven other city council members have previously requested the DA's office to investigate the NYPD tactics used at Critical Mass while Mayor Bloomberg continues to remain silent on the subject. "Mayor Bloomberg's tacit endorsement of Raymond Kelly's anti-biking policing is out of step with Bloomberg's administration's stated support for a safe environment for cyclists," says plaintiff Brandon Neubauer. "This settlement is a victory for a wide-range of cyclists who realize the potential for a safer, more bicycle-friendly city and keep on riding in the face of years of unjustified harassment and arrests by the NYPD," says Bill DiPaola, Director of Time's Up! Environmental Group.

Chapter 8

1. (1956) "This Land is Your Land."

References

Abramovitz, M. 2000. *Under Attack, Fighting Back*. New York: Monthly Review.

Abu-Lughod, Janet. 1999. *New York, Chicago, Los Angeles: America's Global Cities*. Minneapolis, MN: University of Minnesota Press.

———. 2007. *Race, Space, and Riots in Chicago, New York, and Los Angeles*. New York: Oxford University Press.

Adams, Ernest. undated. The Construction of Ludic Spaces, www.designersnotebook.com/Lectures/The_Construction_of_Ludic_Spaces.ppt.

Adkins, Warren D. 1997. New York's Free Love Advocates Blast New Puritanism. *Badpubby Gay Today*, June 25,

Agnotti, Tom. 2009. "Speculation and Change: Community Land in New York City" Where We Are Now, accessed on December 2, 2010 from http://wherewearenow.org/vol1/change/speculation-and-change-community-land-in-new-york-city/.

Alinsky, S. 1971. *Rules for Radicals*. New York: Vintage Books.

Allen, Mike. 1998. Vending Ban Widens, *New York Times,* June 2, B1.

Alternatives to the SOB, *Harlem News*, October 1969. In the Schomburg Center Archives.

Amateau, Albert. 2002. Queer Youth Protest, Celebrate, FIERCE Caps a Day of Protest with a West Village Street Fair. *Gay City News*, November 17.

———. 2006. 6th Precinct Denies Gay Youth Charges of Brutality. *The Villager*, December 6–12.

America's Most Expensive Cities. 2009. *Forbes*, October 7.

Amsden, David. 2009. The Billyburg Bust. *New York Magazine*, July 12, http://nymag.com/realestate/features/57904/.

Aqueno, Frank. 1996. Queer Pier, http://members.aol.com/Qxbin/QUEER-PIER.html.

Arendt, Hannah. 1963. *Eichmann in Jerusalem*. New York: Penguin.

Aronowitz, Stanley. 2003. A Mills Revival? *Logos*. 2, no. 3, www.logosjournal.com/aronowitz.htm.

Aronowitz, S. and H. Gautney, eds. 2003. *Implicating Empire*. New York: Basic Books.

Arreorla, Guadalupe, Alicia Schwartz, James Tracy, and Tom Wetzel. 2011. *Dispatches Against Displacement: From the Global Economy to the Eviction Notice.* Oakland, CA: AK Press.

Askew, Fred. 2005. Images: Bike Lane Liberation Day. Bicycle Clown Brigade, http://nyc.indymedia.org/en/2005/08/55910.shtml.

Associated Press. 2004. "Judge Dismisses New York's Bid to Force Bike Rally to Get Permit." *New York Newsday*, December 24.

Association of the Bar of the City of New York (2006). Statement of the Association of the Bar of the City of New York Concerning the Proposed New York City Parade Regulations, November 27, accessed on December 6, 2010 from www.nycbar.org/pdf/report/Parade_Regs_ Statement.pdf.

Aufheben . Undated. What Ever Happened to the Situationists? Accessed on January, 27, 2006 from http://www.geocities.com/aufheben2/auf_6_ situ.html.

Bagli, Charles V. 2009. "Court Bars New York's Takeover of Land for Columbia Campus." *New York Times* December 4.

Bakhtin, M. 1984. *Rabelais and His World.* Bloomington, IN: Indiana University Press.

Baldwin, James. 1960. *Another Country.* New York: Vintage International

Barbara. 2005. "Send in the Clowns: Bicycle Clown Brigade to Shame Cars out of Bike Lanes. 16 December," www.NYC Indymedia.*org*.

Barnett, Jonathan. 1982. An Introduction to Urban Design. New York: Harper & Row.

Barrett, Wayne. 2009. A Bloomberg Scorecard: The Mayor's Hits and Misses. *Village Voice.* October 13, www.villagevoice.com/2009-10-13/news/a-bloomberg-score-card-the-mayor-s-misses-but-also-his-biggest-hits/.

Berlant, Laura and Michael Warner. 1999. Sex in Public. In *The Cultural Studies Reader*, 2nd ed., ed. Simon During, 354–70. New York: Routledge;

Berlant, Lauren and Elizabeth Freeman. 1993. Queer Nationality. In *Fear of a Queer Planet*, ed. Michael Warner, 193–229. Minneapolis, MN: University of Minnesota Press.

Berman, Marshall. 1982. *All That is Solid Melts into Air.* New York. Penguin.

———. 2006. *A Times Square for the New Millennium.* New York: Random House.

———. 2007. Introduction. In *New York Calling: From Blackout to Bloomberg*, eds. Marshall Berman and Brian Berger, 9–38. London: Reaktion Books.

Bernstein, Nina. Decline Is Seen In Immigration. *New York Times*, September 28, Accessed on December 5, 2010 from http://query.nytimes.com/gst/ fullpage.html?res=9901E1DB1230F93BA1575AC0A9639C8B63.

Bérubé, Allan. 1997. On the Gay Waterfront (slide show). A SexPanic! Event New York City Lesbian and Gay Community Services Center, September 5.

Besser, Howard. 2002. Victorious Critical Mass Lawsuit. In *Critical Mass: Bicycling's Defiant Celebration*, ed. Chris Carlson, 219–22. Oakland, CA: AK Press.

Bey, Hakim. 1985. *The Temporary Autonomous Zone, Ontological Anarchy, Poetic Terrorism*. New York: Autonomedia, accessed on December 5, 2010 from http://hermetic.com/bey/taz_cont.html.

Bike4peace@aol.com, 2009 "Re: [xup-core] dance ride last night." Email message. August 21.

Black, John, 1981. *Urban Transport Planning: Theory And Practice*. London: Croom Helm.

Block, Dorian. 2006. New York City finishes 200 miles of bike lanes at Grand Concourse ceremony. *New York Daily News*. July 9. accessed on December 3, 2010 from www.nydailynews.com/ny_local/bronx/2009/07/09/2009-07-09_rollin_to_a_record_city_finishes_200_miles_of_bike_lanes.html#ixzz178z8Atcg.

Boal, Augusto. 1979. *Theatre of the Oppressed*, New York : Urizen Books.

Bogad, L. M. 2005. *Electoral Guerrilla Theatre*. New York: Routledge.

———. 2006. A Place for Protest. In *Performance and Place*, eds. Leslie Hill and Helen Paris, 170–79. New York: Palgrave Macmillan.

———. 2007a. Upstaging the Establishment. *UC Davis Magazine* 24, no. 3.

———. 2007b. Carnivals Against Capital: Radical Clowning and the Global Justice Movement, *CalArts Magazine*, Spring.

Boghosian, Heidi. 2007. Punishing Protest. Government Tactics that Suppress Free Speech. National Lawyers Guild, accessed on December 5, 2010 from http://www.scribd.com/doc/38157022/Punishing-Protest-Government-Tactics-that-Suppress-Free-Speech-NLG-2007.

Bonilla-Silva, Eduardo. 2003. *Racism Without Racists: Color-Blind Racism and the Persistence of Racial inequality in the United States*. New York: Rowman and Littlefield.

Brain, David. 1991. Practical Knowledge and Occupational Control: The Professionalization of Architecture in the United States. *Sociological Forum* 6, no.2: 239–68.

Bray, Rebecca, Thomas Stephanos, Justi McSimov, Dan Fennessey and Allen Regar vs The City of New York, Raymond Kelly, Police Commissioner. United States District Court of New York. Filed December 12, 2004. William Pauley District Judge.

Brechner, J, T. Costello, and B. Smith. 2000. *Globalization from Below*. Boston: South End Press.

Buettner, R. and R. Rivera. 2009. A Stalled Vision: Big Development as the City's Future. Sweeping Rezoning and Billions in Cash Yield Uneven Results. *New York Times*, October 29, A1.

Burr, Thomas. 1998. Sleazy City: 42nd Street Structures and Some Qualities of Life. October 85: 90–105.

Butters, S. 1983. The Logic of Inquiry of Participant Observation. In *Resistance through Rituals*, eds. S. Hall and T. Jefferson, 253–73. London: Hutchinson University Library.

Byers. Jack. 1998. The Privatization of Downtown Public Space: The Emerging Grade-Separated City in North America. *Journal of Planning Education and Research* 17: 189–205.

Campbell, Andy. 2009. Cyclist Killed by Trucker in Greenpoint! and Williamsberg Culture Clash. Bike Battle Rages. *The Brooklyn Paper*, December, 14, 1.

Campo, David. 2002. Brooklyn's Vernacular Waterfront. *Journal of Urban Design* 7, no. 2: 171–99.

Carr, C. 1993. Portrait of an Artist in the Age of AIDS—David Wojnarowicz. In C. Carr, *On Edge*, 294. Middletown, CT: Wesleyan University Press.

Carr, Stephen, Mark Francis, Leanne G Rivlin, and Andrew M. Stone. 1992. *Public Space*. New York: Cambridge University Press.

Castells, Manuel. 1989. *Informational City*. New York: Blackwell.

Congressional Budget Office. 2010. Report on the Troubled Asset Relief Program. A CBO Report. March.

Chambliss, W. J. 1995. Control of Ethnic Minorities. In *Ethnicity, Race, and Time*, ed. D. Hawkins, 235–58. Albany, NY: SUNY Press.

Charas. Undated. Charas Website, www.charas.org.

Christian, Nichole M. 1998. "War of the Paintbrushes; Near the Metropolitan, Police Confiscate Art Daily," New York Times, March 22.

Chung, Jen. 2006. Clowns Take Back the Bike Lanes. *The Gothamist*, May 12, Accessed on December 5, 2010 from http://gothamist.com/2006/05/12/clowns_take_bac.php.

Chvasta, Marcyrose. 2006. Anger, Irony, and Protest: Confronting the Issue of Efficacy Again. *Text and Performance Quarterly* 26, no. 1: 5–16

"City Hall, Behind Barricades." 1998. *New York Times*, December 03.

City Planning Commission. December 20, 1993. Calendar no. 7 N940013 ZRM, with reference to a 1989 report, Regulating Residential Towers and Plazas: Issues and Options.

City Record. 1999. Parks and Recreation: Amendment to Chapter 1 of Title 56 of the Official Compilation of the Rules of the City of New York. August, 16.

Clark, Carly and Aaron Naparstek. 2009. The Street of the Future is a Livable Street. *Good Magazine*, accessed on December 5, 2010 form http://awesome.good.is/transparency/web/0904/livable-streets.html

Cohen, Lizabeth. 2003. *A Consumer's Republic: The Politics of Mass Consumption in Postwar America*. New York: Knopf,

Cohen-Cruz, Jan. 1998. *Radical Street Performance*. New York Routledge.

Conaway, Laura. 2007. Sick of Cars in Your Bike Lane? *Village Voice Blogs,* May 25, www.villagevoice.com/blogs/runninscared/archives.

Crimp, Douglas. 2002. *Melancholia and Moralism: Essays on AIDS and Queer Politics*. Boston: MIT Press.

———. 2007. Action Around the Edges. 16th Annual Kessler Lecture. Center for Lesbian and Gay Studies, November, 2.

Crimp, Douglas, Ann Pelligrini, Eva Pendleton, and Michael Warner. 1998. This is a SexPanic! *Fountain* 6, no. 2: 22–24.

Cross, Kenneth D., and Gary Fisher. 1977. A Study of Bicycle/Motor-Vehicle Accidents: Identification of Problem Types and Countermeasure Approaches, accessed on December 5, 2010 from ntl.bts.gov/lib/25000/25400/25439/DOT-HS-803-315.pdf.

Crowly, Michael. 2009. Honk, Honk, Aaah. *New York Magazine*, May, 17, http://nymag.com/news/features/56794/.

Dangerous Bedfellows. 1996. *Policing Public Sex: Queer Politics and The Future of AIDS Activism*. Boston, MA: South End Press.

Daniel, Jamie Own. 2000. Rituals of Disqualification: Competing Publics and Public Housing in Contemporary Chicago, in *Masses, Classes, and the Public Sphere*, ed. M. Hill and W. Montag, 62–82. London: Verso.

Davey, J. 1995. *The New Social Contract: America's Journey from Welfare State to Police State*. Westport, CT: Praeger.

Davis, Mike. 1990. *City of Quartz: Excavating the Future in Los Angeles*. New York: Verso.

———. 2007. *Planet of Slums*. New York: Verso.

De Toqueville, Alexis. 1994. *Democracy in America*. New York: Knopf.

Delany, Samuel R. 1999. *Times Square Red, Times Square Blue*. NY: New York University Press.

Desert, Jean-Ulrich. 1997. Queers Space. In *Queers in Space: Communities, Public Spaces, Sites of Resistance*, eds. Gordon Brent Ingram, Ann-Marie Bouthillette, and Yolanda Retter, 17–26. Seattle: Bay Press.

Dewey, John. 1954. *The Public and Its Problems*. Athens, OH, Swallow Press.

Dijkstra, Lewis. 2000. Public Spaces: A Comparative Discussion of the Criteria for Public Space. In *Constructions of Public Space: Research in Urban Sociology*, vol. 5, ed. Ray Hutchinson, 1–22. Stamford, CT: JAI Press.

Dobbs, Bill. 2004. Quotes, http://thinkexist.com/quotes/bill_dobbs/.

Domhuff, G. W. 1998. *Who Rules America? Power and Politics in the Year 2000*. Mountain View, CA: Mayfield.

Doody, Tim. 2007. Quinn Sidesteps Real Issues of Parade Permits. Letter to the Editor. *New York Blade News*, accessed on October 12 from http://www.nyblade.com/2007/10-12/viewpoint/letters/letters.cfm

Dorn, Paul. 1998. Pedaling to Save the City, *The Quarterly* (Spring).

Duany, Andres and Elizabeth Plater-Zyberk. 1994. Downcity Providence: Master Plan for a Special Time. Providence, Rhode Island Department of Planning and Development.

Duncombe, Stephen. 1997. *Notes from Underground: Zines and the Politics of Alternative Culture.* New York: Verso.

———. 2002a. *Cultural Resistance: A Reader.* New York: Verso.

———. 2002b. Stepping off the Sidewalk: Reclaim the Streets/NYC. In *From ACT UP to the WTO: Urban Protest and Community Building in the Era of Globalization*, eds. Benjamin Shepard and Ron Hayduk, 215–29. New York: Verso.

———. 2007. *Dream.* New York: New Press.

Duneier, Mitchell. 1999. *Sidewalk.* New York: Farrar, Straus and Giroux.

Dunlap, David. 1999a. Commercial Property; Courtyard Is Rising With New Look. *New York Times*, June 30, B6.

———. 1999b. Filling in the Blanks at Battery Park City," *New York Times*, February 7, Section 11, 1.

Dunn, C. et al. 2004. Arresting Protest—A Special Report of the NYCLU on New York City's Protest Policies at the February 15, 2003 Antiwar Demonstration in New York City, www.rncprotestrights.org/pdf/arrestingprotest.pdf.

Dwyer, Jim. 2006. City Rebuffed in Trying to Bar Mass Bike Rides. *New York Times*, February 16.

———. 2008. One Protest, 52 Arrests and a $2 Million Payout. *New York Times*, August 20, B1.

Earth Celebrations. 2004. Fourteenth Annual Rites of Spring Procession. Flyer. May 22.

Ehrenreich, Barbara. 2007. *Dancing in the Streets.* New York: Metropolitan Books.

Eliade, Mercia. 1957. *The Sacred and the Profane.* New York: Harcourt Brace & Co.

Ellen. 2007. Message to [xup-outreach] Report—Roving Garden Party! June 17.

Elevald, Kerry. 2006. Christopher Street Compromise: More officers plus youth services ease West Village tensions. *New York Blade News.* August 21, accessed on November 29, 2010 from www.fiercenyc.org/index.php?s=100&n=17.

Engels, Frederick. 1883. *Dialectics of Nature*, www.marxists.org/archive/marx/works/1883/don/index.htm.

Eyerman, Ron and Jamison, Andrew. 1998. *Music and Social Movements.* Cambridge: Cambridge University Press.

Fainstein, Susan S. 2001. *The City Builders: Property Development in New York and London, 1980–2000.* Lawrence, KS: University Press of Kansas.

Feeney, Michael and Jane H. Fursee. 2009. Cyclists Give Their Lost Bedford Ave Bike Lane Mock Funeral in Brooklyn. *Daily News*, December 14.

Ferguson, Sarah. 1998. Your Right to Party. *Village Voice*, October 13, 113.

————. 1999. A Brief History of Grass Roots Gardening on the Lower East Side. In *Avant Gardening: Ecological Struggle in the City and the World*, eds. Peter Lamborn Wilson and Bill Weinberg. Brooklyn, NY: Autonomedia.

————. 2000. New York Mayor's War On Community Gardens Backfires. *JINN*, February 21, accessed on December 5, 2010 from http://www.pacificnews.org/jinn/stories/6.04/000221-garden.html.

————. 2004a. Earth Angels: Eight-Hour Pageant Fetes East Village Gardens Earth Celebrations' 14th Annual Rites of Spring Procession. *Village Voice*. 17 May.

————. 2004b. Partying for Your Right to Fight: Get Down and Battle Bush. *Village Voice*, July 20, accessed on November 2005 from http://www.villagevoice.com/2004-07-13/nyc-life/partying-for-your-right-to-fight-get-down-and-battle-bush/..

————. 2006. Peaceful Gnome Clowns Take Manhattan. *Village Voice*. January 16, accessed December 5, 2010 from blogs.villagevoice.com/runninscared/2006/01/peaceful_gnome.php.

————. 2007. Brooklyn Bridge Art Party Turns to Naked Coney Carousing. *Village Voice*. July 16, blogs.villagevoice.com/runninscared/2007/07/brooklyn_bridge.php..

Fernandez, Luis. 2008. *Policing Dissent*. New Brunswick, NJ: Rutgers University Press.

Ferrell, Jeff. 2001. *Tearing Down the Streets*. New York: Palgrave/St. Martin's Press.

FIERCE. Save Our Space Campaign. 2007, http://www.fiercenyc.org/index.php?s=115.

Filler, Martin. 2009. Up in the Park. Review of Designing the High Line: Gansevoort Street to 30th Street, ed. Friends of the High Line. *The New York Review of Books* 56, no. 13, Accessed on December 5, 2010 from www.nybooks.com/articles/archives/2009/aug/13/up-in-the-park/.

Fine, Gary Allen. 1995. Public Narration and Group Culture: Discerning Discourse in Social Movements. In *Social Movements and Culture*, eds. Hank Johnson and Bert Klandermans, 127–43. Minneapolis, MN: University of Minnesota Press.

Fitch, Robert. 1993. *The Assassination of New York*. New York: Verso.

Fitzharris, Dustin. 2007. Speaker Quinn's Stonewall Riots. Protestors Banners: Cops Should Not Write Laws and Quinn Betrays Queers. *New York Blade*, September 28, http://nyblade.com/2007/9-5/local-news.cfm.

Flusty, Steven. 1995. *Building Paranoia: The Proliferation of Interdictory Space and the Erosion of Spatial Justice*. Los Angeles, CA: Los Angeles Forum for Architecture and Urban Design.

Flynn, Kevin. 1998. Protesters Say Politics Dictate Parade Permits. *New York Times*, November 25, A1.

Frampton, Kenneth. 1980. *Modern Architecture: a Critical History.* London: Thames and Hudson.

Fraser, Kate. 2002. E-mail correspondence with the Shepard. December 18.

Freeman, Joshua. 2000. *Working-Class New York: Life and Labor Since World War II.* New York: Free Press.

Freire, P. 1970. *Pedagogy of the Oppressed.* New York: Continuum.

Friedan, Bernard J. and Lynne B Sagalyn. 1989. *Downtown, Inc.: How America Rebuilds Cities.* Cambridge, MA: MIT Press.

Friedmann, John and Goetz Wolff. 1982. World City Formation: An Agenda for Research and Action. *International Journal of Urban and Regional Research* 6: 309–44.

Fyfe, Nicholas R. and Jon Bannister. 1998. The Eyes Upon the Street: Closed Circuit Television Surveillance and the City. In *Images of the Street: Planning, Identity and Control in Public Space,* ed. Nicholas R. Fyfe, 254–76. New York: Routledge.

Fyfe, Nicholas. 2004. Zero Tolerance, Maximum Surveillance? Deviance, Difference and Crime Control in the Late Modern City. In *The Emancipatory City? Paradoxes and Possibilities,* ed. Loretta Lees, 40–58. Thousand Oaks, CA; Sage Publications.

Gans, Herbert J. 2002. The Sociology of Space: A Use-Centered View. *City and Community* 1, no. 4, 329–39.

Gans, Herbert. 2006. "Jane Jacobs: Toward and understanding of 'Death and Life of Great American Cities.'" *City & Community* 5, no. 3: 213–15.

Gidden, Elizabeth. 2007. Parks on a Lark. *New York Times,* September 23, CY5.

Gieryn, Thomas 2000. A Space for Place in Sociology. *Annual Review of Sociology* 26: 463–96.

Gladstone, David and Susan Fainstein. 2003. The New York and Los Angeles Economies. In *New York & Los Angeles: Politics, Society, and Culture: A Comparative View,* ed. David Halle, 79–98. Chicago: University of Chicago Press.

Goldberger, Paul. 2001. The Malling of Manhattan. As Distinctions between City and Suburb Blur, a Steep Urban Price is Paid, as the Public Realm Shrinks. *Metropolis Magazine.* March, accessed on December 6, 2010 from www.metropolismag.com/html/content_0301/nyc.htm.

Goldstein, Richard. 2002. Street Hassle: New Skool Versus Old School in Greenwich Village. *Village Voice,* April 24–30.

Gonzalez, David. 2007. Carving Out Havens and Facing Down the Skeptics. *New York Times,* May 8.

Goodman, Andrew. 1998. A Shrinkage of Public Space: Notes on the New Regulatory Infrastructure. Comment on Liora Salter and Rick Salter, *The New Infrastructure. Studies in Political Economy* 57 (Autumn): 149–62.

Gothamist. 2008. Rides Go Up for Sale as Astroland Closes Shop Today. September 7, http://gothamist.com/2008/09/07/rides_go_up_for_sale_as_astroland_c.php.

Graham, Stephen and Alessandro Aurigi. 1997. Virtual Cities, Social Polarization, and the Crisis in Urban Public Space. *Journal of Urban Technology* 4, no. 1: 19–52.

Greenberg, Miriam. 2008. *Branding New York: How a City in Crisis Was Sold to the World.* New York: Routledge.

Grutzner, Charles. 1961. Lefkowitz Asks End to "Terror." *New York Times,* October 6, 23.

Guthrie, Woody. 1956. "This Land is Your Land," accessed on September 29, 2008 from http://www.arlo.net/resources/lyrics/this-land.shtml

Habermas, J. 1971. *Knowledge and Human Interests.* Boston: Beacon Press.

Hagan, John and Bill McCarthy. 1997. *Mean Streets: Youth Crime and Homelessness.* Cambridge, MA: Cambridge University Press.

Hales, Linda. 2004. 2004. "At Columbus Circle, Going Round & Round Over A Building's Fate." *Washington Post,* May 29, p. C1.

Hall, S. et al. 1978. *Policing the Crisis.* New York: Holmes and Meier Publishers.

Hammett, Jerilou and Kingsley Hammett, eds. 2007. *The Suburbanization of New York: How America's Greatest City Became Just Another Town.* New York: Princeton Architectural Press.

Harcourt, Bernard. 2001. *Illusion of Order: The False Promise of Broken Windows Policing.* Cambridge, MA: Harvard University Press.

Hardt, Michael. 2000. The Withering of Civil Society. In *Masses Classes and the Public Sphere,* eds. Mike Hill and Warren Montag, 158–78. London: Verso Press, 2000.

Harlem News. 1969a. Alternatives to the SOB, October.

———. The Meaning of Reclamation Site 1, October.

Harrington, Mark. 2005. Interview with Benjamin Shepard.

Harstock, N. 1998. *The Feminist Standpoint Revisited and Other Essays.* Boulder, CO: Westview Press.

Harvey, David. 1973. *Social Justice and the City.* Baltimore, MD: Johns Hopkins University Press.

———. 1990. *The Condition of Postmodernity: An Enquiry into the Origins of Cultural Change.* Cambridge, MA: Basil Blackwell.

———. 1994. Flexible Accumulation through Urbanization: Reflections on 'Post-modernism' in the American City. In *Post-Fordism: A Reader,* ed. Ash Amin, 361–86. New York: Blackwell.

———. 2005. *A Brief History of Neoliberalism.* New York: Oxford.

———. 2008. The Right to the City. *New Left Review,* 53 (September–October): 23–40.

Hauser, Christine and Diane Cardwell. 2004a. Judge Blocks Central Park Protest. *Newsday.* August 25, www.uslaboragainstwar.org/article.php?id=6282.

———. 2004b. Judge Lets City Bar Convention Protest on Park's Great Lawn. *Newsday.* "Judge Blocks Central Park Protest," August 2

Hawkneswood, William. 1996. *One of the Children: Gay Black Men in Harlem.* Berkeley, CA: University of California Press.

Hayduk, R. and K. Mattson, eds. 2002. *Democracy's Moment: Reforming the American Political System for the 21st Century.* New York: Roman and Littlefield.

Hebert, Bob. 1999. The Giuliani M.O. *New York Times,* January 3, accessed on December 6, 2010 from www.nytimes.com/1999/01/03/opinion/in-america-the-giuliani-mo.html?scp=1&sq=The%20Giuliani%20M.O., %E2%80%9D%20New%20York%20Times,&st=cse.

———. 2007. Arrested While Grieving. *New York Times,* May 26. http://query.nytimes.com/gst/fullpage.html?res=9F0DEFDD1730F935 A15756C0A9619C8B63&sec=&spon=&pagewanted=all.

———. 2009. No Cause for Arrest. *New York Times.* April 18, Accessed on December , 2010 from www.nytimes.com/2009/04/18/opinion/18herbert.html?_r=1&scp=1&sq=No%20Cause%20for%20Arrest&st=cse.

Hines, Ayelet and Craig Evarts. 1998. Worldwide Parties Reclaim Streets: Lighten Up! Globalization Ain't So Bad. *Earth First! Journal* 18, no. 6 (June–July).

Holtzman, Benjamin Craig Hughes, and Kevin Van Meter. 2007. Do It Yourself . . . and the Movement Beyond Capitalism. In S. Shukaitis, D. Graeber, and E. Biddle. *Constituent Imagination,* 44-61. Oakland, CA: AK Press.

Holtzman, Benjamin Craig Hughes, and Kevin Van Meter. 2007. Do It Yourself . . . and the Movement Beyond Capitalism. *Radical Society* 31, no.1: 7–20.

HRPT. 2002, www.hudsonriverpark.org/welcome.html, accessed January 15, 2003.

Huizinga, Johan. 1950. *Homo Ludens: A Study of the Play Element in Culture.* Boston: Beacon.

Hume, Lynne and Jane Mulcock. 2004. Introduction: Awkward Spaces, Productive Places. In *Anthropologists in the Field,* eds. Lynne Hume and Jane Mulcock, xiv–xxvii. New York: Columbia Press.

Hunter, Chalayne. 1970. Harlem Building Fight Ebbs, *New York Times.* April 16, 43.

Hunter, Aina. 2005. Keep Moving, Son. Cops in Carroll Gardens are Hussling School Kids onto Trains. Police call it Protection. Parents Call It Harassment. *Village Voice,* August 3–9, 32.

Huxtable, Ada Louise. 1970. Tale of a few cities—Everywhere. *New York Times,* March 9, 36.

Illich, Ivan. 1973. *Tools for Conviviality.* London: Marion Boyers.

Illson, Murray. 1963. Parks Fears Scored as Exaggerated: Police Aide Says Impression of Public Is Erroneous, *New York Times,* September 28, 21.

Indy Media. 2007. Eviction of Danish Social Centre Fuels Anger Across Europe, January 3, accessed January, 3, 2007 from www.indymedia. org.uk/en/2007/03/363973.htm.

Jacobs, Jane. 1961. *The Death and Life of Great American Cities.* New York: Vintage Books.

————. 2005. Letter to Mayor Bloomberg and the City Council. *Brooklyn Rail,* http://brooklynrail.org/2005/5/local/letter-to-mayor-bloomberg/.

Javits, Eric M. 1961. *SOS New York: A City in Distress.* New York: Dial Press.

Johnson, M. 2003. *Street Justice: A History of Police Violence in New York.* Boston, MA: Beacon.

Jordan, John. 1998. The Art of Necessity: The Subversive Imagination of Anti-road Protest and Reclaim the Streets. In *DiY Culture,* ed. George McKay, 129–51. London: Verso.

Juris, Jeffrey. 2007. Practicing Militant Ethnography. In *Constituent Imagination: Militant Investigations // Collective Theorization in the Global Justice Movement,* eds. S. Shukaitis and D. Graeber, 164–78. Oakland, CA: AK Press.

Karmazin, Eugene. 2005. Riding for Critical Mass. *Guernica: A Magazine of Art and Politics,* May, accessed May 25, 2005 fromwww.guernicamag.com/features/riding_with_critical_mass/index.php.

Kasinitz, Philip, Gregory Smithsimon, and Binh Pok. 2005. Disaster at the Doorstep: Battery Park City and Tribeca Respond to the Events of 9/11. In *Wounded City: The Social Impact of 9/11,* ed. Nancy Foner, 79–105. New York: Russell Sage Foundation.

Kauffman, L. A. 2000a. The New Unrest. *The Free Radical* #1, accessed September 23, 2003 from www.free-radical.org/issue1.shtml.

————. 2000b. Hot Spring. *The Free Radical* #20. February, accessed September 23, 2003 from www.free-radical.org/issue1.shtml.

Kaufman, Michael T. 1999. William H. Whyte, "Organization Man" Author and Urbanologist, Is Dead at 81. *New York Times,* January 13, accessed on November 11, 2009 from www.nytimes.com/1999/01/13/arts/william-h-whyte-organization-man-author-and-urbanologist-is-dead-at-81.html?sec=&spon=&pagewanted=1.

Kayden, Jerold, Municipal Arts Society, and New York Department of City Planning. 2000. *Privately Owned Public Spaces: The New York City Experience.* New York: John Wiley.

Kharakh, Ben. 2007. The Wildman Steve Brill, Naturalist. *Gothamist,* www.gothamist.com.

Kifner, John. 1999. Giuliani's Hunt for Red Menaces: From Transit Union to Gardeners, Mayor Sees Marx's Shadow. *New York Times.* December 20, B3.

Kihss, Peter. 1969. Governor Calls for Start on Harlem Office Building. *New York Times,* September 22, 1, http://select.nytimes.com/gst/abstract.html?res=F40F13FA345E1B7493C0AB1782D85F4D8685F9.

Kim, Jinai. 1987. Privatization Of Public Open Space: Public Process And Private Influence. PhD diss., The Massachusetts Institute of Technology.

King, Anthony D. 1990. *Global Cities: Post-Imperialism and the Internationalization of London.* New York: Routledge.

Klein, Naomi. 2002. *Fences and Windows.* New York.

————. 2003. Reclaiming the Commons. In *Movement of Movements*, ed. Tom Mertes, 219–29. Verso: New York.

————. 2007. *The Shock Doctrine*. New York: Metropolitan Books.

Kohn, Margaret, 2004. *Brave New Neighborhoods: The Privatization of Public Space* New York: Routledge.

Kowinski, William. 1985. *The Malling of America*. New York: William Morrow.

Kridger, Alex. 1995. Reinventing Public Space. *Architectural Record* 183, no. 6 (June): 76–77.

Kruks, Gabe. 1991. Gay and Lesbian Homeless/Street Youth: Special Issues and Concerns. *Journal of Adolescent Heath* 12: 515–18.

Ladamado. Kathleen. 2008. "Bloomberg to democracy: Drop Dead": Protestors—and supporters—speak out at term limits hearing. *New York Daily News*, October 17, www.nydailynews.com/ny_local/2008/10/17/2008-10-17_bloomberg_to_democracy_drop_dead_protest.html.

Lee, Trymaine. 2007. Arrest of 30 Leads Youths to Organize in Brooklyn. *New York Times*, June 6, accessed on October 12, 2009 from www.nytimes.com/2007/06/06/nyregion/06arrests.html?fta=y.

Lees, Loretta. 1998. Urban Renaissance and the Street: Spaces of Control and Contestation. In *Images of the Street: Planning, Identity and Control in Public Space*, ed. Nicholas R. Fyfe, 236–53. New York: Routledge.

LeFebvre, Henri. 1974. *The Production of Space*. Cambridge, MA: Blackwell, 1991. Trans Donald Nicholson-Smith, first published in French, 1974.

————. 2003. *The Urban Revolution*, Minneapolis, MN: University of Minnesota Press.

Levinson, Marc. 2008. *The Box*. Princeton, NJ: Princeton University Press.

Levitt, Leonard. 2009. *NYPD Confidential: Power and Corruption in the Country's Greatest Police Force*. St. Martin's Press: New York.

Lichterman, Paul. 2002. Seeing Structure Happen: Theory Driven Participant Observation. In *Methods of Social Movement Research*, ed. B. Kandermands and S. Staggerborg, 118–45. Minneapolis, MN: University of Minnesota Press.

Lipton, Robert. 2004. Guiliani, Selling Public Image, Branches Out for Private Profit. *New York Times*, February 22, A1 and 30.

Loew, Karen. 2009. What the High Lines Success Can Teach Us. *City Limits* #600. June 15, accessed on June 15, 2009 from www.citylimits.org/content/articles/viewarticle.cfm?article_id=3760.

Logan, John. R. and Harvey L. Molotch. 1987. *Urban Fortunes: The Political Economy of Place*. Berkeley, CA: University of California Press.

Long, Louella Jacqueline and Vernon (Ben) Robinson. 1971. *How Much Power to the People?*. New York: Urban Center at Columbia University.

Low, Setha. 2003. *Behind the Gates: Life, Security, and the Pursuit of Happiness in Fortress America*. New York: Routldge.

Low, Setha and Neil Smith, eds. 2006. *The Politics of Public Space*. New York: Routledge.

Lueck, Thomas J. 1998. Cabdrivers Go to Court Seeking To Restage a Quashed Protest. *New York Times,* May 23, B1.

Lynch, Kevin. 1981. *A Theory Of Good City Form.* Cambridge, MA: MIT Press.

Make The Road By Walking. 2008. Charges Against Innocent Young People Are Dropped. March 6, www.maketheroad.org/article.php?ID=510.

Marcos, Subcomandante Marcos. 2001. *Our Word is Our Weapon. Selected Writings.* Seven Stories Press: New York.

Martinez, Miranda J. 2002. The Struggle For The Gardens: Puerto Ricans, Redevelopment, And The Negotiation Of Difference In A Changing Community. PhD diss. New York University.

Marx, Karl. 1978. Manifesto of the Communist Party. In *The Marx-Engels Reader,* 2nd ed, ed. Robert C. Tucker, 469–500. New York: W.W. Norton.

Marzulli, John. 2009. Judge Jack Weinstein Rips NYPD on False Arrests as Brothers Sue for $10 Over Wrongful Narcs Bust. *Daily News,* November 30, www.nydailynews.com/news/ny_crime/2009/11/30/2009-11-30_judge_rips_nypd_on_false_arrests.html.

Massey, Douglass S. and Nancy A. Denton. 1993. *American Apartheid: Segregation and the Making of the Underclass.* Cambridge, MA: Harvard University Press.

McAdam, Doug. 1996. The Framing Function of Movement Tactics. In *Comparative Perspectives on Social Movements,* eds. Doug McAdam, John D. McCarthy, and Mayer N. Zald, 338–55. Cambridge, UK: Cambridge University Press.

McAdam, Doug, John D McCarthy, and Mayer N. Zald. 1988. Social Movements. In *Handbook of Sociology,* ed., N. J. Smelser, 695–730. Newbury Park, CA: Sage.

McArdle, A and T. Erzen, eds. 2001. *Zero Tolerance.* New York: New York University Press.

McCormack, Lindsey, 2008. In Summer time, The Street is for Park-ing. *City Limits Magazine,* July 28, www.citylimits.org/content/articles/viewarticle.cfm?article_id=3598.

McGrath, Ben. 2006. Holy Rollers. *The New Yorker,* November 13, www.newyorker.com/archive/2006/11/13/061113fa_fact.

McKay, George, ed. 1996. *DiY Culture: Party and Protest in Nineties Britain.* New York: Verso.

McQuiston, John T. 1988. Edward Sulzberger Is Dead at 80; President of Real Estate Concern. *New York Times,* July 1, B8.

Mele, Christopher. 2000. *Selling the Lower East Side: Culture, Real Estate, and Resistance in New York City.* Minneapolis, MN: Minnesota University Press.

Melendez, Mickey. 2003. *We Took the Streets: Fighting for Latino Rights with the Young Lords.* New York: St. Martin's Press.

Merrifield, A. 2002. *Metromarxism.* New York: Routledge.

Mertes, Tom, ed. 2003. *The Movement of Movements: Is Another World Really Possible?* London and New York: Verso.

Mindlin, A. 2008. On the Waterfront, Locked Gates and Grumbling. *New York Times*, June 8, 6CY

Mitchell, Don and Lynn Staeheli. 2006. Clean and Safe? Property Redevelopment, Public Space, and Homelessness in Downtown San Diego. In *The Politics of Public Space*, eds. Setha Low and Neil Smith, 143–76. New York: Routledge.

Mitchell, Don. 1995. The End of Public Space? People's Park, Definitions of the Public and Democracy. *Annals of the Association of American Geographers* 85: 1.

———. 2003. *The Right to the City: Social Justice and the Fight for Public Space.* New York: Guilford Press.

Monroe, James A. 2003. *Hellfire Nation.* New Haven, CT: Yale University Press.

Moody, Kim. 2007. *From Welfare State to Real Estate: Regime Change in New York, 1974 to the Present.* New York: New Press.

Mooe, Patrick. 2004. *Beyond Shame.* Boston: Beacon.

Moynihan, Colin. 1999. Still Mourning, Latino Group Loses 2 Treasured Murals. *New York Times*, November 21, section 14, 8.

———. 2004. Judge Refuses to Halt Mass Ride and Forbids Police to Seize Bicycles. *New York Times*, October 29, B3.

———. 2008. Bike Lanes, Intended for Safety, Become Battlegrounds. *New York Times*, May 4, Metro Section, www.nytimes.com/2008/05/04/nyregion/04bikes.html?_r=1&oref=slogin.

———. 2009. Protesters Dispersed After G-20 Meeting. *New York Times*, September 29, www.nytimes.com/2009/09/27/world/27protest.html?_r=1.

Naparstek, Aaron. 2005. Smolked Out. *New York Press*, May 11–7, 11.

Nardi, Peter. 2006. Sociology at Play, Or Truth in the Pleasant Disguise of Illusion. Presidential Address to the. Pacific Sociological Association. *Sociological Perspectives* 49, no. 3: 285–95.

Nelson, Katie. 2009. Hunter College Survey Finds Car Drivers Block Bicycle Lanes in Manhattan. *New York Daily News*, December 3, accessed on December 29, 2009 from www.nydailynews.com/ny_local/2009/12/03/2009-12-03_survey_finds_drivers_block_bicycle_lanes.html.

Nepestad, Sharon Erickson. 2002. Creating Transnational Solidarity: The Use of Narrative in the US-Central America Peace Movement. In *Globalization and Resistance*, eds. Jackie Smith and Hank Johnston, 133–52. Lantham, MD: Roman and Littlefield.

Neuman, William. 2006. City Hall Promises Major Increase in Bike Lanes on Streets. *New York Times*, September 13, http://query.nytimes.com/gst/fullpage.html?res=9E0CE6D91531F930A2575AC0A9609C8B63..

———. 2007. A Busy City Makes Room for Bikes. *New York Times*, September 23, N37

New York City. 2009. Zoning Resolution, Article III Chapter 7 Section 70.

New York Civil Liberties Union. 1999, New York Civil Liberties Union vs. Giuliani: First Amendment Cases, www.nyclu.org/news/nyclu-v-giuliani-first-amendment-cases.

———. 2006. Tens of Thousands Still Detained Longer than Law Allows, NYCLU Study Finds, January 31, www.overbrook.org/newsletter/feb_06/NYCLU_ChargeOrRelease.pdf.

———. 2006. Justice Delayed, Justice Denied: A Study of Arrest-to-Arraignment Times in New York City www.overbrook.org/newsletter/feb_06/NYCLU_JusticeDenied.pdf.

New York Times. 1969. Plazas, Nice for Strollers, Give Builders Problems, August 24, S8, 8.

———. 1992. Strong Words for a Police Riot, September 30, A22

———. 1998. City Hall, Behind Barricades, December 3, A30.

———. 2000. Free Speech at City Hall, April 7, A22.

———. 2009. Police Stop More Than 1 Million People on Street. *New York Times*, October 8.

Newman, Andy. 2009. No Charges for Most of the 32 Arrested on Way to Wake. *New York Times*, January 29, www.nytimes.com/2008/01/29/nyregion/29arrest.html.

Newman, Oscar. 1972, *Defensible Space: Crime Prevention Through Urban Design.* New York: Macmillan Company.

Nichols, Jack. 1997. Sex Panic! Marches Angrily Thru Manhattan Streets, Protests Giuliani Administration's Elimination of City's Cruising & Gay Social Zones; Veteran NYC Activists Randy Wicker & Sylvia Rivera React Differently. *Badpuppy Gay Today*, September 8, accessed on October 10, 1999from www.gaytoday.com/garchive/events/090897ev.htm.

NYCStories. 2006. Bicycle Clown Brigade, August 23, accessed on August 28, 2006 fromwww.nycstories.blog-city.com/bicycle_clown_brigade.htm.

Ollman, Bertell (2003) *Dance of the Dialectic: Steps in Marx's Method.* Champaigne-Urbana, IL: University of Illinois Press.

Olshan, Jeremy. 2009. Biker Brawl Goes Global. *New York Post*, December 10, 4.

O'Neil, Michael. 2004. Please Steal Christmas! 12/15 at St. Marks. December 12. E-mail announcement to norncarts@mediajumpstart.net, December 12.

October 22 Coalition to Stop Police Brutality, Repression and the Criminalization of a Generation. 2009. At Least 174 People Have Been Killed By NYPD Since Amadou Diallo, Poster, accessed on October 20, 2009 from http://october22-ny.org/SLP/KilledbyNYPDsinceDiallo1009.pdf.

Orum, Anthony M. and Zachary P. Neal. 2010. *Common Ground? Readings and Reflections on Public Space.* New York: Routledge.

PedalPowerPete. 2009. Mayor signs pedicab bill into law. Email message, August 19.

Piven, Frances Fox. 2006. Commentary. New Spatial Scales of Democracy and Resistance. CUNY Graduate Center. May 4.

Plant, Sadie. 1992. *The Most Radical Gesture: The Situationist International in a Postmodern Age.* New York: Routledge.

Prestin, Terry. 2002. Veni, Venti, Grande; Starbucks Strikes Deep in a Wary Land of Pushcarts and Delis. *New York Times,* April 29, www.nytimes.com/2002/04/29/nyregion/veni-venti-grande-starbucks-strikes-deep-in-a-wary-land-of-pushcarts-and-delis.html.

Project Universal Access. n.d. Implications of Universal Access Principles for Bicycle-Specific Roadway Markings, accessed on October 21, 2009 from www.humantransport.org/bicycledriving/library/uastripes/uastripes.htm.

Project Universal Access. n.d. Principles of Universal Access, accessed October 21, 2009, from http://www.humantransport.org/universalaccess/page2.html.

Purcell, Mark. 2003. Excavating Lefebvre. *GeoJournal* 58: 99–108.

Putnam, Robert. 2001. *Bowling Alone.* New York: Simon and Schuster.

Rashbaum, William K. 2009. Buildings Dept. Woes Have Persisted Despite Bloomberg's Overhaul. *New York Times,* October 31, accessed on December 5, 2009 from www.nytimes.com/2009/10/31/nyregion/31buildings.html?_r=1&pagewanted=print.

Reclaim the Streets, New York. 1998a. The Evolution of Reclaim the Streets, October 29, http://www.gn.apc.org/rts/evol.htm.

———. 1998b. Propaganda, December 1,www.gn.apc.org/rts/prop01.htm.

———. 1998c. Reclaim the Streets! How To Start a Street Party, December 1, www.gn.apc.org/rts/sortit.htm.

———. 1998d. Beneath the cobble stones, the beach. From the London RTS web site "Propaganda," December 1, 1998, http://www.gn.apc.org/rts/prop01.htm.

———. New York 1999.

———. 2001. Save Charas. Flyer, December. Reclaim The Streets, London.

Reed, T.V. 2005. *The Art of Protest.* Minneapolis, MN: University of Minnesota Press.

Ribey, Francis. 1998. Pas de pieton pas de citoyen: marcher en ville un manifeste de citoyennete. *Revue des Sciences Sociales de la France de l'Est* 25: 35–41.

Rieder, Jonathan. 1985. *Canarsie: The Jews and Italians of Brooklyn against Liberalism.* Cambridge, MA: Harvard University Press.

Rubin, Gayle. 1984. Thinking Sex:. In *Social Perspectives in Lesbian and Gay Studies: A Reader,* eds. P. Nardi and B. Schneider, 100–133. New York: Routledge.

Sachs, S. 1998. Giuliani's Goal of Civil City Runs into First Amendment, *New York Times,* July 6, www.nytimes.com/1998/07/06/nyregion/giuliani-s-goal-of-civil-city-runs-into-first-amendment.html.

Samuels, David 1997. The Real-Estate Royals. End of the Line?, *New York Times*, August 10, section 6, 37.

Sanders, Barry. 1995. *Sudden Glory: Laughter as a Subversive History*. Boston: Beacon.

———. 1998. *The Private Death of Public Discourse*. Boston: Beacon.

Santos, Fernanda. 2008. Neighbors Use City's Street Closings as a Way to Expand Their Park. *New York Times*, August, 4, accessed on December 6, 2010 from www.nytimes.com/2008/08/04/nyregion/04jackson.html.

Sassen, Saskia. 2001. *The Global City*. Princeton, NJ: Princeton University Press.

Schaper, Donna. 2007. *Grassroots Gardening*. New York: Nation Books.

Schechner, Richard. 2002. *The Performance Studies Reader*. New York: Routledge.

Schwartz, Samuel I. 2006. Rolling Thunder. *New York Times*, November 5, accessed on December 6, 2010 http://query.nytimes.com/gst/fullpage.html?res=9902E4DB103FF936A35752C1A9609C8B63.

Scott, Allen and Edward W. Soja, eds. 1996. *The City: Los Angeles and Urban Theory at the End of the Twentieth Century*. Berkeley, CA: University of California Press.

Sennett, Richard. 1992. *Fall of Public Man*. New York: W. W. Norton & Company.

Shepard, Benjamin. 2001. Queer and Gay Assimilationists. *Monthly Review*, May, 49–62.

———. 2002. Community as a Source for Democratic Politics. In *Making Democracy Work: Reforming the American Political System for the 21st Century*, ed. R. Hayduk and K. Mattson, 109–20. New York: Roman and Littlefield.

———. 2003. Absurd Responses Versus Earnest Politics. *The Journal of Aesthetics and Protest* 1, no. 2, 95–115.

———. 2004. Sylvia and Sylvia's Children. In *That's Revolting*, ed. M. B. Sycamore, 97–112. Brooklyn, NY: Soft Skull Press.

———. 2005. Creative Direct Action in the Era of the Patriot Act: Arrested for Stickerring, Biking and Other Misadventures. *Counterpunch*, June 18–19.

———. 2006. Toward a Ludic Counter-public: Play, Creativity, and the New Street Activism. *Drain—A Journal of Contemporary Art and Culture*, Theme *Play*, 6.

———.2008a. Union Square is Not for Sale Declare Activists. *Brooklyn Rail*. June, www.brooklynrail.org/2008/06/local/union-square-is-not-for-sale-declare-activists.

———. 2008b. Defending Democracy, History and Union Square. *OnNYTurf* (one zap at a time), June 29, www.onmyturf.com

———. 2009. *Queer Political Performance and Protest: Play, Pleasure, and Social Movement*. New York: Routledge.

————. 2011. *Play, Creativity and Social Movements: If I Can't Dance Its Not My Revolution.* New York: Routledge.

Shepard, Benjamin and Ronald Hayduk, eds. 2002. *From ACT UP to the WTO: Urban Protest and Community Building in the Era of Globalization.* New York: Verso.

Shepard, Benjamin and Kelly Moore. 2002. Reclaim the Streets for a World without Cars. In *Critical Mass: Bicyclings's Defiant Celebration*, ed. C. Carlsson. Oakland, CA: AK Press.

Shevory, T. 2004. *Notorious HIV.* Minneapolis, MN: University of Minnesota Press.

Shindler, Paul. 1997. Is It a Gay Thing or a Giuliani Thing? *LGNY*, August 3.

Shively, Charley. 1974/2001. Indiscriminate Promiscuity as an Act of Revolution. In *Come Out Fighting*, ed. C. Bull. New York: Nation Books.

Siegel, Jefferson. 2005a. With Lawsuit, City Keeps Chasing Critical Mass. *The Villager* March 30–April 5, 1 and 14.

Siegel, J. 2005b. Clowns Serious about Parking in Bike Lanes. *The Villager*, August 31, accessed on December 3, 2010 from www.thevillager.com/villager_122/clownsesriousabout.html.

Siegel, J. 2006. Stanton St. Kids' Garden is in Need of Some Magic. *Villager.* October 25, accessed December 3, 2010 from www.thevillager.com/villager_182/stantonstkids.html.

Siskind, Peter. 2001. "Rockefeller's Vietnam?": Black Politics and Urban Development in Harlem, 1969–1974. Paper presented at Gotham Center Conference on New York City History, October 5–7.

Sites, William. 1997. The Limits of Urban Regime Theory: New York Under Koch, Dinkins, and Giuliani. *Urban Affairs Journal* 32, no. 4, (March), 536–57.

Sites, William. 2003. *Remaking New York.* Minneapolis, MN: University of Minnesota Press.

Smith, Adam J. 1998. New York City Mayor Giuliani is Caught Suppressing Report Of His Own Aids Commission On Needle Exchange. In The Week Online with DRCNet, Issue 26, January 23, accessed on April 19, 2004 from www.drcnet.org/rapid/1998/1-23.html#giuliani.

Smith, Neil. 1996. *The New Urban Frontier.* New York: Routledge.

Smithsimon, Gregory. 2011. *Battery Park City as Urban Citadel: How an Exclusive Enclave was Created in Lower Manhattan* New York: New York University Press.

Soja, Edward W. 1989. *Postmodern Geographies: The Reassertion of Space in Critical Social Theory.* New York: Verso.

————. 1996. *Thirdspace: Journeys to Los Angeles and Other Real-and-Imagined Places.* Cambridge, MA: Blackwell.

Solnit, David, ed. 2004. *Globalize Liberation: How to Uproot the System and Build a Better World,* San Francisco, CA: City Lights Press.

Soloski, A. 2004. Street Scenes: In Anticipation of the RNC, Activists Pound the Pavement, Theatrically. *Village Voice*, August 3, www.village voice.com/2004-07-27/news/in-anticipation-of-the-rnc-activists-pound-the-pavement-theatrically/1/.

Somers, Margaret. 1994. The Narrative Construction of Identity. *Theory and Society* 23, 613–14.

Sorkin, Michael, ed. 1992. *Variations on a Theme Park: The New American City and the End of Public Space*. New York: Hill and Wang.

Sottile, Alexis. 2001. Best Place to Rally Around and/or Resuscitate— Charas/El Bohio. *Village Voice*, Accessed 1 January 2002 from www.villagevoice.com/bestof/2001/award/best-place-to-rally-around-and-or-resuscitate-494589/.

Sparkles, Sarah. 2007. Parades, Parties, and Protests. Unpublished Paper.

Spitzer, Elliot. 2002. Memorandum of Agreement between Attorney General and Community Gardeners, accessed on May 23, 2004 from http://www.nyccgc.org/Docs/2010/community_gardens_agreement.pdf.

Stallman, Honorable Michael D. 2006. Supreme Court of the State of New York. The City of New York against Times Up, Inc. Index # 400891/05 Decision and Order, accessed on January 12, 2009 from http://times-up.org/uploads/pdf/2006-02-14-decision.pdf.

Still We Speak, 2005. Still We Speak: Rally to Protect Free Speech and Decry First Amendment and Decry First Amendment Abuses in New York City. Press Release, accessed on October 4, 2008 from www.stillwespeak.org/images/speakrelease2.pdf.

Streetsblog. 2006. New York Gets First Ever Physically Separated Bike Path. September 20, accessed on October, 16, 2007 from http://www.streetsblog.org/2007/09/20/nyc-gets-its-first-ever-physically-separated-bike-path.

Sutton-Smith, Brian. 1997. The Ambiguity of Play: Rhetorics of Rate. In *The Performance Studies Reader*, ed. H. Bial, 132–38. New York: Routledge.

Swan, Cathryn. 2009. Email to saveunionsquareplanning@googlegroups.com Subject: [SUS planning] Fwd: Assemblymember Glick's Community E-Update (Union Sq), November 7.

Sweeny, Matthew. 1998. Marching Against Gay Violence: Protesters Say Mayor Giuliani Is To Blame Thanks to His "tone." *The Brooklyn Papers*, October 2.

Symes, Arthur. 2003. Interview, May 22.

Talen, Bill (aka Reverend Billy). 2003. *What Should I Do if the Reverend Billy Is in My Store?* New York: Free Press.

———. 2005. Push Back Starbucks! *The Stop Shopping Monitor*, accessed on February 14, 2005 from http://stopshoppingmonitor.journurl.com/index.cfm/mode/article/entry/1004 (9 February).

Tarleton, John. 2002. Pete Seeger Joins Fight to Save Harlem Garden, June 30, accessed on November 11, 2009 from www.johntarleton.net/gardens.html.

Tedlock, Barbara. 1991. From Participant Observation to Observation of Participation: the Emergence of Narrative Ethnography. *Journal of Anthropological Research* 47: 69–94.

Thompson, Kenneth. 1998. *Moral Panics: Key Ideas.* New York: Routledge.

Thompson, Mildred. 2008. Powerful PBS Documentary Shows Where You Live Affects How You Live. Email announcement, April 3.

Thompson, Nato. 2004. Trespassing Relevance. In *The Interventionists: User's Guide to Creative Disruption of Everyday Life*, ed. Nato Thompson and Gregory Sholette, 13–22. Boston: Mass MOCA. .

Tilly, Charles. 1999. *Durable Inequalities.* Berkeley, CA: University of California Press.

Time's Up. 2007. NYC Concedes Defeat and Drops Major Lawsuit Against Time's Up! Press Release, March 27.

———. 2009. Bicycle Clowns Declare: Ain't Biking Grand Celebrate Grand Street Bike Lane as a Part of the Solution to a Chaotic City, January.

Tonkiss, Fran. 2005. *Space, the City and Social Theory.* Malden, MA: Polity Press.

Trebay, Guy. 1998. Hemp and Circumstance. *Village Voice*, May 12, 57.

Turner, Victor. 1969. *The Ritual Process.* Chicago, IL: Aldine Publishing Company.

Urban Justice Center. 2010. Stuck in the System: Expanding the Public Health Access by Reconciling the Penal Code with Public Health Law, accessed on December 14, 2010 from www.urbanjustice.org/pdf/publications/Stuck_in_the_System.pdf.

Van Kleunen, Andrew. 1994. The Squatters: A Chorus of Voices. . . . But is Anyone Listening? In *From Urban Village to East Village*, ed by J. Abu-Lughod, 285–312. Oxford: Blackwell.

Vanderbilt, Tom. 2009. What Would Get Americans Biking to Work? Decent Parking. *Slate*, August 17, www.slate.com/id/2225511/.

Vaneigem, Raoul. 1967, 2003. *The Revolution of Everyday Life.* London: Rebel Press.

Varon, Jeremy. 2004. *Bringing the War Home.* Berkeley, CA: University of California Press.

Vaughan, Diane. 1996. *The Challenger Launch Decision: Risky Technology, Culture, and Deviance at NASA.* Chicago: University of Chicago.

Vega, De La. 2006. Bike Lanes Are a Great Start, But Add Barriers. *The Villager* 24, 20–26.

Villager. 2006. They've Got to Get Themselves Back to the Gardens. 76, no. 1. *The Villager*, May 24.

Vitale, Alex. 2008. *City of Disorder: How the Quality of Life Campaign Transformed New York Politics.* New York: New York University Press.

Vitale, Alex and Keith McHenry. 1994. Food Not Bombs. *Z Magazine.* (September): 19–21.

Wagner, D. 1997. The Universalization of Social Problems. *Critical Sociology,* 23, no. 1: 3–23.

Wagner, James. 2007. Apparently Sylvia Rivera Still Scares the Cops. Blog entry, September 28, accessed on October 9, 2007 from http:// jameswagner.com/mt_archives/006679.html.

Wallace, Deborah and Rodrick Wallace. 1998. *A Plague on Your Houses: How New York Was Burned Down and National Public Health Crumbled.* New York: Verso.

Warehouse Newsletter 1, no. 6. July 31, 1975, 2 (no author).

———— 1, no. 8, August 14, 1975, 1 (no author).

Warner, Michael. 1999. *The Trouble with Normal.* New York: Free Press.

————. 2002. *Publics and Counterpublics.* New York: Zone Books.

Weiser, Benjamin. 1998. Ban on Big Gatherings at City Hall Is Ruled Unconstitutional. *New York Times,* July 21, B1.

Weissman, H. 1990. *Serious Play.* Silver Spring, MD: NASW Press.

WEWANTyou. 2007. Message to rha@lists.riseup.net [rha] 9/29 Parade Without a Permit Reportback, Oct 1.

Whalen, Richard J. 1965. *A City Destroying Itself.* New York: Morrow.

White, Rob. 1996. Sanitary Cities: How Designers Banish the Young and the Poor from the Public Realm. *Architecture Australia* v 85, no. 3 (May-June): 82–85.

Whyte, William H. 1988. *City: rediscovering the center.* New York: Doubleday.

————. 1972a. Conversation with Architect. Unpublished. From the archives of William Whyte's work at the Project for Public Space, April 28.

————. 1972b. Talk with Mel Kaufman 1/8/72. From the archives of William H. Whyte, at Project For Public Space.

Wilder, Craig. 2000. *A Covenant with Color: Race and Social Power in Brooklyn.* New York, NY: Columbia University Press.

Will, Brad. 2003. Cultivating Hope: the Community Gardens in New York City. In *We Are Everywhere,* ed. Notes from Nowhere, 134–39. New York: Verso.

Will. 2006. Clowns Liberate Bike Lanes, May 22, accessed on July 1, 2007 fromwww.onnyturf.com/articles/read.php?article_id=264.

Williams, Howard, 2002. "Critical Mass March Madness! Hale Bopp! Hail Bob!" in *Critical Mass: Bicycling's Defiant Celebration,* ed. Chris Carlson (Oakland, AK Press).

Williamsburg Waterfront 197-A-Plan, www.nyc.gov/html/dcp/html/pub/ 197will.shtml.

Wilson, James and George L. Kelling, 1992/2001. Broken Windows. In *The City Reader,* 2nd ed, ed. Richard T. LeGates and Frederich Stout, 251-63. New York: Routledge.

Winnicott, D. W. 1971. *Playing and Reality.* Philadelphia: Routledge.

Wockner. Rex. 1997. Sex-Lib Activists Confront "Sex Panic". Badpuppy Gay Today, November 17, accessed on July 11, 2003 from http://gaytoday.badpuppy.com.

Wojnarowicz, David. 1991. *Close to the Knives.* London: Serpent's Tail.

Wolfe, Tom. 1981. *From Bauhaus to Our House.* New York: Pocket Books.

World Urban Forum. 2004. World Charter for the Right to the City. Elaborated at the Social Forum of the Americas (Quito, Ecuador, July) and the World Urban Forum (Barcelona, Spain, September), http://portal.unesco.org/shs/en/ev.php-.

Xavier, Emanuel. 1997. *Pier Queen.* Piers Queen Productions. New York : New York.

Zimmer, Amy. 2007. Cyclists Want Cars Out of Their Lanes. *Metro New York*, November 2, 1.

Zukin, Sharon. 1982. *Loft Living: Culture and Capital in Urban Change.* Baltimore, MD: Johns Hopkins University Press.

———. 1991. *Landscapes of Power.* Berkeley, CA: University of California Press.

———. 1995. *Cultures of Cities.* Cambridge, MA: Blackwell.

———. 2004. *Point of Purchase.* New York: Routledge.

———. 2010. *Naked City: The Death and Life of Authentic Urban Places.* New York: Oxford University Press.

Index